FERRY PILOT

Nine Lives Over the North Atlantic

By

Kerry McCauley

Printed in the United States of America

First Printing, 2020

EBOOK: ISBN 978-1-7353390-0-9
PAPERBACK: ISBN 978-1-7353390-1-6

www.kerrymccauley.com

DEDICATION

To my friends with wings, who never made it home.

Kathy
JQ
Quazy
Kurt
Gary
Kristy
Jim
Peter
Grant
Will
Neal
Todd
Eric
Mark
John
Ryan
Monty
Lex
Brad
And Pete

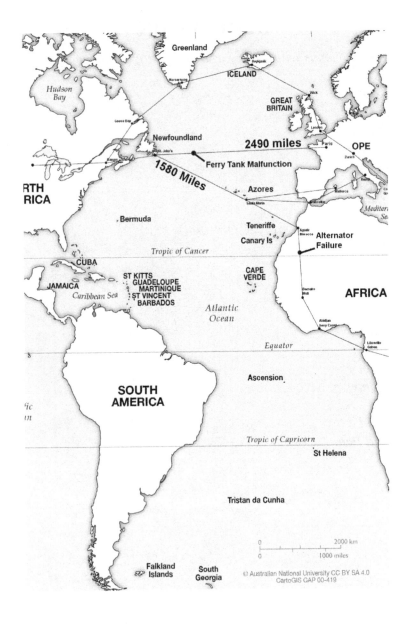

Greenland

ICELAND

GREAT
BRITAIN

Hudson
Bay

2490 miles

Newfoundland

Ferry Tank Malfunction

OPE

1580 Miles

RTH
RICA

Azores

Bermuda

Mediter
Se

Teneriffe

Canary Is

**Alternator
Failure**

Tropic of Cancer

CUBA

CAPE
VERDE

AFRICA

ST KITTS
GUADELOUPE
MARTINIQUE
ST VINCENT
BARBADOS

JAMAICA

Caribbean Sea

Atlantic
Ocean

Equator

SOUTH
AMERICA

Ascension

Tropic of Capricorn

St Helena

Tristan da Cunha

0   2000 km

0   1000 miles

Falkland
Islands

South
Georgia

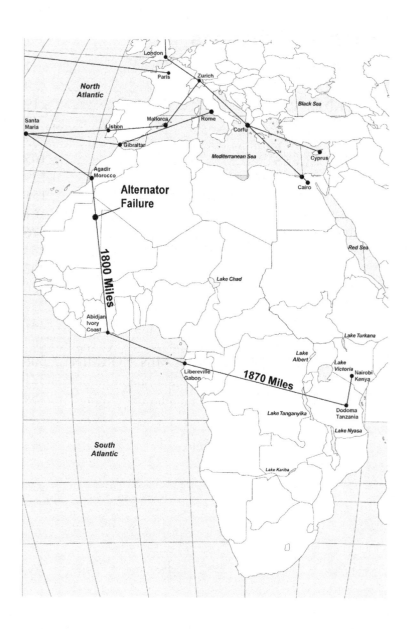

Table of Contents

PREFACE..7
SCARY...9
LEAP OF FAITH...19
ORIENT AIR..47
BLUE SKIES..83
POWERLESS..105
210 TO DODOMA...129
THE SOUND OF SILENCE....................................151
PRESSURE...161
ILLUSTRATIONS..176
I SUPPOSE THAT WAS YOU...............................184
402 DOWN...202
PYRAMID SCHEME..226
RING OF FIRE..239
THE BANK JOB..247
THE SHAH'S REVENGE..264
THE RESCUE OF THE STORMIN' NORMIN......308
ST. ELMO'S FIRE...321
ABOUT THE AUTHOR...354

PREFACE

In any given year an average of three pilots die ferrying small aircraft over the North Atlantic. What kind of a pilot . . . what kind of a man does such a job? What makes him head out over the ocean again and again when he knows the odds are so stacked against him?

July 17, 1991
Africa

My mood darkened as I stared out at the massive light show laid out in front of me. I didn't bother looking at the map for an escape path, there was none. And I'd passed the point of no return long ago. I needed to go east and the line of massive thunderstorms was in my way. As I approached the storm wall I felt insignificant, like a tiny ant at the base of a skyscraper. The boiling mass of dark gray towered above me, topping out at 40,000 feet? . . . 50? . . . higher? The unreachable tops of the powerful storm front didn't matter to me though. (The tiny Cessna I was flying could barely make half that altitude on its best day.) I was heading for the middle. Tightening my seat belt I studied the flashing clouds, looking for a weakness, a gap, anything that might increase my chances of survival. Not seeing any breaks in the wall I picked an area with the least amount of flashes, kicked off the autopilot and dove in.

Strong turbulence slammed into the plane as soon as I penetrated the cloud wall. I fought for control as I was tossed around like a rag doll. The sound in the cockpit was deafening as heavy rain pelted the windshield and airframe. Then, without warning, the floor gave way as I plunged over a thousand feet in just seconds. The strong downdraft made it feel like a trapdoor opened beneath me. Loose items floated around the cockpit as I shoved the throttle to the stops and hauled back on the yoke, trying to arrest the uncontrolled descent. In spite of my efforts I was still going down at over two thousand feet per minute. Then a sudden updraft grabbed the plane and pushed me down in the seat as the altimeter spun back the other way. This cycle repeated several times while lightning flashed in the cockpit like a crazy strobe light show. I was almost completely out of control on a crazy roller coaster ride that I couldn't get off of. The plane was being slammed around so much that I was worried the wings might come off. I slowed my airspeed down as much as possible and tried to dampen the crazy gyrations as the term "in-flight breakup" echoed in my mind.

SCARY

*"An adventure is misery and discomfort,
relived in the safety of reminiscence."*
- Marco Polo

A life of adventure, that's all I ever wanted. Unfortunately I had the misfortune of growing up in the most unadventurous environment imaginable, the suburbs. And not just any suburb, a suburb of Minneapolis, Minnesota. It's about as far from any mountains, oceans, jungles or deserts as any place on earth. About the only dangerous thing you can do in Minnesota is go outside in the winter and try to freeze off various body parts. Good fun.

Despite the cotton bunting, white bread and mayonnaise environment, or perhaps because of it, I was born with my eyes on far horizons. From the time I could walk, my parents had a devil of a time keeping track of me. As a toddler I frequently went AWOL. Usually found blocks from home exploring the neighborhood on my own. Once, when I was three years old, the police brought me home from over a mile away. I was equipped for adventure, with my new cowboy hat, boots and shiny plastic six shooters. Ready for action. At five, they couldn't find me at the local pool one summer day. Then they spotted me, on the high dive board just before I jumped. As I got older I expanded my range to include the densely wooded shoreline and cold deep waters of the Mississippi River. In addition to that natural playground, there was a large decommissioned hydroelectric dam for me to play on. My constant wingman for my adventures was a neighbor boy named Lee Wolfgram. The two of us grew up on the river like Tom Sawyer and Huck Finn, spending countless summer days climbing all over that dam. We fished for carp with canned sweet corn next to the old powerhouse and swam in the dangerous waters under the massive spillways. (I never said we were smart.) Of course trespassing on the dam was strictly forbidden and we played a constant cat and mouse game with the park rangers who constantly chased us. As we got older Lee and I traded in our ten speed bikes for beat up cars that we raced up and down a dirt road that ran along the river.

As time wore on the itch for adventure became a burning obsession in me. Whenever I wasn't out having adventures of my own I was devouring books that took me beyond the horizon. Visions of trackless jungles, Arctic ice fields, mountains, valleys and exotic countries filled my dreams. I couldn't wait to get started. One of my favorite topics to read about was the military, especially flying. I devoured dozens of books about the Green Berets, great tank battles in North Africa, the Flying Tigers and MiG Alley. I built dozens of model airplanes and hung them from the ceiling in my bedroom in a huge plastic dogfight.

At seventeen I'd finally had enough dreaming about adventure. It was time to actually get started. I'm not sure whose idea it was but one day Lee and I headed down to the local recruiting office to join the Army National Guard. We were still in high school at the time, but the Guard had a program that allowed us to go to basic training in-between our junior and senior years and finish our training after graduating.

Because I was only 17 I had to get my parents' approval to join the Army. At first my mother refused to sign the papers. She had no intention of letting her baby boy go off to war. Even though in 1979 things around the world were pretty quiet. But my father took her aside and somehow persuaded her to let me go. So while the rest of our friends were getting ready for a summer of drinking beer and chasing girls, Lee and I were off to Army basic training in Fort Leonard Wood, Missouri.

I loved every minute of it. The screaming drill sergeants, the push-ups, the running, the obstacle course, I was in hog heaven. I especially loved the weapons training. Shooting machine guns and throwing hand grenades was a blast! (Pun intended.) It was a life changing event for me. I was finally out in the world doing the things I'd always dreamed of. My father said my body returned home that fall but my mind never did. When I got back to high school everything just seemed so small and unimportant. I'd had a taste of the real world and having to go back to what I considered childhood really grated on me.

But I somehow made it through one more school year and I was off to Fort Rucker, Alabama, for the twelve week UH-1H Huey helicopter crew chief school. I loved the school and being out on my own. Finally, a man of the world! Okay, I'd only made it as far as Alabama, but at least I was on my way.

When I returned to Minnesota from crew chief school, I went on an adventure binge. I talked my friends into joining me on all kinds of crazy adventures. I got into spelunking, worming my way into caves hundreds of feet underground, and rock climbing, scaling the tall cliffs on the North Shore of Lake Superior. And while everyone else went to Florida for spring break, my college buddies and I hopped freight trains to Seattle and back. The crazier stuff I did, the more I needed the adrenaline rush that it gave me. It was about then I got the nickname "Scary Kerry".

Then I started taking flying lessons. IT. WAS. AMAZING! My life's passion for so many years was finally a reality! I couldn't believe I'd waited so long. I loved everything about flying, and I was good at it, a natural some might say. After each lesson I would eagerly sign up for another. In no time at all I was cleared to solo and on my way to becoming a pilot.

I was having the time of my life and it didn't look like I was ever going to stop. But like millions of adventurous young men before me I was slowed down by the one thing I couldn't fight, a woman. I met Kathy at a frat house toga party in St. Paul. We immediately hit it off. She was a petite brunette with big dark eyes that I got lost in. Kathy was amazing. She was game for almost anything. She joined me on hunting and fishing trips and even came with me when I went spelunking in the deep caves in southern Minnesota. Her small frame allowed her to worm her way into the smallest cracks that frustrated the rest of us. We moved in together after only a few months and were married shortly after.

I really hadn't planned on getting married so young, and I tried my best to get out of it. I told Kathy that it wouldn't work because I was a free spirit. She said she wouldn't tie me down. I told her any woman I married would have to be just as crazy as I was, and would have to be willing to hunt, fish, camp, rock climb, anything I could think of. She said she would love to do all of these things with me. I was stuck. Kathy had defeated all my reasons for not getting married by agreeing with everything I said. I couldn't think of any other arguments so I started a new adventure and became a married man.

During my first year of marriage my life changed quickly. Lee had lucked into a job as the property manager of a new office building in downtown Minneapolis and asked me if I wanted to be his assistant. I would have my own office, wear a suit to work and help Lee run the entire building. It was too good a job to pass up so I dropped out of college and joined the corporate world. I loved it, for a while. I wore suits, went to staff meetings, attended managers retreats and generally fell right into the life of a big shot property manager's assistant. But while I liked how seemingly important and successful I'd suddenly become, the silk ties were starting to chafe. Somehow my life of adventure had been sidetracked and down deep I knew this wasn't where I belonged.

* * *

I didn't know it when I joined the National Guard, but hidden in that organization was the doorway to an adventurous life beyond my wildest imagination. One drill weekend, while working on UH-1H Huey, I struck up a conversation with a fellow crew chief that I hadn't seen for a few months. When I asked him where he'd been, he replied, "I just got back from Africa."

"Africa!" I exclaimed, my interest suddenly piqued. What were you doing in Africa?"

"I flew a Bonanza down to Johannesburg," he said. "My dad owns a ferry company that delivers planes all over the world."

His name was Peter Demos, Jr. He went on to tell me about his job as a ferry pilot flying small planes to their new owners all over the globe. As I listened to him tell me about flying over oceans and deserts, the Greenland icecap and the jungles of the Congo, I realized that my future was in the cockpit. I decided right there and then that being a ferry pilot was what I wanted to do for a living. There was only one little obstacle standing in my way, I didn't have a pilot's license yet. I asked Pete what it took to get hired as a ferry pilot.

"You have to have your commercial, instrument and multi-engine ratings." He said.

"That's doable," I told him. I'd been planning to get those anyway so that didn't seem to be that big of an obstacle. "How much flight time do you need?"

"Most of the guys get hired with at least fifteen hundred hours, some have a lot more."

My optimism disappeared. Without even a private pilot's license in my wallet, getting all the necessary ratings, plus a total of fifteen hundred hours, seemed like an impossible goal. I lacked one key element, money. The private, commercial and instrument ratings would be expensive enough, but renting a plane for fifteen hundred hours would cost over one hundred thousand dollars. Even though I'd somehow lucked into a good paying job, that much money was way more than I could ever hope to come up with. But talking to Pete motivated me to keep working toward getting my pilot's license.

Flying took over my life and I quickly progressed in my training, sometimes a little too quickly. Just days after talking to Pete I went out to the airport only to be told by the cute flight school receptionist that my instructor wouldn't be able to make it for my lesson that day. I tried to pretend I was disappointed, but I was really ecstatic. The last time I'd talked to my instructor he told me that I could fly solo even if he wasn't there. I could stay in the landing pattern and do touch and go's but under no circumstances was I to leave the vicinity of the airport. His restrictions didn't bother me at all. This was for the first time I'd be able to just hop in an airplane and go flying, just like a real pilot.

I went out to the little Cessna 152 trainer, climbed in and started the engine. Grinning from ear to ear, I taxied to the runway, and quickly ran through the short takeoff checklist. Then in the most professional voice I could muster, I requested takeoff permission from the control tower. Once the tiny trainer broke free from the runway my grin got even bigger. I was finally flying by myself! I was free! I'd flown solo before, but always under my instructor's supervision from the ground. Now I was responsible for myself, master of my own destiny, the pilot in command. I stayed in the pattern like my instructor told me to and did two touch and go's. Then the little red devil on my shoulder showed up.

"Hey Kerry, let's leave the pattern and go do some REAL flying!"

It was tempting. The guys in the control tower had no idea that I was supposed to stay in the pattern and there was nobody at the flight school that day but the receptionist. No one would have any idea, or care, that I'd strayed. I looked for the angel on my other shoulder, but he was a no-show.

"Crystal tower, Cessna six five tango, departing the pattern to the west."

"Roger six five tango, frequency changed approved, have a good day."

And just like that I was free. I flew west to the flight school's practice area and immediately started screwing around. Steep banks, wingovers, stalls, the works. I was in heaven. I'd grown up listening to my Uncle Kerry tell me flying stories about his life as a naval aviator and dreaming about flying fighters off an aircraft carrier into combat. I had thousands of hours of flight time in my daydream logbook. Now I finally had the chance to prove I was as good of a pilot as I thought I was. I swooped, dove and banked as aggressively as the under-powered trainer would let me. After a few minutes of aerobatics, that I was sure would have made my uncle proud, I decided to try something new. I pulled back on the control yoke and climbed steeply. Just before I lost all my airspeed, I pushed on the yoke as hard as I could putting the plane into a steep dive and floating me out of the pilot's seat in a negative G maneuver. Like a roller coaster going over the top and heading down the big drop.

The whoop of delight died on my lips quickly. Instead of gently floating off the seat and hanging there in zero gravity for a few seconds, my body fell forward into the control panel, trapping the yoke under my chest in the full down position. In a flash I realized why pilots wear their seat belts tight. The Cessna continued diving at the farmland below as I desperately tried to pull on the yoke and level the plane out. Being trapped against the control panel I couldn't get any leverage. A cascade of loose items from the back of the plane flew past my head as I pushed on the instrument panel and forced myself back into my seat. I held myself there with one hand and tightened my seat belt with the other. As soon as the belt was holding me in place again, I frantically hauled back on the yoke with both hands and pulled the Cessna out of the dive. More than a little shaken, I decided to cut my airshow short and head back to the airport.

After landing and shutting the plane down I sat in the cockpit for a few minutes thinking about what a dumb shit I'd been. On one hand, I was very angry with myself for making such a boneheaded mistake and almost getting myself killed. On the other hand, I was kind of proud of myself for not panicking in an emergency situation. With the two attitudes conflicting with each other, I decided to go with pride. After all, I told myself, all the great pilots did dumb stuff early in their careers. The trick was to learn from your mistakes. At least that's what I told myself.

Then I remembered something my Uncle Kerry told me when I started flying lessons.

"Every pilot has two bags, an experience bag and a luck bag. When he first starts out his experience bag is empty and his luck bag is full. Every time the pilot survives doing something stupid or dangerous, he takes a little out of the luck bag and puts it in the experience bag. The trick is to fill the experience bag before the luck bag runs out."

Those words rang true in my head as I realized I'd just made my first withdrawal from my luck bag. I hoped it was a deep bag.

LEAP OF FAITH

"I hope you either take up parachute jumping
or stay out of single motored airplanes at night."
- Charles A. Lindbergh to Wiley Post, 1931

Not long after getting my pilot's license a friend asked me
if I wanted to take skydiving lessons with him. As you can
imagine, he didn't have to work very hard to persuade me
to join him. Kathy wasn't thrilled with the thought of me
spending even more of our hard-earned money on another
crazy hobby. She also wasn't surprised and didn't try and
hold me back. She knew what she signed up for when she
married me.

Early the next Saturday morning my buddy and I rode
our motorcycles out to the middle of dairy country in
western Wisconsin. I was sure that we'd taken a wrong turn
when we pulled onto a rutted, muddy driveway that looked
to lead to an empty field. Then we saw a small, beat up
white building with an even smaller and more beat up plane
parked out front. We'd found the home base of the St.
Croix Valley Skydivers. I didn't know it at the time but it
was to become my home for the next ten years.

As soon as I walked into the clubhouse, I was in love.
The large open room was filled with unpacked parachutes
and stained couches piled high with beer cans.

Posters and faded black and white photographs covered the walls and there was a jumpsuit clad mannequin leg complete with a jump boot sticking out of a hole in the ceiling. Hilarious. Half a dozen young men and women sat on a long carpet covered table that ran the length of the far wall. They were a motley looking crew that looked like they really needed the steaming cups of coffee they were clutching. Despite the obvious effects of the previous night's festivities there was an excited expectation in their voices as they talked about getting ready for another day of jumping.

My instructor was a skinny young woman named Vicky Churches who promised us that if we didn't pay attention or each donate the traditional case of beer to the general fund we wouldn't be jumping that day. She explained that in skydiving, whenever a jumper does something for the first time they owe a case of beer to the dropzone. It was clear to us that the beer rules were the most important part of our training. Safety third they said. The first jump class was six hours long and mostly covered what to do in case of a parachute malfunction. It seemed that there were more ways for things to go wrong than right. After class was over I was given a faded jumpsuit, helmet and goggles. Then a jumpmaster strapped a bulky, grass stained parachute on me and walked me and two other first timers out to the plane. Then the four of us crammed into the small plane we'd seen driving up and we were off! My jumpmaster was a long-haired hippie with a scraggly beard and John Lennon glasses named Miles Hubbard. Miles, along with his old lady, traveled the country every summer when he wasn't teaching calculus at St. Cloud State. I was more than a little nervous as the little Cessna bounced down the uneven dirt runway, but I was also incredibly excited. I was going to jump out of a plane! One of the adventures I'd been dreaming about my whole life, was about to come true.

In what seemed like no time at all, the small Cessna was at 2800 feet above the ground and Miles was telling me to climb out of the open door. Clinging to the wing strut I stepped onto the small homemade metal step covering the right wheel, inched my way to the edge and looked over at the hippie.

"GO!" He smiled and yelled.

I let go of the airplane and my life changed. Trying to describe the feelings and sensations of someone's first jump is impossible. It's literally another world up there. By the time I'd steered the canopy back to the dropzone I knew I was hooked.

But skydiving isn't free, and if I wanted to continue jumping and stay married, I'd have to do something to help pay for my new addiction. When I'd quit taking flying lessons I was about halfway done. My new plan was to finish up and get my license, then talk the chief pilot into hiring me to fly skydivers. I'd not only make enough money to keep skydiving, but build flight time as well. It was the perfect plan.

The chief pilot's name was John Quist, but everyone called him JQ. He was the "Sky God" of the St. Croix Valley Skydivers, and sort of a local legend. A short, heavyset man, JQ had literally grown up at the dropzone in Wisconsin. He got his first job packing parachutes before he was old enough to drive. He then moved up the skydiving ladder steadily, becoming a jumpmaster, parachute rigger, then finally a pilot. When I met him, he had over five thousand hours of flight time and almost three thousand skydives. JQ was not only the head of our little ragtag band of jumpers, but also flew jets as a corporate pilot. To say that he was the most experienced skydiver and pilot on the dropzone was a huge understatement. Even though he scared the hell out of me, I knew he was the man I needed to impress. So I promptly proceeded to screw that up.

I'd just finished my ninth training jump, and was extremely pleased with myself at what I perceived as my complete mastery of the sky. I might have been a little too pleased with myself. My jumpmaster agreed that I'd done a great job, he also thought I should do one more jump from 7,500 feet before moving up to 9,500 feet. I argued and pleaded with him to let me jump from the higher altitude but his decision was final. I was to do one more low altitude jump before moving up, and that was that. The jumpmaster then left the dropzone to go to his "normal" job, leaving me frustrated and not just a little annoyed. Didn't he realize that I was a natural?

Another jumpmaster walked into the clubhouse a few minutes later and asked me where I was in my training. I innocently told him that I did right and left turns and a back flip from 7,500 feet on my last jump. I added in the fact that the jumpmaster told me I'd done a great job. The way I phrased my answers might have made it sound like I'd been cleared to 9,500 feet. I sort of forgot to tell the new jumpmaster that Tom had insisted I do one more jump from

7,500 feet. I wasn't really lying to the jumpmaster, it was just an honest mistake, it could happen to anyone.

"KERRY!"

The icy shout from behind me stopped my mouth in mid-lie. I turned around, and there was JQ. He was standing next to a parachute packing table wearing bright red shorts, a tie-dyed t-shirt and a look of stone-cold fury. In a flash I realized that JQ had been working on a reserve parachute all morning, and even though the table was on the other side of the room, he'd undoubtedly overheard my conversations with both jumpmasters.

"Come here!" JQ said, standing next to the packing table with his hands on his hips.

I slunk over to him knowing I was busted.

"Didn't Tom tell you he wanted you to do another jump from 7,500 feet?" JQ said while poking me in my chest with his finger.

"Yes," I said with a sheepish head bob.

"Then don't go telling the very next jumpmaster you see that you're cleared to jump from 9,500 feet!"

I nodded my head and looked down at the dirty carpet remnants that covered the packing floor.

"Look Kerry, you're doing great up there but I'm afraid you're going to get yourself killed with that attitude of yours."

More head nodding and foot shuffling.

"When someone who's been jumping for as long as your jumpmaster has, tells you to do something, maybe you should listen to him!"

I felt like Tom Cruise in *Top Gun* getting bawled out for buzzing the tower.

"If you wise up, slow down and listen to what your instructors are trying to teach you, you might live long enough to learn something!"

The longer he yelled at me the smaller I felt. And worse yet, the man screaming at me was the one man I needed to impress the most. *Great.*

"Now go do another jump from 7,500 feet! And if I ever hear about you lying to one of your instructors again, you're out of here!"

I wasted no time getting out of there and telling the waiting jumpmaster that my next jump would be from the lower altitude. The next training jump went well. The instructor tested my free fall skills by varying his fall rate, and seeing how well I adjusted. After landing I slunk back into the clubhouse to drop off my gear. Happy about my performance but still smarting from the ass chewing I'd received earlier.

I tried to sneak past JQ, who was still working on the emergency chute, but he stopped me and asked how the jump went. Reluctantly, I told him about the jump. I thought I'd done a really good job but bragging didn't really seem like a good idea at the time, so I just stuck to the facts.

JQ didn't say anything for a few seconds, judging me. Then he told me if it was okay with the instructor, I was cleared off student status, and allowed to jump solo from 9,500 feet. I was shocked at the change in his attitude. I thought that I'd put myself on JQ's permanent shit list, but now he was letting me skip the last two training jumps and go solo. I didn't waste time wondering why, I got the hell out of there before he changed his mind.

Becoming a skydiver opened up a whole new world for me. Mastering the ability to control my body in the air became an all encompassing obsession for me, and much to my surprise I quickly found out that I was a natural. Jumping out of an airplane, sweeping my arms back and diving down to catch up to a formation of skydivers, was by far the most fun thing I'd ever done. I couldn't get enough.

One sunny Saturday afternoon a group of us were just sitting around outside the clubhouse watching the first timers jump and land. We heard the plane fly overhead and watched as another first jump student left the plane and his parachute opened wide. I casually watched as he flew the canopy down into the landing pattern to set himself up for landing. Suddenly, at about 90 feet, his body detached from the parachute and plummeted to the ground. Instinctively, I jumped up and ran over to spot in the tall grass where he landed. Or, I should say, where his body landed, because when I got there it was obvious he was dead. I turned him over, and started working on him anyway. He didn't have a pulse so I began doing CPR, but when I started compressions I could feel all of the bones in his chest were broken. I knew it was a waste of time but I continued to work on him until the ambulance came.

When JQ inspected the student's gear he could find nothing wrong with it. Apparently, he'd thought he had some kind of malfunction, and pulled his emergency release handle. But he'd done this far too low, and his reserve chute didn't have time to open. This was my first introduction to the deadly side of skydiving and aviation. It wouldn't be my last.

* * *

I'd racked up almost one hundred jumps when Kathy decided that it was time to join the fun. As soon as she made her first training jump, she was hooked. The first weekend she made five jumps, and couldn't stop talking about them all the way home. I was almost as excited as she was. Even though we did a lot of things together, I could tell we were going to have a lot of fun being a skydiving couple.

Not being able to wait for the next weekend, Kathy insisted we head out to the dropzone the next Wednesday after work so she could get a couple of training jumps in. On her first jump that afternoon she flew a little too far downwind over a large stand of trees and barely made it back to the field for landing. As she was walking back into the clubhouse, both her jumpmaster and I commented on her flight path. She definitely took the coaching from her instructor better than from her husband. We packed up her parachute and took Kathy up for another jump.

After opening her canopy on that jump, Kathy made the same mistake flying her parachute. Only this time, she didn't make it back over the trees. As I watched, her yellow and blue parachute disappeared into the tall oaks behind the clubhouse.

The jumpers and I who'd been watching, ran into the woods and found her dangling sixty feet in the air, suspended by the parachute lines that were tangled in the branches above her. I was worried that she'd been hurt coming through the treetops, but when I saw the disgusted look on her face, I knew that she was okay.

The other jumpers and I immediately started trying to figure out how to get Kathy safely down from her perch. A coil of rope was found and I started climbing up the massive oak tree she was hung up in. The climb was very difficult due to the size of the tree and lack of branches to grab. I was making slow progress. Suddenly, I saw Kathy's yellow helmet fall past me and land on the ground beneath me. Confused, I looked up and was horrified to see that Kathy had somehow managed to get out of her harness, and was hugging the branch above me, and inching her way to the tree trunk. I couldn't believe what I was seeing. I told her to stay put but she refused, telling me that she could get down on her own. Unhappy with the situation, but unable to persuade Kathy to wait for me to reach her, I frantically tried to make my way higher. Then I heard a slight gasp, and looked up to see Kathy dangling under the branch, trying desperately to wrap her legs around the main tree trunk. The massive trunk was leaning slightly towards her making hanging on all but impossible. I knew she was going to fall. There was just no way she could hang on, and get her arms wrapped around the large tree trunk. I made a desperate lunge for her arm as her hands slipped off the tree. I missed.

Kathy fell hard and landed on her neck and back and was knocked unconscious. We called an ambulance and she was airlifted by helicopter to a St. Paul hospital. I had one of my friends fly me there in one of our jump planes. I called my parents, who came down to wait with me for news of Kathy's condition. When the doctor came in I stood up and steeled myself for bad news. I knew before he said anything. Kathy had suffered a serious head injury, and due to swelling of the brain she wasn't expected to survive. Kathy died two days later.

The following period of my life was almost too painful to bear. Kathy was the love of my life, and losing her left a hole in my soul that took a long time to heal. I blamed myself for the accident, but I couldn't just crawl into a hole and die. Kathy would want me to go on and live my life. I made myself go back into skydiving; the only thing that made any sense in my life. The dropzone family and its crazy band of jumpers became my life. I spent every weekend, holiday and most days after work, out at the DZ. I literally threw myself into the sport, making just over 200 jumps that summer alone.

At the same time many of Kathy's friends and co-workers sort of adopted me. Refusing to let me sit at home feeling sorry for myself. If I wasn't skydiving I was out with Kathy's friends. As the months went by I began to spend more and more time with one particular girl in the group, coincidentally also named Cathy.

Cathy was a beautiful Finnish farm girl from the Upper Peninsula of Michigan. She was as much fun to hang around with as the other girls in the group but there was something about her that impressed me and made me want to spend more and more time with her. One afternoon I had the brilliant idea to take Cathy for an airplane ride. It wasn't really a date, but I hoped it might turn it into one. There was only one small problem with my idea, I hadn't actually taken my private pilot's check ride yet. So no pilot's license. I was close, but as they say, close don't count. I could fly by myself all I wanted, but taking passengers was completely forbidden. So of course I did it anyway. What could possibly go wrong?

It was simple really. I took off alone from the airport where I was taking lessons, and picked Cathy up at a nearby airport where nobody knew me. It worked perfectly. I flew us around Minneapolis, showing her the sights and hopefully impressing the heck out of her. Before taking her back, I asked if she wanted to grab a burger after the flight. When she said yes I suggested we land at the airport where my car was, and after we ate I'd drive her back to her car. I was feeling pretty good as I landed and taxied back to the flight school. Maybe I was feeling too good. I completely forgot that I wasn't supposed to have passengers until I started to taxi past the big glass windows of the flight school.

"Oh crap! You're not supposed to be in here!" I yelled. "DUCK DOWN!"

To her credit, Cathy didn't hesitate and ducked quickly. I went right by where I would normally park the plane and continued down past two rows of hangars before stopping. I had Cathy get out and run around back to where my car was parked, while I went back to the flight school and parked the plane like nothing happened. No one suspected a thing. After that Cathy and I started to spend even more time together. We weren't exactly a couple yet but I tended to hang out with her more than any of Kathy's other friends.

A few weeks later I passed my check ride and finally achieved my goal of getting my pilot's license! I immediately asked JQ to teach me how to fly skydivers.

After mumbling something about rookie pilots being a pain in the ass, he walked me out to his beat up Cessna 182, and began the long and painful process of teaching me how to haul jumpers. JQ told me he would start me off with ten hours of classroom training. We'd be covering aerodynamics, jumper relations, fluid dynamics, Newton's third law, the theory of gravity and practical applied physics. But then somebody wanted to make a jump so he tossed me into the plane and taught me how to fly jumpers by kneeling on the floor behind the pilots set and barking orders over my shoulder instead. The training session was short. JQ showed me how to get the plane to ten thousand feet without cooking the engine, how to set up a jump run so the jumpers stood a reasonable chance of making it back to the DZ and how to get the plane down quickly without supercooling the cylinders. It was the busiest twenty minutes of my life. On the way down JQ had me level off at two thousand feet over the DZ.

"Think you can get on the ground without breaking anything?" He asked.

When I told him I thought I could He popped the door open and jumped. My Career as a diver driver had begun.

Dropping meat bombs taught me volumes about flying and maintaining what some would call, extremely rustic airplanes. Others would call them pieces of junk. Shabby paint and no interior is the hallmark of a jump plane. Large gaping holes in the instrument panel, where critical flight instruments used to live, are common. Sometimes these were removed to save weight, and sometimes the owner was just too broke to fix them and deemed them "unnecessary." Either way I never saw a jump plane that had all of its instruments in place. I also think it's an FAA regulation that all jump planes have at least two and a half rolls of duct tape holding them together.

We would typically cram four skydivers into a Cessna 182. The skydivers sat toboggan style and tried, mostly unsuccessfully, to be comfortable. Starting the engine sometimes required the help of jumper cables and a pickup truck, but we usually got it running. Then we'd taxi the beat up and muddy old Cessna down the bumpy cow path to the relatively smooth section of a farmer's field that served as our runway.

Every takeoff was an adventure. The so-called runway was so short that you had to line the plane up at the very end with your tail in the weeds, stand on the toe brakes, and run the engine up to full power before popping the brakes. Wasting even an inch of precious runway wasn't a good idea if you wanted to build up enough speed to clear the barbed wire fence at the far end. As I rattled down the worn dirt path, I'd dodge what potholes I could and splash through the ones I couldn't. It was always a relief to finally break ground and get the plane into the air where it belonged.

After takeoff I'd circle the dropzone while coaxing the tired old bird up to 10,000 feet as efficiently as possible. Once over the dropzone, the jumpmaster would open the jump door, stick his head out and give me heading corrections until he was satisfied with the spot. Then all four jumpers would climb out, stand on the landing gear and hang onto the wing strut before all jumping together. It took a lot of aileron and rudder control to keep the plane stable and pointed in the right direction with the weight and drag of four skydivers hanging outside. With a little practice I got pretty good at it. That little 182 would give quite a lurch as a thousand pounds of skydivers all left at once, but I had gotten used to that too. Once the jumpers were gone, I'd kick the rudder to close the door, do a wingover, and dive for the ground. The object was to get down as fast as possible so I could pick up the next load and do it all over again. I'd fly as many as 25 loads on a really busy day and I got one free jump for every load I flew. Both my flying and jumping logbooks filled up rapidly. It was tough and demanding work that would leave me completely wrung out at the end of the day. I loved every minute of it. It was also like getting a masters degree in stick and rudder skills, which was a good thing because it wasn't long before I'd need them.

My first big test came on a cold fall day 9,000 feet over the quiet Wisconsin countryside. The club decided that for the last jump of the weekend they would try to get twelve skydivers together in a complicated freefall formation. We launched all three of our planes at the same time. The plan was to fly in close "V" formation over the dropzone where the jumpers would exit as quickly as possible and attempt to link up in free fall.

Formation loads were a lot of fun for the jumpers, but they were more fun for the pilots. Having another plane in the sky and seeing just how well you could maintain a position just off his wing was just the kind of challenge we loved. The goal is to stay in formation with the lead plane by making constant throttle and control inputs. A good pilot can make it seem like the other plane was just suspended in mid-air. Of course, skydivers being skydivers it wasn't unusual to see someone's bare butt pressed up against the window in the classic salute.

That day I was chosen to fly the left side of the formation, Shirley Christensen, our only female pilot, flew right chase, and JQ flew lead. He led our little formation in a winding path around the tall white cumulus clouds that had been building in the area all afternoon.

As we got closer to 10,000, feet I started to get a little concerned that we might not be able to make it over the dropzone. The clouds seemed to have gotten a lot bigger and looked to me like they were blocking our way. But what did I know? I was just a snot-nosed rookie and JQ was, well, he was JQ.

Flying into the clouds even for a short time was out of the question for three reasons. Number one: It would be illegal, not that we cared, but we were flying VFR (visual flight rules) and weren't even supposed to get within 2,000 feet of clouds let alone fly through them. But the cloud clearance law was one we broke regularly so that aspect didn't bother me much.

Number two: If our formation entered thick clouds the three of us wouldn't be able to see each other and there'd be a good chance of collision. Always considered bad form.

But for me, the third reason was the biggest. Being low man on the totem pole, the plane I was flying was the least equipped and most beat up plane of the fleet. Not only was the turn and bank indicator broken, but there was a big hole in the instrument panel where the artificial horizon should be. Without either of these instruments it would be impossible to maintain control of the plane if I flew into the clouds for any length of time. So, yeah, I wanted to stay out of the clouds.

But a good wingman doesn't question his lead, at least that's what I thought at the time. I didn't take my eyes off JQ's plane as he made the final turn to jump run. We were trying to keep the formation as tight as possible to give the skydivers the best chance of getting together once they exited the planes. I was concentrating hard, making tiny power changes with the throttle to stay in position. Out of the corner of my eye I could see the clouds getting closer and I risked a quick glance out front to see what we were flying into. The huge cloud barring our way confused me. Why was JQ taking us right into it? Why wasn't he turning us away? I didn't have time to think about that right then as I went back to concentrating on keeping my position in the formation. I was just going to have to trust that JQ knew what he was doing.

Suddenly, JQ's plane disappeared in a flash of white as we plunged into the cloud.

"Shirley, go right! Kerry, go left! I'll go straight ahead!" JQ yelled over the radio.

The three of us frantically split up our tight formation to avoid running into each other in the bright white clouds. I turned my yoke to the left for a two count then brought it back to neutral, hoping to keep the plane's wings level while I waited to break out of the cloud. Without an artificial horizon, turn and bank indicator, or even a directional gyro compass (DG) to give me attitude information, I was forced to keep the plane under control with nothing but the airspeed indicator, a bouncing alcohol compass and the seat of my pants.

Instead of thinning, the clouds started getting darker. Turbulence started bouncing the plane around as I desperately prayed for clear sky. A glance at the airspeed indicator showed my speed increasing dramatically, inching dangerously close to the red "never exceed" line. I pulled back on the yoke, trying to bring the plane out of the dive and slow down. I was reluctant to pull too hard, because without an artificial horizon, I had no idea what attitude the plane was in. If I was in a steep bank, or even inverted, pulling hard on the yoke would tighten the spiral and put the plane into a high-speed stall, which would then quickly develop into a spin.

The situation only worsened as ice started pelting the Cessna, building up on the wings and windscreen. Real fear began to take hold as I desperately continued pulling on the yoke trying to somehow regain control of the plane and the situation. The airspeed and G forces built up rapidly, pushing me down into my seat and making pulling back on the yoke even more difficult. The whiskey compass was spinning crazily and lacking any outside frame of reference I became convinced the plane was in a spin.

Running out of ideas and getting desperate, I yanked the throttle back to idle as the altimeter spun crazily through 5,000 feet. I was shocked when I saw that I'd lost 4,000 feet in less than a minute. *I'm halfway to the ground! DO SOMETHING! Impact is in less than one minute, unless the wings come off first! DO SOMETHING!*

But I didn't dare pull back any harder on the yoke. I was already pulling almost as hard as I could and was afraid that if I pulled any harder, I'd overstress the airframe and rip the wings right off. I was wearing an emergency parachute and all four of my passengers were skydivers so if the wings did come off, we'd at least have a chance to bail out. But a pilot is supposed to bring the plane back when he's done with it, so jumping didn't even cross my mind.

With no other options or ideas, I decided to hold the yoke where it was and pray. The airspeed indicator needle continued to creep toward the red line of 195 knots when suddenly we burst through the bottom of the dark gray cloud in a sixty degree dive. One second, the windscreen showed nothing but dark gray clouds, the next it was filled with bright green farmland coming up fast. Finally able to see again, the whole world sprang back into place.

In addition to the dive, the plane was in a steep right bank but thankfully not in a spin. I quickly leveled the wings and hauled back hard on the yoke. I prayed that the wings would stay on while the nose of the little Cessna started to slowly come up. The needle of the altimeter had wound down to 1,200 feet before I was back in level flight.

With the aircraft back under control I breathed a huge sigh of relief. Then I remembered that I wasn't alone. I looked back at the jumpers huddled on the floor in the back of the plane. Amazingly, not one of them had said a single word during the whole ordeal. I could tell by the look on their faces and their wide eyes, that they'd been just moments from leaving me to deal with the problem by myself.

When I got back on the ground I thought about how I'd handled the emergency situation. Like every pilot, I'd always wondered just how well I'd perform if I was ever in a life or death situation. Pilots like to think they'll handle their first real emergency like Chuck Yeager. Saving the day with their amazing flying skills, then heading to the bar to tell everyone how cool you were under pressure while ordering another round of tequila. But every new pilot knows that they really have no idea how they'll handle their trial by fire. You'll never know until you're there, facing the beast.

After my own session of self-analysis and tequila shooters with my fellow jumpers and pilots, I concluded that my big mistake was not saying anything when it looked like we were heading for the clouds. But speaking up would have meant questioning the actions of a vastly more experienced pilot, not something easy to do. Nevertheless, I told myself that next time I think someone is wrong, I was going to speak up, no matter how much flight time they had in their logbook. Either way, it was a chip out of the luck bag and into the experience bag.

Flying skydivers was helping me build total flight time in my logbook. I was making slow but steady progress towards becoming a ferry pilot, but I still needed more of what most struggling young pilots were lacking, multi-engine flight time.

Pete told me that I would need about 200 hours of multi-engine time before I'd even be considered for a job as a ferry pilot. The problem was that the cheapest twin-engine plane I could rent was well over $100 an hour. Getting the required amount of multi-engine time was going to cost me over $20,000, which I didn't have. Two hundred hours of multi-time seemed far away.

That's when Lee Wolfgram came up with the brilliant idea of finding three or four pilots who also needed multi-engine time and buy a cheap twin-engine plane together. We could all get our multi-engine ratings in it, fly the hell out of it for a year or so to build up our flight time, and then sell it. He reasoned that if we didn't lose too much money on the resale, we should be able to get our multi-engine time for less than half of what it would cost us to rent a plane. Lee argued his case nonstop for an hour but he could've saved his breath. He had me at "Let's buy a plane."

To make things even cheaper we talked another budding young pilot and National Guard officer into joining us. Together the three of us begged, borrowed and scraped together enough money for a down payment on a small, four passenger, twin-engine plane. I couldn't believe it; I was an airplane owner.

Our new pride and joy was a 1967 Piper Twin Comanche, and it was perfect for us. The Twin Comanche is a wonderful little plane. It's easy to fly, easy to maintain, and best of all, cheap to operate. I was thrilled. There was just something deeply satisfying about flying my own plane. To be able to go out to the airport, open the hangar door and see that beautiful sleek red and white steed waiting for me was a dream come true. It even had a painting of Snoopy on the tail, complete with helmet, scarf and goggles, sitting atop his Sopwith Camel/doghouse. Not being particularly imaginative, we christened our first airplane Snoopy.

Lee and I hired an instructor and we quickly got our multi-engine ratings. With my goal in sight, I was happier than I'd been in a long time. I had no idea that ten months later I'd be sitting in that plane, knowing exactly how I was about to die.

Lee and I flew Snoopy every chance we got until Lee, and our third partner John, who although owning a third of an airplane still hadn't gotten around to getting his pilot's license, were selected to go to the Army's helicopter flight school in Ft. Rucker, Alabama.

The US Army's flight school program is an extremely difficult course where they somehow take a student whose feet have never left the ground and turn him or her into a supposedly competent helicopter pilot, in the incredibly short time of twelve months. It's a difficult and demanding training course with a high washout rate, but not even the Army is heartless enough to keep the students in the classroom over Christmas.

Lee and John were issued a six-day pass. Being short on time, they begged me to fly the Twin Comanche down to Alabama and bring them home. They didn't have to beg very hard to convince me to make a long cross country flight in my new plane. I flew Snoopy down to Alabama, picked up the two fledgling rotor heads and flew them back to Minnesota.

After Christmas we all met at the St. Paul Downtown Airport to fly back to Alabama. Joining us was another officer who was in flight school with Lee and John. He'd somehow missed his commercial flight back and asked if he could hitch a ride to Ft. Rucker.

It was snowing lightly outside as the four of us stood around the flight planning room studying a giant aviation wall map of the United States trying to decide what to do.

The FAA weather briefer had told us over the phone that a large area of snow was moving into central Minnesota and was scheduled to dump six to eight inches of snow over the entire area before it passed. The weather in St. Paul was currently still VFR but that wasn't going to last long as the snow showers intensified.

This news was a big problem for Lee, John and the other pilot candidate. The three of them were due back in Ft. Rucker first thing the next morning. If they didn't make it they might be considered AWOL and could potentially be kicked out of flight school.

"We have to go, there's no other option," Lee said, sounding very determined. "the briefer said that the system is moving east at thirty miles an hour." Lee said, tracing the route with his finger. "We fly a lot faster than that. If we head straight east, we can get ahead of it. Then we can turn south and be home free."

"We'll have to go almost to Chicago to get around the low ceilings. That's pretty far out of our way." I said staring at a large wall map.

"There's no choice, it's either that or stay here for two days, and we can't do that." Lee said with a tone like the decision had already been made.

I didn't like the sound of that, but I wasn't the one with the deadline to make. "What do we do if the weather gets worse and we have to land? We'll be stuck in some small town until the storm passes." I asked.

"If that happens, we'll just land, put him up front and file an instrument flight plan." Lee said pointing at the officer hitchhiking with us.

Our last-minute passenger was the only one of us who had his instrument rating that allowed him to legally fly in clouds and bad weather.

I tried to persuade Lee and John to put the guy with the instrument rating up front right off the bat, but I'd done all the flying from Alabama to Minnesota so it was Lee's turn to fly. John hadn't even gotten a chance to fly the plane so he also wanted to sit up front. Both Lee and John seemed to have this invincible opinion about their flying skills because they'd been flying Army helicopters for the incredibly long period of four months.

Lee, John and I had a heated argument about delaying the flight or putting the instrument rated pilot up front, but their minds were made up. Lee and John would be in the cockpit, and the only instrument rated pilot onboard would be crammed in the back.

We were all ready to go, but not without a maddening 45 minute delay getting everyone's bags loaded into the plane, last minute hugs from their girlfriends and anything else they could think of to waste time. The longer we sat on the ground the worse the weather got. Time was our enemy.

When we were finally ready to leave the base of the dark gray clouds had dropped down to 1,200 feet. Visibility was down to three miles and a light snow had started to fall, covering everything with a thin layer of white powder. Thoroughly pissed off at the delay and not getting to sit up front, I squeezed into the backseat, buckled up and watched over his shoulder as Lee started the engines and took off. Lee leveled off almost immediately to keep us below the clouds and pointed Snoopy east in search of better weather.

But better weather proved hard to find. The dark base of the overcast kept dropping, forcing us lower and lower while pockets of heavy snow continually herded us eastward, away from the direction we wanted to go.

After less than an hour the base of the clouds had forced down to under 800 feet and the falling snow had cut visibility down to less than a mile. It was starting to look like we were in way over our heads. The final straw was when a radio tower that no one had seen flashed by our right wingtip. Lee didn't take much convincing when I suggested for the third time that we land at the nearest airport and switch pilots before we really got into trouble.

Checking the map, we saw that Tomah, Wisconsin, was only fifteen miles away and had a 5,000 foot runway. If the clouds stayed high enough for just a few minutes more we would be able to get down safely. Not being a very trusting backseat pilot, I watched over Lee's shoulder as he dodged around a heavy snow shower trying to find a snow-covered runway hiding in the snow-covered farmland. Finally, the green flash of a rotating beacon appeared out of an almost complete whiteout. With the visibility dropping fast Lee banked Snoopy over hard to keep the life-saving beacon in sight as the four of us searched for the runway. Lee clicked the microphone switch seven times to activate the runway lights. Like magic, a double row of white lights appeared in front of us marking the runway.

For the last twenty minutes I'd had my head up in between the two pilots up front, monitoring our progress and making sure they didn't miss anything. Once we were lined up on the runway I sat back in my seat, relieved that we'd made it out of the rapidly deteriorating situation.

The sound of the engines dropped and the runway lights flashed past as Lee began the landing flare. I looked out my side window and watched as the plane's nose pitched up to allow the wheels of the main landing gear to touch down first. As the nose continued to pitch up, I thought to myself how strange it felt sitting in the backseat on landing. I'd never been in the back of the Twin Comanche for a landing before, and I thought it almost seemed as if the tail was going to hit the runway first instead of the landing gear.

The sudden horrible sound of the tail cone scraping the concrete runway jolted me out of my premature relief. Unbelievably, the tail of the aircraft had hit the runway before the main wheels. The tail bounced once, came up slightly, then quickly hit again as the nose of the plane pitched up dramatically. I frantically grabbed the back of the front seats, hauled myself up and screamed "POWER!" Lee's right hand slammed forward as he jammed the throttles to the stops, and the Comanche's engines screamed as fuel poured into the cylinders. The plane immediately rolled violently 45 degrees to the left with the nose pointed at the tree line along the edge of the runway. Then time stopped like someone hit the pause button.

I could see everything as clearly, as if I was studying a photograph in a book. I could see Lee's hands on the yoke and throttles, knuckles white with strain. John was holding onto the glare shield with his both hands and bracing himself for the impact. And I could see exactly what was about to happen. In a cool dispassionate inner voice I ran through the coming sequence of events to myself.

Let's see, we're heading off the runway in a steep left bank. The left wingtip is going to hit that snowbank running along the edge of the runway. We're going to cartwheel over the ditch on the other side and continue to cartwheel across that small field before smashing into those trees on the other side . . . we're dead. These thoughts went through my mind as slowly as if I was having a casual conversation with someone. Then my brain hit play and time started again. I released my death grip on the front seats, put my head down, and brought my fists up to protect my face. As I tensed up and waited for impact, I had one final thought. *I'm about to be in a plane crash and I'm not even wearing my seat belt.*

Then a Christmas miracle happened and Lee saved our lives. The instant after I buried my head in my hands and accepted my fate Lee chopped the power to the screaming engines and slammed the yoke hard over to the right, leveling the airplane a split second before we hit the side of the runway. Instead of catching the left wingtip on the snowbank and cartwheeling, Snoopy's belly hit the ridge of snow catapulting us back into the air. We flew sickeningly sideways through the air, all control gone, heading for the next impact. Luck was with us that snowy evening because there was no reason for an aircraft tossed into the air like that to remain upright, but it did. We hit the ditch hard and sheared the landing gear off. We bounced back into the air briefly before slamming back to earth, violently sliding and spinning around on our belly three times before slamming to a stop.

None of us moved or said anything for a few eternal seconds. The incredible noise and violence of the crash became stunned silence. The only sound was the slight ticking of the cooling engines. Each of us began to realize that …we weren't dead …our stories didn't end there …we were still alive. The four of us looked at each other in shock.

"HOLY SHIT!" someone said.

We all looked out at the curled propellers and crumpled wings. An eerie calm prevailed in the cabin as each of us came to grips with what had just happened. Then someone noticed a thin stream of white smoke from the ruined right engine, curling upward like a cobra rising from a snake charmer's basket.

"FIRE!"

That got our attention. We all scrambled into action, unbuckling our seat belts (those of us that were wearing them) and waited for John to get the only door open. The door resisted his first attempt and the level of anxiety in the cabin began to climb as the big Lieutenant rammed his shoulder against the door three or four times before it finally gave way. The four of us set a new world speed record evacuating the wrecked aircraft. We frantically scrambled out of the cabin and out over the wing. Once out of the plane we madly threw handfuls of snow into the smoking engine to put the fire out.

After the chaos was over, we found out just how lucky we'd been. The Twin Comanche had impacted and spun through a field filled with fresh cut tree stumps. The stumps shredded the underside of the aircraft but miraculously didn't flip it over. Even more amazing, we found out later, was the fact that those trees had been cut down just two months prior. Had those trees still been there when we crashed instead of a stump-filled field we would've been killed for sure. The four of us stood in the falling snow, silently staring at the wreckage, our baptism into the dangerous world of aviation.

ORIENT AIR

"I owned the world that hour as I rode over it . . .
free of the earth, free of the mountains, free of the clouds,
but how inseparably I was bound to them."
- Charles A. Lindbergh (1902-1974)

Losing the Twin Comanche was a tragedy, but at least it
had fulfilled its purpose. Before the crash I'd managed to
cram over two hundred hours of priceless multi-engine
time into my logbook. Those hours, along with the time
spent flying skydivers, brought my total up to around
fourteen hundred hours. My dream of becoming a ferry
pilot was finally within reach. All I had to do was convince
Pete Demos Sr. that I was experienced enough to fly for
Orient Air.

Pete was a second generation Greek with thinning salt
and pepper hair and a small pot belly set on impossibly
skinny legs. A self-assured and opinionated man, Pete
never hesitated to speak his mind. If he thought you were
an idiot, his most common conclusion, he never failed to let
you know. Pete was one of those rare individuals who
never left you wondering what he really thought about you.

A former Marine pilot and member of Pappy
Boyington's famed Black Sheep squadron VMF-214, Pete
was never one to do things in moderation. After leaving the
Marine Corps in 1965 he was hired to ferry a single engine

Cessna to Africa and Pete was immediately hooked. The adventure and romance of flying small planes around the world got into Pete's blood and he started ferry flying any chance he got. After making a few dozen trips for other people Pete started his own international aircraft delivery company and Orient Air was born.

Pete's new business was immediately successful. A lucky break got his new company off the ground when he landed a contract to deliver modified Cessna Skymasters to Vietnam for the US military. Pete quickly made Orient Air one of the more reliable companies to do business with. But Pete's claim to fame was stealing Idi Amin's jet.

In 1976, Pete was contacted by agents for the Israeli government to see if he would be willing to go to Uganda and attempt to repossess an Aero Commander jet worth over one million dollars. Idi Amin owed the Israelis a considerable amount of money for the plane and for building him two airports. But after their famous raid on Entebbe Airport the Israelis didn't think the African dictator was going to be in a hurry to pay them back. The Israelis also figured it would be a whole lot easier to repossess a jet than an airport.

Always a pirate at heart, Pete accepted the job and flew to Uganda posing as a technician hired by the aircraft's manufacturer to modify the wheel brakes on the jet. After pretending to work on the brakes for an hour Pete told Amin's chief pilot that he needed to do a high speed taxi run to test the repairs. Being suspicious, the head of security insisted armed soldiers accompany Pete in the jet as he ran up and down the runway "testing" the brakes.

After the fake test run Pete told the official that the brakes were still not quite right. He tinkered with the landing gear for another few minutes before declaring the plane ready for another test run. There was more than a little grumbling from the soldiers as they piled into the cramped business jet for the second trip down the runway. Their displeasure was understandable because number one; soldiers bitch a lot (it's their job), and number two; the plane had been sitting in the hot equatorial sun all day turning the interior of the aircraft into an oven. It was hot. Stiflingly hot. Face melting hot. Africa hot.

By the time Pete told the guards that he needed to make a third test run the soldiers had had enough of climbing into the hot cramped jet and told Pete that he could make that test run by himself. Finally alone in the cockpit Pete roared down the runway and instead of testing the brakes, lifted off and headed north leaving his dumbfounded guards behind to face the wrath of Idi Amin.

When Pete landed in Sudan he firmly cemented his place in aviation rogues' history by charging the fuel back to the dictator.

After hearing all the stories about Pete, I had to admit I was a little nervous when I asked his son to arrange a meeting for me. When I sat down in Pete's office, he said in no uncertain terms that even if he needed another ferry pilot, which he did not, what made me think that I was qualified to fly solo over the Atlantic Ocean? Didn't I know that it was the most difficult and dangerous flying in the world? Didn't I know that every year men with far more experience went down in the North Atlantic, never to be seen again? No, Pete told me, he didn't have any room for another snot-nosed pilot.

I was pretty bummed after the meeting. But Pete Jr. told me that his father must have liked me because if he hadn't he would've kicked me out of his office much sooner. He told me to keep building flight time and bugging Pete, because sooner or later there would be an opening and I'd have a shot at getting a job. Little did we know just how soon that opening would come.

Just two weeks after meeting his father, Pete Jr. called to tell me that one of Orient Air's pilots had been killed. The pilot had just departed the South St. Paul Airport when his engine quit over the Mississippi River. Not having sufficient altitude to glide back to the airport, the pilot elected to ditch the disabled plane in the river. Unfortunately, just before touch down he clipped a street light on a road that ran along the river bank. The plane hit the water hard and the pilot was knocked unconscious. A passerby jumped in and tried to pull the pilot to safety but was unable to get him out before the Bonanza slipped beneath the surface.

The NTSB investigation discovered that the pilot had not correctly positioned the fuel selector valve on the ferry tank installed to give the Bonanza the range to cross the Atlantic. Apparently after testing the ferry system the previous day, the pilot left the valve open on the almost empty tank. When the nose of the airplane came up on takeoff, the small amount of fuel left in the ferry tank rushed to the back allowing air into the system, killing the engine and ultimately the pilot.

When I heard the news I wasn't exactly sure how to feel. Here at last was my chance to realize my dream of becoming a ferry pilot. But I'd been hoping there would be an opening in the company because one of the pilots moved up to an airline job or retired, not because he got killed. It just didn't seem right for me to go up to Pete and say, "Hey Pete, I hear you're short one ferry pilot, how about a job?" But I was also afraid that if I didn't do it, someone else would.

I decided to wait until Jr.'s upcoming wedding to approach Pete about flying for him. It would be two weeks after the accident, long enough not to seem ghoulish but hopefully soon enough that he wouldn't have filled the position yet. Besides if he had a few drinks in him it might be easier to talk him into giving me a shot.

Jr.'s wedding day came, and after the reception had been under way for a few hours I made my move. It was very intimidating walking up to the table filled with Pete and a bunch of ferry pilots. Encouraged by the impressive number of empty beer bottles and drink glasses on the table I once again made my case to become Orient Air's newest ferry pilot. Obviously feeling no pain, Pete turned to the other pilots sitting at the table and asked them what they thought. It was the perfect set up for a bunch of drunk pilots. There were the usual comments about being wet behind the ears and not being able to find my ass with both hands let alone Europe. The hazing went on for about five minutes while I just stood there and took it with an embarrassed smile on my face. In the end they decided if I was brave enough, or stupid enough, to want to fly small planes over the ocean, it was good enough for them. Pete told me to pull up a chair. Then he and the other ferry pilots proceeded to tell me stories about bad weather, corrupt airport officials, shitty airplanes and friends they'd lost. My education as an international ferry pilot had begun.

A week later Pete's wife Barb called and asked me if I was available to fly a Beechcraft Duchess from St. Paul to Portugal. Here it was, the day I'd been dreaming about for three years. Yes, or no Kerry, do you have the guts to fly a small plane across the Atlantic? The conflict between safety and adventure took about two milliseconds to resolve.

"Sure," I said, committing myself, "I can do that."

The decision had been an easy one. Of course sitting 1,500 miles away from the ocean in nice safe Minnesota wasn't the same as sitting on the runway in Canada. That test would come later.

At least I wouldn't be completely alone on my first trip. Barb told me that Pete would be flying another plane to Switzerland and that he'd stick with me all the way to Portugal. He'd be in the same sky with me and would help me as much as he could but I'd still be alone in the cockpit.

Joining us on this trip would be Jim Bell, one of Orient Air's most senior pilots. Jim was ferrying a Cessna 210 to Africa and would leave us in the Azores. Pete always tried to group his pilots together whenever he could in order to save money on taxis and hotel costs. They could also support each other in case one of them ran into trouble. But it was mostly to save money.

The day before we were to leave, Pete took me to Orient Air's hangar and showed me the plane I'd be flying over the ocean. The Beechcraft Duchess is a small four passenger twin engine plane commonly used for training. It had two meek 180 horsepower engines that pushed it along at a blistering 150 knots. The engines were just powerful enough that if one of them failed the other would get the pilot all the way to the scene of the crash.

Pete showed me the two 90 gallon ferry tanks they'd installed behind the cockpit, increasing the plane's range from 780 to almost 2000 miles. In addition to the ferry tanks, there was a HF (high frequency) radio that was secured to the top of one of the ferry tanks with bungee cords and duct tape. The HF radio is essentially a portable ham radio and was the only way to stay in contact with the controllers in Canada and Europe when dealing with the vast distances of the Atlantic.

We spent a few minutes going over the operation of the ferry tanks and radios before I brought up the fact that I'd never flown a Duchess before.

"Don't worry," he said, "you'll have plenty of time to practice on the way to Newfoundland."

Early the next day the three of us took off for Portland, Maine, where we dropped Jim's plane off at an avionics shop to get a radio looked at that was giving him trouble. The technician told us he'd have it fixed by morning so we headed to the hotel to spend the night before continuing on to St. John's, Newfoundland.

Once checked in, the three of us sat in Pete's room drinking whiskey while Pete and Jim continued my education in the mystical art of ferry flying. They taught me how to chart a course across the Atlantic, how to make position reports to oceanic control, and most importantly, every trick they'd ever learned about how to stay alive in a small plane over a big ocean. I learned a ton that night, including the fact that ferry pilots have a tendency to drink too much and stay up too late. What a shock.

When we got to the airport the next morning we found out that Jim's plane wasn't done yet. So we waited. And waited. And waited. There is nothing more frustrating and boring than sitting around an airport waiting for a mechanic to fix your airplane. To say Pete was upset at the delay would be an understatement. The sun was low on the horizon by the time Jim's plane was finally declared fit for service. Our late departure meant that we'd be getting to St. John's well after midnight. And to make matters worse, the weather in Newfoundland was looking like crap. Not only would we be tired after a late start and a long day of flying, but we'd have to deal with some truly terrible weather when we got there. *Great.*

There are two types of pilots in the world. Recreational pilots and professional ones. A recreational pilot has the option of not going flying for almost any reason. If the plane has even the smallest thing wrong with it or the weather looks a little iffy, he can just say screw it and go see a movie instead. But the professional pilot is expected to go flying unless it looks like he might die in the process, and sometimes even then.

Up until this point I'd been a recreational pilot and my flying experience in really bad weather was limited. Sure, I'd gone out and played with my instrument rating here and there but I'd never flown in really terrible weather before. But now I was a ferry pilot. And a ferry pilot is expected to fly in all but the absolute worst weather. And St. John's is famous for the worst weather. Newfoundland is the eastern most province in Canada and St. John's is the eastern most point on the island. Perched on the end of a long peninsula, St. John's was perfectly positioned for pilots crossing the North Atlantic or to catch the strongest winds and worst weather coming off the ocean. When we arrived at St. John's the weather there was the worst I'd ever flown in. Low clouds, strong crosswinds and blowing snow made the approach and landing one the most challenging, scratch that, THE most challenging approach and landing I'd ever done. To quote John McClain in the movie *Die Hard*, "Welcome to the party, pal!"

What I was about to do really hit me when I walked into the FBO and saw the giant map of the Atlantic on the wall. I was in St. John's Newfoundland, jumping off point for crossing the Atlantic. From there pilots could fly to Greenland, Iceland, the Azores, or if they're feeling lucky, all the way to Ireland. Hundreds of pilots had taken off from St. John's. Many didn't make it. Orient Air had lost four. This was as real as it gets. The three of us would be heading to Santa Maria the next day. Santa Maria is an island in the Azores located 900 miles west of Portugal and is a popular refueling stop for pilots on the way to Europe or Africa. The distance from St. John's to Santa Maria is 1,700 miles which is far beyond the normal range of small aircraft. The ferry tanks we had installed would give us the extra fuel needed to make the ten hour flight. Hopefully.

With a proposed takeoff time of 5:00 AM Pete and Jim didn't think it was worth wasting time driving into town to get a hotel room so they decided we'd sleep on the couches in the airport pilot's lounge. That is, Pete and Jim slept on the two couches in the pilot's lounge. I got to sleep on the threadbare carpet under the coffee machine table.

Sunrise was still hours away when we got up, had a quick cup of coffee, and went out to the planes on the cold windswept ramp. The temperature was hovering around twenty degrees below zero Fahrenheit with a wind chill of forty below. It was pretty brutal fueling the planes and getting ready to go.

When temperatures are below freezing a plane needs to have its engine preheated for twenty minutes with a portable torpedo heater to have any chance of getting it started. The problem at St. John's was that they only had one engine heater working. That meant it would take over an hour to get all three planes running at the same time.

The ground crew got Jim's plane started first. Then after another long, cold twenty minutes the mighty Duchess sprang to life. But Pete and the ramp guys had some trouble getting his plane started and it took a lot longer than twenty minutes. While we were waiting for Pete to get his plane running Jim's preplanned departure time came up and Pete told him to takeoff.

I desperately hoped Pete could get his plane running soon. My departure time was coming up and I didn't want to miss it. I was also freezing my ass off and wanted to get the heater going. It was so cold!

Unlike single engine planes which got their cabin heat directly from the engine, most light twins have a gasoline fueled heater mounted in the nose of the aircraft. And those heaters aren't supposed to be used on the ground, because without a strong airflow they can easily trip the overheat safety switch. I knew all this but I'd been sitting in an unheated plane with my teeth chattering for over an hour. I had to do something. Hoping that the outside air temperature was low enough to avoid tripping the safety switch I turned the heater on trying to get just a little heat in the cabin.

Just a few seconds of heat. Then I'll turn it off before it overheats. That should be okay . . . . I think.

I flipped the heater switch and was instantly rewarded with blessed warm air flowing into the cockpit.

Oh my God! That feels soooo good! Ten seconds, that's it. Then I'll shut it off.

Just as I was reaching for the off switch the air flow from the heat vents suddenly turned cold as ice; I'd run the heater too long and blew the overheat switch.

OH NO! NO! NO! NO! CRAP!

What a boneheaded move! I couldn't believe I'd been so stupid! I said a few other choice words to myself as I desperately paged through the pilots operating manual, trying to find out how to reset the switch. Unfortunately, the manual confirmed what I already suspected, the switch couldn't be reset in flight or from the cockpit.

DAMN IT!

I looked up and saw that they'd just gotten Pete's engine running. I sat there shivering in the cockpit wondering what to do. It was bitterly cold sitting on the ground and I knew as soon as I took off and climbed up to altitude the temperatures would get downright dangerous.

I took stock of my situation. I was already frozen to the bone and it would only get worse as I climbed into the colder air up at fifteen thousand feet. I'd only gotten maybe an hour of fitful sleep on the floor of the pilot's lounge that night, and the trip was going to take ten long hours. The forecast at Santa Maria was for low clouds and rain, so I'd have to shoot another instrument approach when I got there. And to top it all off, it was going to be my first solo flight across the Atlantic Ocean.

Can I do all this on no sleep while I'm freezing my ass off? Is it safe? Well, no, obviously. But is it safe enough? Can I do it?

All of these factors together sounded like an accident report waiting to be written. Taking off in those conditions would be stupid. I had to get the heater working.

Reluctantly I keyed the mike and called Pete. He wasn't very happy when I told him I had to shut down and reset the overheat switch before I could takeoff. But he agreed that I needed the heater. He pointed out one aspect that I'd missed; if I ran into any ice I'd need the defroster to keep the windscreen clear. Lack of sleep was already having a negative effect on my thought process.

I shut the engines down and climbed out of the Duchess. MAN, it was COLD! I opened the nose compartment for the first time on the trip and found that it was jammed full of aircraft parts! Pete later told me that the parts were hidden in my plane in order to, shall we say, avoid any Imperial entanglements (customs and import tax) on their way to a buyer in Spain.

I quickly pulled the parts out of the nose and desperately tried to find the heater reset switch with my flashlight before I froze completely. It wasn't helping that I was wearing my good Nomex Army flying gloves. They were nice and thin, perfect for pushing buttons and flipping switches in a moderately chilly cockpit. They were absolute crap on a subzero ramp. Pete shut down his plane and came over to help. We searched for as long as we could stand it on the cold, dark ramp but we finally had to admit defeat. The ramp guy helped us haul the plane into a heated hangar where we could dig out the maintenance manuals to find the missing switch.

By the time we located the switch and put the plane back together, both Pete and I were too cold and exhausted to think about trying to fly ten hours to Santa Maria. We called the control tower and had them relay Jim to that we weren't coming. Then we got a cab and headed into town to find a hotel, tired and disappointed.

The next morning was just as cold as the day before but I had put on more clothes so I was ready. We got both planes started without incident and it wasn't long before I heard the St. John's control tower give Pete takeoff clearance. I watched as his light blue Cessna 206 roared down the runway and disappeared into the black predawn sky. I was next.

Canadian regulations required a fifteen-minute separation between transatlantic departures. Apparently, Gander Control didn't want those little planes clacking into each other as they wandered aimlessly over the North Atlantic.

I had to watch a pilot with well over three hundred crossings and twenty years of ocean flying experience, disappear into the haze while I waited to make my first trip alone. At that point I was sure wishing I could've made at least one crossing with someone experienced sitting next to me rather than on a radio lifeline thirty miles ahead of me.

Fifteen minutes to wait until my departure time. I went over my before takeoff checklist again. I paid particularly close attention to the ferry system. The pilot I replaced was killed on takeoff because he had the fuel selector valve on the ferry system set incorrectly. I didn't want to make that same mistake.

I double-checked that I had the correct maps and instrument approach plates handy. My HF radio was working and set to the first frequency I would use. I checked that the ditch bag with survival gear was accessible in case I was forced down at sea. Life raft on top of the ditch bag.

If I only have time to take one thing it had better be the raft.

As I got everything in the cockpit ready for takeoff it felt like I was preparing for a NASA space shuttle launch. And in a sense I was, because once out over the open ocean I was on my own, virtually unreachable. I might as well be on the way to the moon.

Finally convinced the plane was as ready as I could make it I checked my watch to see how much longer I had to wait.

Twelve minutes left? Are you kidding me? AAAAARRRG!

The anticipation was killing me! Time seemed to drag on forever. I tried not to think about just how big the Atlantic Ocean was and what I was about to do, but it was impossible.

Another check around the cockpit: snack bag clear of the rudder pedals on the right side, a twelve pack of diet soda within reach, fresh batteries in my Walkman, cabin door secure. Everything all set. I adjusted the orange neoprene survival suit I was wearing. I only had on up to my waist and wondered if I should put it on all the way. If I lost an engine on takeoff, I might not have time to finish putting it on and get it zipped up before I was in the water. But I'd have a hard time flying with my hands inside the thick neoprene gloves. I decided to leave it just pulled up to my waist and take my chances.

Ten minutes.

It's not too late. I still have time to change my mind. All have to do is taxi back to the ramp, lock up the plane and catch a flight back to Minneapolis. Heck, if I got lucky, I could be back home by dinner time.

Pete had told me about lots of guys who'd gotten this far and chickened out, or come to their senses.

This is CRAZY! What am I thinking? I'm not ready for this!

I thought about how many men were at the bottom of the Atlantic, sitting in planes just like the one I was in. Their skeletons picked clean by crabs, at the controls for eternity.

And what was even doing this for? Fame? Even though Charles Lindbergh became a living legend for doing almost exactly the same thing, no one outside my small group of friends will ever know of my flight. Money? Hell, a ferry pilot would have to fly his ass off to make twenty-five thousand dollars a year. There were easier and safer ways to make a living. Glory? What is glory? There would be no parades. Women wouldn't swoon when they met me. There would be no commemorative stamp with my picture on it. (That would be cool though.) I guessed that I was doing it just for the challenge and adventure of it. In the end that would have to be enough.

"November six seven one eight delta, clear for takeoff, fly runway heading until two thousand feet then contact Gander on one two six point zero five, have a good flight."

It was time.

I acknowledged the tower and moved into position on the runway. All I could see off the end of the concrete strip in front of me was the faint glow of the approaching sunrise. The Atlantic Ocean was out there waiting for me.

Show time.

I pushed the throttles to the stops, gave the engine instruments one final check and released the brakes. The overweight Beech didn't exactly snap my head back as it reluctantly began moving down the concrete runway.

It had only been three years since I'd heard Jr. telling me about ferry flying. And here I was, finally racing down the runway toward my first Atlantic crossing.

Once the needle on the airspeed indicator approached normal liftoff speed I eased back on the yoke and the overloaded plane staggered into the air. It was the first time I'd taken off with full ferry tanks and I was very careful to keep my speed up and fly smooth. Pete and the other ferry pilots of Orient Air had made sure I understood the importance of flying overloaded aircraft at a higher airspeed than normal, especially on takeoff. He even warned me that retracting the landing gear too soon on a plane loaded with so much weight behind the center of gravity could cause it to stall and crash. He'd seen it happen to another light twin on that very runway years before and had included the story as part of my training. I found Pete's tragedy filled method of instruction very inspiring.

When the speed built up to a point I hoped would keep the little trainer staggering skyward I retracted the landing gear and waited for the plane to stall or roll over, but the Duchess just continued to wallow upward. I carefully brought the nose up just a little, gingerly coaxing the aircraft into a slight climb. With the dangerous takeoff behind me I turned south east and continued the shallow ascent.

Before I knew it I was crossing the rocky shoreline of Newfoundland and heading out over the open ocean.

There's no turning back now.

Or was there? I could still come up with some fictitious mechanical problem that would give me a reason to abort the flight and return to the safety of land. A rough running engine, low oil pressure or any number of excuses could be used to justify my retreat from the vast expanse of ocean stretched out before me. It'd be easy. Except for the fact that I wouldn't have been able to live with myself if I'd chickened out, and besides, I didn't want to turn around. I wanted to fly over the ocean!

Even though I was a little apprehensive about the trip I was also very excited and really looking forward to the adventure.

After all, what could possibly go wrong?

Climbing for what seemed like an eternity, the poor overloaded Duchess finally reached the cruising altitude of fifteen thousand feet. I reduced the power and RPM and leaned the mixture out to the max range settings like Pete had shown me. With full wing tanks and the extra fuel in the ferry tanks the long range power setting might mean a low true airspeed but it would keep the Duchess in the air for a butt-numbing thirteen hours. My estimate for Santa Maria in the Azores was just under eleven hours so I should have over a two-hour reserve. Not quite the three hour reserve Pete told me I should shoot for, but hopefully enough.

With the plane at the final cruising altitude and established on course I checked my heading and speed against what I had calculated based on the winds aloft forecast. I was still receiving the St. John's VOR which would give me accurate heading and ground speed readings until I was out of range. I was pleasantly surprised that my heading and speed matched almost exactly what I was expecting. Apparently the Canadian weather service knew what they were talking about when it came to forecasting the winds aloft.

Unlike Lindbergh who got only the crudest form of weather forecast, the weather packet and briefing that Pete and I received was quite detailed and impressive. When we showed up in the weather office for our early morning appointment the briefer had a big blue folder for each of us containing a map of the Atlantic with any significant weather drawn on it, the latest satellite image of our route, the forecast for the Azores for the day and a printout of the winds aloft for the entire Atlantic Ocean.

The briefer went over the information in great detail and answered any questions. I listened intently to the briefer and nodded my head knowingly at the appropriate times. He told us that most of the route was going to be clear all day with a favorable tail wind to help us along.

The only problem was Santa Maria was forecast to be IFR (instrument flight rules) with low clouds and fog around the time of our arrival. That last bit of information got my attention. Forecast for low clouds at our destination? What if the weather was worse than forecast and we couldn't get in? It wasn't like we could just continue on to another airport in Portugal or Africa. We didn't have enough fuel to make it anywhere but the Azores. But Pete didn't seem to think it was a big deal. I guess I'd trust him, after all he had done this over three hundred times.

Ninety miles out to sea the warning flag on the VOR flipped on and off a few times before staying red for good. Bye, bye VOR. I was out of range of St. John's and would have to navigate by compass alone until I picked up the Lajes NDB (non-directional beacon) 1,400 miles away.

The Lajes NDB is a powerful beacon that broadcasts a radio signal that can be picked up as far as three hundred miles away. That meant I had a target six hundred miles across to hit, theoretically. My navigation would have to be WAY off for me to miss that! Unless of course if my ADF (automatic direction finder) receiver broke.

The night before Pete had told me for the third time, over his third Scotch, that the big danger in making the long 1,500 mile trip from Canada to the Azores was the ADF failing. If that happened my navigation based on the winds aloft forecast would have to be perfect. I'd have to hit the nail on the head to find the island. And even if I was perfect, if there were low clouds over the islands when we arrived, finding Santa Maria would be impossible. If that happened I'd be forced to circle helplessly until my fuel finally ran out. Followed by ditching into the cold Atlantic ocean, at night, in the dark, when I couldn't see. I looked again at the cloudy, rainy forecast for Santa Maria and knew that my life literally depended on the ADF continuing to work.

Losing contact with the St. John's VOR had a surprising effect on me. With my last tenuous link with land broken I was truly on my own. I'd been worried about how I would feel and react at this moment. Was I really as brave as I thought I was? Did I actually have the courage to press on over the vast empty ocean stretching out in front of me? You can never know how you'll react in a situation like this until you're there. Just like you can never know how you'll handle an emergency until you are thrust into one headfirst. Instead of fear or apprehension I felt excitement! It was the moment I'd worked so hard for over the previous three years and it was finally here. I felt like the king of the world.

With nothing much to do until my first position report in two hours I turned on the autopilot, pulled a paperback book from my flight bag and started reading to help pass the time. I was kind of surprised how calm I was and how quickly the trip had become almost routine, but even the beautiful but frightening view of miles and miles of open ocean can only hold your attention for so long.

Every few hours I was required to call Gander control on the HF radio and make a position report. I'd tell them my altitude, how much fuel I had left, what time I'd crossed the reporting point and what time I expected to be over the next one.

Telling Gander exactly what time I was over one particular point in the ocean and my estimate for the next seemed a little disingenuous to me. I really had no way of knowing what my position was or how fast I was going. For all I knew I was miles off course and hours behind schedule. If I went down anyone looking for me would have only the roughest of guesses as to where I might be. But I diligently made the required reports and hoped for the best.

As the hours wore on, sitting in the cockpit seemed more like hanging out in a really small dorm room than flying. I listened to music on my Walkman, drank can after can of diet soda, and ate Ritz crackers with sardines and Cheese Wiz for lunch. The bright sun shining in through the windshield forced me completely out of the survival suit and I turned it into a seat cushion, which didn't help much because my rear end had started to feel like it was filled with molten lead.

At the four hour and twenty-eight minute mark I approached the infamous point of no return, once I passed that I would no longer have enough fuel to turn around and return to St. John's if anything went wrong. I looked the engine instruments over for any signs of impending doom. Nothing. All the needles were in the green and the engines sounded smooth and strong. Eliminating any mechanical reasons to abort the flight left only the human factor in the equation. Did I have the guts to press on knowing that from this point on I either made it to the tiny speck of land in the middle of the big wide ocean or go for a swim? It really wasn't much of a choice at all. I picked up my book and went back to reading.

From time to time Pete would call me on the radio to check up on me and make sure I was okay. About five hours into the flight he called me for a very different reason. He'd lost his vacuum pump. This news really got my attention because without the vacuum pump his gyroscopic compass and artificial horizon wouldn't work.

Not having an artificial horizon wasn't a big problem at the time because it was the middle of the afternoon with hardly a cloud in the sky. However, by the time we got to Santa Maria it would be well after sunset. That, along with the low clouds and fog we were expecting, would make things really interesting with two of your most important instruments not working.

Flying an approach without an artificial horizon is the emergency that every pilot trains for when getting his instrument rating. Without the artificial horizon a pilot has to use the needle and ball on the turn and bank indicator to tell him if his wings are level and his airspeed indicator to tell if he's climbing or diving. It can be done if you're careful and fly smooth, but God help you if you get even a little bit out of control because without a working artificial horizon it's virtually impossible to regain control. It's a skill every instrument pilot has, but rarely practices. Especially those pilots who've been flying forever and think they're above practicing such mundane skills, like Pete.

Losing your vacuum pump is considered an emergency situation and the standard procedure is to land as soon as possible. Unfortunately for Pete, as soon as possible was seven hundred miles away.

When Pete told me about his problem I said to myself, Boy, that sucks! I felt a little guilty but I couldn't help feeling relieved that it was Pete's problem and not mine. I sure wouldn't want to have my only two options being, land in bad weather, at night, on a small island in the middle of the ocean or run out of fuel and crash into the cold, dark Atlantic.

But Pete hadn't survived that long without having a few tricks up his sleeve. He told me over the radio that he'd wait for me over the Island of Flores. We'd then link up and fly close formation the final 360 miles to Santa Maria. His plan was to fly as close as he could to me and use my aircraft as his artificial horizon when we hit the low clouds that were forecast over Santa Maria. He told me that he and another pilot had done the same thing years before and it worked out well. He neglected to add that they'd done it in daytime but he figured that was a detail I didn't need to know.

I wasn't crazy about the idea of Pete trying to fly close formation with me through a few hundred miles of bad weather, especially at night. I had enough to worry about without the added risk of a midair collision. Ending the night with an instrument approach down to minimums didn't make me feel any better, even if I didn't have my boss flying right off my wingtip. To top off the list of things that made me nervous about that plan was Pete would be tired after flying all day, that and the fact that he wasn't very current in formation flying. (If he ever had been.) So there was a long list of reasons to say no to Pete's plan. . . . I agreed in an instant.

As we approached the Azores I turned on my ADF radio and tuned in the Lajes NDB beacon. The ADF needle spun in lazy circles indicating that I was still too far out to receive the signal. But a half an hour later the needle stopped its wandering and pointed twenty degrees to my left, I had a signal! My relief was like releasing a breath I didn't know I'd been holding. For eight hours I'd been crossing the ocean with nothing but a compass to follow. No better than Columbus. Now I had something concrete to hang onto. Barring mechanical difficulty, or Pete running into me, I was now reasonably certain I could at least reach the Azores. Dealing with Pete's problem had almost made me forget just what I was doing.

The Island of Flores is the western most island in the Azores chain. It's the first tiny speck of land a pilot in trouble could reach if he was coming from St. John's. Flores is a small volcanic cone that poked out of the ocean, creating just enough room for a few hundred lost souls to scratch out a living herding sheep or doing God knows what. It also has a tiny airport with a short black runway carved out of lava alongside the dormant volcano. The airport doesn't have fuel, a mechanic or services of any kind. But it's three hundred sixty miles closer than Santa Maria and to a pilot in trouble it's like a life ring to a drowning man.

Due to the government-imposed separation Pete arrived first and had been circling the cloud topped volcano for fifteen minutes before I was able to spot the island through the haze.

Feeling cocky and trying to keep Pete's spirits up I bet my boss the first drink at Santa Maria that I would spot his plane before he could spot mine, a small point of pride but important to pilots nonetheless.

After only one orbit my eyes were drawn to movement and focused on the blue Cessna circling off my right wing.

"TALLY HO! BANDIT IN SIGHT!" I cried into the microphone, and pulled the plane around in a steep right bank to intercept my prey. I make no secret that I, like most pilots, am a frustrated fighter pilot at heart.

"I'm at your five o'clock coming around hard! I'm too close for missiles, switching to guns!" I said cheerfully in my best *Top Gun* voice, happy to have "won" the engagement.

"Knock it off McCauley and pull ahead of me." Pete replied rather shortly. He was either pissed that he had lost our little wager or the challenge looming in the coming darkness had him worried.

At this point Pete had a choice to make. He could easily land at Flores while it was still daytime and the weather was good or he could press on to Santa Maria and attempt to fly a dangerous partial panel approach at night. I knew what the smart move was, but I had a feeling that Pete wouldn't take the safe way out.

"What's your plan, boss?" I asked.

"Same as we talked about before. I'll fly on your wing all the way to Santa Maria."

"You know we could land here and finish the flight tomorrow morning."

"We could, but there's nothing on Flores, no fuel, no maintenance, not even a hotel."

"So you'd rather fly a no gyro approach at night?" I asked.

"Yes, I'd rather do that than try to sleep in the plane all night. Now shut up and fly."

I eased the Duchess up next to Pete's plane then slowly pulled ahead to lead him east toward Santa Maria and the clouds we could see building on the horizon.

Pete had trouble keeping a stable formation at first, lagging behind then adding too much power and shooting ahead of me before he could get slowed down. But after a while the gyrations became smaller and smaller until I was only moderately concerned that he was going to hit me instead of being certain that he was. As the sun slipped below the horizon the ocean and sky turned a deep orange just as our two ship formation plunged into the clouds.

Once the sky disappeared I went on instruments and switched on my navigation lights for Pete to focus on. I left the strobe lights off so as not to blind Pete as he concentrated on keeping me in sight.

It was a good thing that Pete had a chance to practice his formation flying in clear air because when we entered the thick clouds it took him a while to settle down and fly smoothly. Well, smoothly-ish. I got a crick in my neck looking over my shoulder to make sure he didn't run into me.

It wasn't long before we left any lingering glow from the setting sun behind us and the clouds turned from dark gray to a black sky so totally devoid of light it was hard to believe the bright sunshine had ever existed. I tried to evenly split my concentration between flying smooth and steady for Pete and keeping track of the dim position lights on his aircraft. The red and green lights on his wing tips gave off a misty glow in the clouds and Pete's face was dimly illuminated by the cockpit instrument lights. It was very strange. I could look back and see Pete clearly. But even though we were only feet apart our situations were vastly different.

When we got closer to Santa Maria my VOR came alive and I finally had a good navigation aid to home in on. I should have been happy my first long ocean leg was almost behind me. All I had to do is make it another 70 miles, shoot an approach and it would be over. At least that had been the original plan, but now I was flying in thick clouds, at night, in formation with my cranky boss behind me flying a plane that didn't have all its instruments working. Did I mention that Pete was struggling at formation flying and getting tired? Yeah, I was having a good time.

I called Santa Maria to check in and get the current weather and was told that the clouds were variable down to 500 feet, and visibility was two miles with light rain. After hearing this, Pete decided it was time to let the control tower know what the situation and our plan was.

"Santa Maria approach, Cessna one Juliet Bravo, the Duchess and I are currently a flight of two and request that we remain a flight of two through approach and landing."

"Negative One Juliet Bravo, formation approaches are not allowed at Santa Maria."

"Santa Maria, the reason for the request is that I have lost my vacuum pump and the Duchess is leading me in."

"One Juliet Bravo are you declaring an emergency at this time?"

There was a long pause before Pete answered, "Stand by."

Pete switched frequencies and gave me a call. "What do you think, McCauley?"

Why the hell is he asking me? He's the one with all the experience.

"It's up to you, Pete. It all depends on how comfortable you are flying the approach like that. But I'll do it either way."

"I really don't want to declare an emergency. They'll jerk us around for days then charge me a ton of money for emergency services. I tell you what we'll do. You fly the approach first and tell me what the cloud base is. If it's not bad I'll just descend under the clouds a few miles away from the island. I should be able to see the lights of Santa Maria and fly to the airport visually."

"What if it's really low?" I asked.

"Then I'll declare an emergency, we'll both climb until we're out of the clouds. We form up again then you can lead me down."

It sounded like a crazy idea to me, but at least I wouldn't have to worry about Pete running into me while flying the approach, and what could I say anyway? He was the boss.

With my heart pounding I started flying the ILS approach into Santa Maria. The approach and landing at St. John's had been my first really low approach and I was still pretty green. I certainly hadn't done any at night, over the ocean, with no alternate airports to divert to in case I couldn't land. Still, at least my vacuum pump was working. I managed to get set up on the published approach and was descending down the invisible glideslope when I broke out of the clouds 600 feet over the ocean and was greeted by the beautiful sight of the runway lights of Santa Maria laid out before me.

The relief that flowed over me as the wheels of the Duchess kissed the asphalt was almost a physical thing. I'D MADE IT! Well, not all the way across the ocean but at least the first and most dangerous leg. I was ecstatic but Pete was still out there, fighting for his life in the darkness. Taxiing across the massive ramp I called Pete and told him that the bottom of the clouds was ragged at about 600 feet.

After shutting the plane down I climbed out onto the ramp and looked back at the runway waiting for Pete to land. The airport lights reflected off the empty wet asphalt ramp and the bottom of clouds making a surreal and silent stage. There was no sound but the soft pings of my engines cooling. A long ten minutes later flashing strobe lights appeared out of the darkness a few miles west of the island. The blinking light curved around to the runway, landed and morphed into a plane as Pete taxied onto the dimly lit ramp.

When Pete squeezed his way out of the cockpit he looked a bit shaken. "Jesus Christ, McCauley!" He yelled, "You told me the bases were at 600 feet!"

"Yeah, I also told you that the bases were ragged. Why? What happened?"

"What happened was I didn't break out until 400 feet and almost hit the water!" Pete said as he grabbed his suitcase out of the plane and shut the door. "I sure as hell never want to do that again! Let's go, I need a drink!"

After getting our passports stamped by a sleepy customs agent we were greeted by Orient Air's go-to guy in Santa Maria, Lou Victorino. Lou was an American expat who took care of the needs of the ferry pilots who stopped into Santa Maria. He was an interesting fellow who loved telling the story about how he spent six months manning a secret radio relay station in a cave in Libya during WWII. The details of the story changed with each telling but it was always entertaining. Visiting ferry pilots would bring him American magazines and any Country and Western 8-track tapes they could get their hands on.

We spent two days in Santa Maria waiting for a new vacuum pump to be shipped out to us. After installing it out on the ramp ourselves, completely illegal of course, we were on our way again.

Our next stop was Lisbon, Portugal, the final destination for the Duchess I was flying. I wasn't nervous at all about this leg. It was only 875 miles and we would be doing it all in daylight. I was already thinking of myself as an old hand at this ocean flying stuff.

After landing in Lisbon I was ecstatic. I'd made my first Atlantic crossing! The relief of having the ocean behind me was a huge weight off my shoulders. I dug my logbook out of my flight bag and scrawled MADE IT!! THAT'S ONE! In the comments section.

We met the new owner of the Duchess who was very excited to have his new airplane. He was especially happy to have gotten it before the end of the year for tax purposes, and seeing it was December 31st. We'd delivered it just in time.

That night we had a great New Year's Eve dinner at the new owner's house. I spent most of the night talking with the owner's beautiful daughter, Maria. Before we left she gave me a tiny metal statue of Saint Maria for good luck. I put the gift in my flight bag thinking that having a good luck charm wouldn't be a bad idea at all.

The next day Pete and I jumped into his 206 and flew to Mallorca, a beautiful island in the Mediterranean off the coast of Spain. There we met Pete's friend Onofre, a Captain for Air Europa and part-owner of a small flight school in Palma.

Before going through customs Pete told me that if anyone questioned the large amount of aircraft parts in the back of the plane I was to tell them that they were spare parts that went with the plane. I'd wondered why we had so many aircraft parts with us. In the nose compartment of the Duchess there'd been boxes of starters, magnetos and other various parts that we'd transferred to Pete's plane when we delivered the plane in Lisbon. Now Pete's warning made me a little suspicious.

"What do you mean, spare parts for the plane? I know that most of those parts are not for this plane. And anyway what difference would it make?" I asked.

"Well you see Onofre and I have a small aircraft parts importing business, and it's a lot cheaper to bring parts over with us rather than shipping them." Pete replied.

"Okay, but why tell customs that there are spare parts for the plane? What difference does it make?"

"The difference it makes is that if we call them spare parts we don't have to pay the import duty on them. So after we clear customs here we're going to fly over to Onofre's airport and unload the parts in his hangar where no one can see."

"So we're smugglers."

"No, we're just saving a little money on the outrageous import duty they charge here."

"Right, that's the definition of smuggling."

"Okay, if you want to get technical about it, we're smugglers." Pete said, staring at me, obviously wondering what I was going to do about it.

I thought about it for a few seconds as I saw the customs agents approaching the plane from across the ramp. Did I have a moral problem with smuggling parts into Spain? No, not really, but I sure didn't want to get thrown into a Spanish prison over it either. At that point I really didn't have much of a choice, did I? Of course I didn't really care. I kind of liked having the title of "international smuggler". It was kind of pirate-ish.

The customs agents gave the plane a brief look over but seeing that we were just in their country for fuel they didn't seem to care very much what was inside. After they left, Pete and I got back into the Cessna and flew the short ten miles to a small airport with no control tower. After landing we taxied the plane right into a large hangar where two men closed the big metal doors immediately after we were inside.

Well that didn't look very suspicious.

As we quickly unloaded the parts and stashed them in a parts locker my heart was beating faster than on the first takeoff from St. John's.

Now I get to add the job title of "smuggler" to my resume.

We pushed the Cessna back out onto the ramp, tied it down for the night and jumped into Onofre's car for a quick getaway. At least it seemed like a quick getaway, it turns out that Onofre always drove like someone's chasing him.

After a fabulous dinner at a seaside restaurant followed by a solid night of drinking some God awful local liquor I finally made it to my hotel room and flopped down on the bed, exhausted from the stress of the long day. As I lay there staring at the ceiling I wondered if every ferry trip was going to be this crazy. I was the one who wanted adventure wasn't I? Well, I sure as hell got one.

As we only had to fly to Switzerland the next day, both Pete and I decided to sleep in for a change, well mostly Pete. He's the boss after all so I deferred to his expertise. Late morning turned into early afternoon and by the time we got in the air it was late afternoon meaning most of the 500 mile flight to Zurich would be at night. Normally it wouldn't have been a big deal, not even any oceans to cross. But there was this little line of hills in our way called the Alps, and snow was forecast for the entire route. Because of course it was.

Flying through solid overcast and snow at twelve thousand feet, Pete and I were within an hour of landing when Center called and told us to intercept a VOR radial and track it inbound to Zurich. Ever since dropping off the Duchess I had been doing the job of a good co-pilot, changing radio frequencies, folding maps, navigating and tuning in any VOR radials we needed to use. I tuned in the next VOR radial on the number two receiver and the needle swung to the left indicating that we were still south of the intersection.

"Shit! We already passed it!" Pete swore as he banked the 206 to the right to turn around and go back to the intersection he thought we missed.

"No we didn't Pete! The needle is supposed to be to the left!" I said pointing at the VOR needle. "We're right where we're supposed to be!"

"No, we're not! The needle should be to the right if we're flying to the station!"

"No, Pete, we're still south of the intersection. Look here," I said as I tuned in the VOR to center the needle to show us what radial we were on. "See? We're on the 240 degree radial and the intersection is on the 280 degree radial."

The dim light from the instruments showed some confusion on Pete's face as he tried to look at the map I was holding, the VOR and fly the plane at the same time. Just then Zurich Center called us on the radio.

"One Juliet Bravo, Zurich Center, where are you going?"

"Sorry Zurich, we passed the intersection. We're turning back now." Pete answered.

"Negative one Juliet Bravo, you are still ten miles south of the intersection. Please return to your original course."

Pete swore and banked the 206 to turn back to the north toward the intersection. I was alarmed to see that instead of turning the plane to the right which would have completed a 360 degree turn and put us back on the airway, Pete turned us to the left. That maneuver put us on a parallel course to the airway we were supposed to be on but an unknown distance to the east.

I opened my mouth to express my opinion about our position but one look at Pete's face illuminated by the lights of the instrument panel made me refrain from pointing out any more of my boss's mistakes. Despite my silence I still wasn't happy about being so far off the airway at night, over the Alps, in a snowstorm.

As I was cross-tuning the VOR's to get our exact position I noticed the needle on the radar altimeter twitch. A radar altimeter is a great instrument to have when shooting low approaches, it is a very accurate way of determining exactly how high above the ground you are. But it has a max range of only five hundred feet, it certainly shouldn't be registering anything up at twelve thousand feet. I stared intently at the instrument to see if it moved again. A few seconds later it twitched again and before I could say anything the needle swung almost all the way around, stopped briefly at the fifty foot mark before returning to its normal position. It only took me a second to realize what had happened, we'd flown right over a mountain top, and just barely missed turning the plane, and us, into confetti.

"Holy crap!" I shouted, "We just flew over a mountain! Turn left and climb! CLIMB!"

This time Pete didn't argue. He'd seen the radar altimeter reading and knew just how close we'd come. We didn't speak as the altimeter showed us slowly gaining altitude. I switched on the landing light and strained forward in my harness, hoping to see any other killer mountains in our way but all I saw was thousands of snowflakes hitting the windscreen at 165 knots. If there was a mountain blocking our way we'd never see it in time. I switched off the landing light and waited. I tensed up and held my breath as the radar altimeter twitched again. Somewhere in the dark, rock and ice passed less than 500 feet below, threatening to blot us from the night sky. But the needle on the radar altimeter dropped back to its normal position and stayed there.

Two minutes later we were back on course and back to having only the normal dangers of flying a small single engine plane over the Alps, at night, in a snowstorm. The incident hung in the cockpit like a shroud. Pete and I both knew what a close call we'd just had. We also both knew who'd been right and who'd been wrong. The embarrassing silence between us was broken only by the necessary radio calls. After a few minutes the tension eased. An unspoken agreement passed between us, we'd had a close call and learned something from it. And more importantly, to me anyway, I'd proven myself as a pilot and gained Pete's respect.

Two days later I was sitting in an Air France jet over the middle of the Atlantic drinking Tuborg beer and looking down at the ocean. It seemed strange that just a few days before I was heading the other way and wondering if I was going to die or not. I spent a lot of time thinking about the trip after dropping off Pete's plane at a cool little 2200 foot airstrip carved into a Swiss mountainside. To say the trip had been interesting and exciting would be the understatement of the century. It was also exactly the kind of adventure I was looking for when I became a pilot. But I couldn't deny that it was extremely dangerous and there was a good chance of getting killed doing it. Was the adventure worth the risk? I tried to tell myself that I was giving it careful consideration, weighing all the options before making up my mind to take another ferry flight over the ocean. But who was I kidding? I signaled the flight attendant for another beer and looked back out the window.

Wild horses couldn't keep me from doing that again.

BLUE SKIES

"Aviation in itself is not inherently dangerous. But to an even greater degree than the sea, it is terribly unforgiving of carelessness, incapacity, or neglect."
- Captain A. G. Lamplugh

When I got back from my first trip I couldn't wait to head out to the dropzone and tell all my friends about it. The skydivers I hung out with were a particularly hard bunch to impress, but I was sure that having flown a small airplane across the Atlantic would do the trick.

As I pulled into the parking lot I saw Quazy takeoff in his Cessna 182. I didn't see anyone in the back so I presumed he was just hopping over to the local airport to pick up a load of jumpers. It was a common practice for us to use the hard surface runway at the Osceola airport whenever the club's runway got too muddy on warm winter days. The skydivers still landed back at the dropzone where they would pack their parachutes before shuttling back to the airport to do it all over again.

I was slightly disappointed because Pat "Quazy" Quasnick was one of my best friends and mentors and I was excited to tell him all about my trip across the ocean. Quazy gave me my very first flying job hauling jumpers in his beat up 1955 Cessna 182. He'd just purchased the land the jump club was located on and was in the process of making it a full-scale commercial operation. The two of us spent a lot of time together, working on his plane and the clubhouse, trying to make his dream of a successful skydiving operation come true. He was also the captain of our competition, eight-way jump team. Quazy taught me almost everything I knew about skydiving.

I walked into the clubhouse and the first person I ran into was JQ. I'd been particularly looking forward to telling JQ about my trip. Not only had he been my flying mentor for the previous three years but just before I left he told me that he was going to hire me as a full-time corporate pilot. I was ecstatic. I'd worked hard to become a professional pilot and while flying small planes around the world would surely lead to some grand adventures, flying a corporate jet would definitely be better for my career in the long run. And I'd get to fly a jet!

As I approached JQ I was just a little full of myself, expecting him to heap praise on me for my incredible achievement. Instead he came up to me and said, "Food, folks and fun."

"What the heck is that supposed to mean?" I asked suspiciously, knowing that it was going to be some kind of dig.

"I hear McDonald's is hiring." He said with a smirk.

"That's got to be a safer way to make a living than flying over the ocean!" he said laughing.

I laughed with him at his joke but inside I was a little hurt that my idol didn't seem very impressed with what I thought was a pretty big achievement.

I talked to JQ for a few minutes about my trip and my upcoming job flying with him in the jet. Then he left with

Curt, Gary, and Christy, three of my skydiving buddies, to drive to the airport to meet Quazy in his 182.

About an hour after the gang left for the airport the phone rang. It was JQ's mother asking if he was there. I instinctively looked out the window while telling her that he was up on a load but he should be down soon. There was an ominous pause before she told me that she'd heard that there had been a plane crash at the airport and would I please have Johnny call her as soon as he got down to let her know he was okay.

After hanging up I realized that my friends had been gone an awfully long time. A few of the jumpers and I went outside to see if we could see the jumpers or hear the overdue plane.

The crystal clear sky was eerily quiet and empty as we stood there straining to hear the faint hum of a Cessna on jump run. A sense of foreboding and unease came over us as the minutes ticked by.

When we couldn't stand it any longer, three of us jumped into my car and sped off towards the airport. As we got close we saw the flashing lights of fire trucks along a road near the runway. There were six or seven firefighters clustered around a crumpled mass of twisted metal in the middle of a snow covered field. I could tell by the way the firefighters were just milling around with no sense of urgency that it was bad. I steeled myself, expecting no survivors.

I parked the car and walked up to the crash scene with my head down, not wanting to see . . . anything. Wishing I was somewhere else. As I got closer I kept repeating to myself "Just let me see paint, just let me see paint."

Because the previous summer Quazy and I had stripped all the paint off the jump plane. If there was any paint on the wreckage, then my friends were alive.

When I got to the wreckage I reluctantly lifted my head and looked at the crumpled mass of metal. A huge flood of relief washed over me. The twisted wing lying on the ground in front of me was painted white. White. It was white. It couldn't be our plane.

"Thank you God." I said.

I felt guilty about being relieved that someone else's friends were dead and not mine as I shifted my gaze to the rest of the twisted and crumpled aircraft. Then I saw something that turned my relief to horror. Perched like a throne on top of the crumpled pile of metal was an aircraft seat with a stained white bottom and an ugly orange back pad. I knew that seat. I knew that seat well. It was the pilot's seat for Quazy's airplane. I'd spent many long hours flying jumpers in that seat. I was confused. How could a seat from an airplane with no paint on it be surrounded by painted wreckage? I took a few steps closer hoping to be wrong about the seat, but my hopes were soon dashed. Lying face down in the wreckage was a body with a red and gray jumpsuit. I knew that jumpsuit well too. It was JQ.

Shock set in as I stared at the body, I couldn't believe what was happening. I looked at the wreckage again and finally figured out why there was paint on some of the metal. The wreckage I was looking at wasn't from one plane, but two. I was looking at the remains of a mid-air collision.

But my time for personal grief had to wait as JQ's brother came running up wanting to know if he was dead. I was immediately transformed from a shocked victim into a grief counselor. I told him the news and tried to help him cope with the loss of his brother as I desperately looked around for survivors. I had to have hope. My friends had all been wearing parachutes and it was reasonable to think that some of them might have gotten out. But no. The fire fighters soon told me that no one had survived. In an instant, five of my best friends were gone. Just like that.

I left John's brother and reluctantly went over to John's house for the hardest job yet, telling his wife and three young kids that JQ wasn't coming home.

Even though JQ's wife was also a skydiver and used to dealing with the high cost of aviation, it still wasn't a pretty scene. At one point I was with John's oldest son who was sobbing in his room. He asked me, now that his dad was dead, who was going to teach him to fly. I looked him in the eye and made a solemn vow to teach him to fly someday.

The FAA investigation revealed what led to the tragedy. Quazy, in his high-wing jump plane, took off from the Osceola airport and began a steep climb to the south in the cool winter air. At the same time a low wing Piper Cherokee being flown by a student and his instructor was approaching the airport from the west, at the unusually low altitude of five hundred feet. The combination of low and high wing put each plane in the other's blind spot. As they approached each other on a collision course neither pilot had more than a second or two to see and avoid the other by the time they came into view. The Cherokee's propeller hit Quazy's plane dead center in the passenger door where JQ was sitting. The impact was catastrophic and none of my friends had time to get out of the twisted mass of aluminum before it crashed to the ground. They never had a chance to use their parachutes.

What followed was once again one of the hardest and most painful periods of my life. It came to be known in the skydiving community as the "Funeral Boogie Week". A boogie is when skydivers get together to jump and party with each other for some sort of special occasion. It's usually a great time with lots of skydives made and gallons of beer consumed. But this time it was a week of funerals. We laughed, we cried, we lifted our glasses to toast our friends and celebrated their lives.

A week later I was back in the air, flying a Cessna 182 to Italy on my second ferry trip. Pete had asked me if I was ready to start flying again or if I needed some time off. I told him that the best place for me to be was back in the air. Pete understood and gave me the next available trip.

My first stop after leaving St. Paul was Moncton, Canada, where I was to get tested for a waiver to ferry single engine aircraft over the ocean. The Canadian government requires pilots flying single engine aircraft over the Atlantic to prove that they know what they're doing, or at least have some clue as to what they're getting themselves into.

When I met the inspector in Moncton he wasted few friendly words on me before sticking his nose into the Cessna and inspecting the fuel system. Typically a small aircraft doesn't have the range to safely make even the shortest legs of an ocean crossing. To extend that range the mechanics at Orient Air would remove the rear passenger seats, install large, metal ferry tanks and connect them to the aircraft's fuel system. The Cessna I was flying had two sixty gallon tanks installed that increased the endurance to fifteen hours.

After he looked over the fuel system the inspector took me inside to quiz me on ocean flying. He made sure I knew about the types of weather I might encounter over the Atlantic and what to do if I ran into adverse conditions such as icing or unexpected headwinds. We covered survival gear, navigation and how to make proper position reports.

It might not seem like it's any of Canada's business if a ferry pilot knows what he's doing while flying over international waters. But since they were the ones sending out the search and rescue aircraft whenever a pilot went down, they decided that anyone departing from one of their airports had to be prepared. I guess they were getting tired of sending their people out on risky rescue missions looking for pilots who had no idea what they were doing.

After convincing the inspector that I sort of knew what I was doing he gave me a temporary single engine waiver to cross the Atlantic.

The requirements for being issued a permanent waiver were simple, survive two crossings in a single engine aircraft. If you made it that far, you either knew what you were doing, or were very lucky, either way was fine with them.

The inspector handed me my paperwork and wished me luck. As I walked back to the plane to head out I wondered how many pilots he'd given waivers to who never made it home. That kind of responsibility had to be hard on a man.

Preparing for a crossing at the St. John's airport was starting to become routine after only one trip. The first thing I did when I landed was fuel up so I didn't have to try and get it done at 5 AM the next morning. This was often easier said than done. The wing tanks were easy, it's the ferry tanks that can be tricky. Getting the large fuel nozzles to fit in between the top of the ferry tank and the roof of the cabin was often difficult and sometimes impossible. In the case of impossible, we'd bring along homemade funnels made out of PVC pipe or whatever we could cobble together. And of course, filling the ferry tanks often resulted in fuel spilled inside the cabin. Another good reason to fuel up the night before. That way the fumes had time to disperse.

After fueling, the next stop was the MET (meteorological) office to get a weather outlook for the next day and to schedule a briefing for the morning. The guys at the St. John's MET office were the best in the business. They would spend as much time as you needed explaining the changing weather patterns and winds aloft that would affect your trip. I was especially grateful for their help on my first few solo trips when I had to make my decisions based on their experience of briefing hundreds of ferry pilots. They wouldn't exactly tell the inexperienced pilots not to go if the conditions were unsafe, but they would conduct their briefing in such a manner as to leave you with no question as to what their opinion was.

After the MET office, it was time to take a taxi to the Radisson Hotel in downtown St. John's. One of the great things about working for Pete Demos and Orient Air was that Pete took good care of his pilots. Most of the other ferry companies gave their pilots a per diem for food and lodging which resulted in guys sleeping in their planes and eating peanut butter to save money. Pete, however, paid for everything. He put us up in good hotels and paid for good meals. He would even allow us to put a few drinks on the dinner tab, although I did see him get pretty mad at a pilot who on one trip put five or six drinks on his dinner bill. Pete wasn't upset about how much the pilot drank. He was upset about the fact that the pilot was in Iceland where drinks cost about eight dollars each.

One of the tips Pete gave me when he trained me was to bring a bottle of my favorite booze with me on the trip. That bottle would come in handy if I got stuck somewhere for a few days due to weather or aircraft problems. I could have a few drinks without breaking the bank. It also came in handy for a nightcap before trying to get some sleep. As I was to learn during my ferry flying career, sleep, or the lack of it, would be a constant battle. The first challenge was to get to sleep the night before a crossing.

After checking into the hotel, and stuffing myself at their wonderful seafood buffet, I went back up to my room to go over my plans for the morning. There was depressingly little to check over. My survival gear and flight gear were in the airplane and I wouldn't get any kind of updated weather forecast until the next morning. I paced around the hotel room trying to think of anything I might have forgotten. Although I had a hard time admitting it, I was still a little nervous about flying over the ocean.

After the experience of my first flight with Pete, I realized that flying over thousands of miles of ocean was anything but a walk in the park. On that trip Pete had lost his vacuum pump in a Cessna very similar to the one I was flying. That problem, although serious, would be minor compared to the fix I'd be in if I developed major engine trouble half way to the Azores.

As much as I tried, I just couldn't get over the fact that it would only take the failure of one of the hundreds of moving parts in my engine to put me in the drink. Despite carrying a life raft and thick neoprene survival suit, I was under no illusions about my chances for survival if I ended up in the Atlantic in the winter time. Pete had two pilots ditch in the ocean in the three years prior to my first crossing. They both had the same survival gear I had. And they were both still at the bottom of the Atlantic.

I had good reason to be concerned about the reliability of the Continental engine in the Cessna 182 I was flying. The previous summer I had lost an engine flying skydivers in a plane exactly like the one I was about to fly over the ocean.

I'd just taken off from our dropzone's dirt strip with a full load of jumpers and was climbing through 2,300 feet when the engine suddenly started shaking violently. Instinctively, I turned back toward the runway and yanked the throttle back to keep the engine from coming off its mounts completely. My mind raced as I tried to think of anything I could do to change the situation but it only took a few seconds to realize we were going down.

As I was looking at the airport trying to determine if I was going to make the runway, one of the jumpers behind me tapped me on the shoulder asked me if they could get out.

"You're still here?!" I yelled.

I was astonished. The horribly violent shaking and my chopping the power should've been a dead giveaway to the fact that we were going down. Most skydivers would've been long gone by now or at least have been ready to jump, but instead, the jumper sitting next to the door was calmly putting his gloves and altimeter on, taking his sweet old time. More importantly, he was blocking the door. I looked at our altitude and was shocked to see that we were passing through 1500 feet and dropping fast. By the time the guy next to the door got his act together and opened the door we'd be below 1000 feet. Too low to jump.

The look on the jumpers' faces when I told them that they would have to ride the plane down with me said it all. Skydivers are scared to death of having to land with the plane under the best of circumstances. A dead stick landing in a disabled plane into a short dirt strip was certainly not something they were looking forward to.

It looked like I'd be able to glide the plane back to the dropzone's short, dirt strip, but that didn't mean I was out of the woods. If I turned in on final too far from the runway I'd come up short and hit the ditch bordering the front of the dirt strip and we'd be dead for sure. If I set up too high and fast, I'd overshoot the runway and end up going through the fence at the end of the runway, into a roughly plowed field and probably flip over. That probably wouldn't kill us. But the post crash fire? That might.

My heart was beating a mile a minute as I lined up for landing. I was a little fast as the ditch flashed beneath my nose. I forced the wheels down with a thump and a splash of mud and got on the brakes as hard as I could without locking them up. It might not have been the smoothest, but it sure was the best landing I'd ever made. I started breathing again as the plane slid to a stop. The jumpers piled out of the plane like puppies, overjoyed at surviving the close call but still pretty mad at the slow poke who'd blocked their escape.

The cause of the engine malfunction turned out to be a piston that self-destructed inside the cylinder. The mechanic who looked at it told me that with the amount of oil the engine was leaking I was lucky to get as far as I did.

So with that incident weighing on my mind I checked my maps and did a few fuel burn calculations for my second ocean crossing. If the winds aloft forecast was accurate, I'd have plenty of fuel to make Santa Maria Island. If not, well . . . . With nothing left to check and satisfied that I was as prepared as I could be, I climbed into bed and turned off the lights.

It soon became evident that sleep might be hard to come by. I just couldn't shut my brain off. What would I do if the engine quit right in the middle of the ocean? How could I improve my chances of survival? I could fly as high as possible so that if I ran into trouble I would have as much time as possible to either fix the problem or call for help. Maybe someone knew the location of any ships in the area. That might be good to know. I told myself to remember to ask someone about that in the morning.

The biggest problem bothering me was ditching. I'd read various opinions about the best method for ditching at sea. Land parallel to the swells, land on the downhill side of a swell or try and stall it in tail first. None of them sounded like much fun.

Over the years I'd seen a lot of videos of pilots ditching their aircraft into the ocean during WWII. The landings never seemed very soft. Most looked fairly violent. And these were highly trained Navy pilots ditching retractable gear aircraft. I was pretty sure that if I had to ditch the 182 it would flip over on its back as soon as its fixed landing gear hit the water. That meant that if I survived the impact and was still conscious I'd have to get my seat belt off, grab my life raft and survival bag, force the door open and worm my way out. I would have to do all this while the airplane was being tossed about in heavy seas, sinking, and probably upside down.

To make matters worse when the ferry tanks were installed, they had to be located as far forward as possible to keep the center of gravity within limits. That meant putting one of the tanks right behind the pilot's seat, which pushed the seat almost all the way up to the instrument panel. Hell, I had a hard time getting out of the plane while it was sitting on the ramp. How was I going to get out of that plane if I had to ditch? I figured my odds of getting out of the 182 with my raft were fifty-fifty at best. Sixty-forty? Less?

As I lay in the dark going over and over the scenarios of doom, the glowing green lights of the clock radio ticked off the sleepless hours.

If I did get out of the plane with the raft, how would I inflate it and keep from drifting away before I could climb in? Would I be able to get in the raft if I was injured? How would anyone find me? I'd definitely need my survival bag because my portable emergency locator transmitter was in it. Without that there would be almost no chance that anyone would find me. Scratch that, no chance. Should I try and zip it inside my survival suit instead?

I could picture myself lying in my raft at night, riding the swells, waiting for rescue that would never come. Or struggling to get out of the plane as it slowly sank beneath, or.........

"AARRGGGG!!! STOP THINKING ABOUT THAT STUFF!!"

If I didn't get some sleep I wouldn't be worth a damn in the morning. I think I was still trying to figure out what heading I would need to sail my raft to Tahiti when the phone rang with my wake up call. I'd gotten maybe four hours of sleep. Not the best way to start an ocean crossing.

Seven hours later I was halfway to Santa Maria, flying along under smooth sunny skies and wondering just what I'd been so worried about. The takeoff and departure from St. John's had gone smoothly. The weather over the Atlantic was great and the plane was running perfectly. I didn't have a care in the world. This ferry flying stuff wasn't that scary once you got used to it. I settled in for a nice relaxing 10 hour flight.

Later that afternoon, I was cleaning up the cockpit after having a delicious junk food lunch when the engine coughed once, then ran smooth again. My head snapped up. The engine then ran very rough for five or six seconds before running smoothly again. I couldn't have jumped higher if you'd jabbed me in the butt with a cattle prod.

"NO! NO! NO! This can't be happening!"

I quickly scanned the engine instruments while frantically pulling my orange survival suit on. My heart was racing as I pulled the heavy rubberized zipper up to my chin and pulled the neoprene hood over my head.

In between instrument checks I tried to figure out my exact latitude and longitude in case I needed to send out a mayday. I kicked myself for being lazy and not plotting my position more often than the mandatory reporting points dictated. But really, what could I have done? There was nothing to fix my position on. All I really knew was that I was 5.7 hours out from St. John's. Without a sextant any position report I gave was pure speculation.

I sat breathlessly waiting for the other shoe to drop while trying to check everything at once. The instruments showed nothing wrong and the sound of the engine was as strong and steady as it had been since leaving Minnesota. As the minutes ticked by I began to relax just a bit. After another hour I pulled the survival suit back down to my waist.

The rest of the trip to Santa Maria was uneventful, except that I was continuously checking the engine instruments and plotting my position every fifteen minutes. I had no idea if the engine was going to quit or not, but if it did I was going to be as ready as I could be.

Once safe on the ramp in Santa Maria, I pulled the cowling off the nose of the plane and inspected the engine. I checked everything I could think of, but I couldn't figure out what might have caused the momentary loss of power in the engine. It might have been just a small amount of water in the fuel or something equally simple. Or perhaps someone just wanted to remind me not to get too cocky and complacent when flying over the Atlantic. Whatever the reason, message received, loud and clear! If you wanted a long career in the ferry business then you'd better stay on your toes.

The next day I left the Azores for another long ocean leg. The scare I had with the engine the previous day was weighing heavily on my mind. I wasn't happy with the fact that I had no idea if anything was really wrong with the plane. With no further information with which to base my decision on whether to go or not, I really had no choice but to press on and hope for the best. The job was becoming a little more stressful than I'd imagined.

The 182 ran great for the nine hour leg from Santa Maria to my next stop, the historic Rock of Gibraltar. Stopping at that landmark reminded me that despite the dangers, being a ferry pilot was pretty damn adventurous.

After landing I noticed the single runway had a unique feature I'd never seen before. Due to the limited space available on the peninsula the British were forced to route the only road to the mainland right through the middle of the runway. Whenever a plane was landing or taking off, barriers came down to stop traffic, just like at a railroad crossing. Seeing two long lines of cars and trucks waiting on either side of you was a great incentive to clear the runway as quickly as you could.

The next day all I had left to cover was a final thousand miles of Mediterranean before I could put my second ferry flight in the completed file. The barriers went down stopping traffic as I taxied onto the runway and brought the 182 up to full power and took off. I made one circuit around the ancient fortress then headed east over the clear blue waters of the Mediterranean. I was really starting to like this job.

The forecast for my route that day called for moderate tail winds above ten thousand feet and a line of scattered thunderstorms in between Mallorca and Corsica. I climbed up to thirteen thousand feet and settled in for what I hoped was an uneventful nine hour flight.

Six hours later my hopes for an easy final leg were gone. The line of thunderstorms I'd been warned about were blocking the route to Italy and didn't look scattered to me. The towering thunderheads weren't nearly as high and menacing as the huge thunderstorms I was used to seeing in the plains of the Midwest but they were still dangerous. I picked a low area between two buildups and plunged in.

The turbulence started almost immediately. I tightened my seat belt and concentrated on the instruments in a futile attempt to keep the plane on its assigned heading and altitude. Shortly after entering the clouds, a frosty haze of ice started building up on the windshield. I looked out the side window and I saw that a layer of rime ice was building up on the leading edge of the wings and the landing gear.

Picking up ice really got my attention because encountering icing conditions in a small plane like the Cessna 182 is considered an emergency situation because the anti-ice systems are almost nonexistent. They consisted of a heated pitot tube to keep the flight instruments functioning and a windshield defroster that will do next to nothing in heavy ice. I wondered if I could open the side window and scrape at it with my fingernails if the ice got too thick.

As ice accumulates on the leading edge of the wings, the airflow gets disturbed, reducing their ability to produce lift. Add to that the increased weight of the ice itself accumulating on the exposed sections of the airframe and it doesn't take long before the plane is going down, whether you like it or not. And if your windshield is still iced over when you break out of the clouds then you won't be able to see anything as you try to pick out a place to crash. I don't know, maybe it's less scary that way.

As I penetrated deeper into the clouds the layer of ice continued to build. Normally, the correct response to flying into icing conditions would be to immediately turn around. But I decided to keep going. I figured if the ice got too bad I could just descend to the warmer air over the Mediterranean where the ice would melt quickly. (Okay, "should" melt quickly). It was a plan. Not a great plan, but a plan.

After being in icing conditions for fifteen or twenty minutes the wings had picked up about two inches of bumpy rime ice. The 182 had been slowed by twenty-five knots, but so far I was able to hold altitude.

Suddenly, there was a sharp BANG from the front of the plane followed by intense vibration.

Oh great! Here we go again!

I quickly scanned the engine instruments for signs of trouble but found nothing wrong. The shaking seemed to be coming from the propeller so I reduced power. The vibration dropped a little, but was still alarming. The lessening of the shaking wasn't the only result of reducing power, the Cessna started losing altitude at about five hundred feet per minute. At that rate I would hit the water in minutes if nothing changed.

Grabbing my map I could see that I was still over one hundred miles from the coast of Sardinia, too far to glide if I lost my engine completely. I wasn't really all that worried yet. I knew that as I descended into the warmer air below, most, if not all, of the ice would melt off quickly. And at the lower power setting the vibration didn't seem all that bad. Maybe I was being too optimistic, but it seemed that I had things under control. Since I was already going down, I called air traffic control and requested permission to descend to a lower altitude. I didn't want to declare an emergency just yet. I was willing to see how the hand played out.

A few minutes later the 182 broke out of the clouds into bright sunshine, leaving the line of thunderstorms and ice laden clouds behind. I descended about two thousand feet and the ice started flying off the wing in big chunks as the warm air worked its magic. My altitude stabilized and things were starting to look up. By the time I started my descent into Rome the ice was completely gone. I'd gotten so used to the slight vibration coming from the front of the airplane that I didn't even notice it anymore.

After landing I inspected the front of the aircraft and discovered the source of the vibration. The cone-shaped spinner attached to the propeller had a two-inch strip of metal missing around the edge of the propeller. The damage was probably caused by ice building up unevenly on the spinner, causing an imbalance. When it finally let go, it took some metal with it. I felt bad about the damage.

Probably shouldn't play around in the ice in someone else's airplane.

My second ferry trip was completed and I was happy to turn the keys over to Ricardo, Pete's longtime friend and customer. Ricardo was the quintessential Italian businessman. Sporting a full head of jet black hair, he always dressed impeccably in expensive suits and couldn't talk at all without waving his hands. He was also a great host. He put me up in a four-star hotel in downtown Rome and took me to a gourmet restaurant where I had a truly amazing seafood dinner. After being treated like a king I was definitely looking forward to delivering more planes to Ricardo, as long as I didn't have to drive with him.

On the morning I was to fly back home to Minnesota, Ricardo was late picking me up from my hotel to drive me to the airport. The ensuing ride was by far the most dangerous part of my trip. The flashy Italian weaved in and out of traffic, cutting cars off and reaching speeds over one hundred miles an hour. While he was driving like a maniac, he was also having a heated conversation on his car phone. He was holding the handset in one hand and waiving a giant cigar around with the other, leaving no hands on the wheel. I was very happy to arrive at the airport in one piece.

On the long flight back from Europe I had time to think about the flying I'd been doing and the options I had. I loved the adventure and romance that went with ferry flying, but realized that it wasn't a job that I could make a career out of. There just wasn't enough money in it. I was being paid one thousand dollars for a trip to Europe. Not a bad amount for doing what you love and having the most exciting job in the world. But I'd be lucky to do two trips a month, even if Pete had the customers to keep me that busy. Also, I wasn't Pete's only pilot, as a matter of fact, I was the low man on the totem pole when it came to bidding trips. It didn't take a math whiz to realize that if I wanted to make enough money to buy a house and raise a family, both things I really wanted to do someday, I was going to eventually have to get a job flying for the airlines or a private corporation. Someone else would have to go on amazing adventures around the world.

When I got back home I immediately went to Horton Manufacturing's flight department to see if there still was a chance of getting a job flying their jet. I hadn't gone in to check on the job immediately after JQ's accident because it just seemed like it would be disrespectful to be concerned about a job when one of my best friends had just been killed. For the second time in one year, I found myself applying for a job to replace a dead pilot. JQ told me he was going to hire me despite my low time and experience because he knew that I was a good pilot. Unfortunately with JQ's death, I had lost my friend on the inside, and the new chief pilot, who had never liked JQ, glanced at my resume and shook his head.

"You might have been John's buddy and maybe he promised you a job as co-pilot but you don't have nearly the experience we're looking for." He handed me back my resume and said without much sincerity, "Maybe give us a call when you have more experience."

I left Horton's flight department dejected. Without a friend on the inside my chances of getting a corporate flying job anywhere were next to zero. And with only fifteen hundred hours of flying time I wasn't going to get hired by the airlines anytime soon. It looked like I was going to be a full time ferry pilot for a while whether I liked it or not. *Oh darn.*

POWERLESS

"A pilot who says he has never been frightened in an airplane is, I'm afraid, lying."
- Louise Thaden

During the summer of 1991 I'd been flying for Orient Air for seven months and was starting to think of myself as an old hand in the ferry flying business. Well, not a complete rookie anyway. I had a large globe at home that I used to keep track of all my flights. I traced the route of each of my flights on the globe every time I returned from a trip. The globe was my pride and joy and was starting to get an impressive spiderweb of black lines across its surface. But there was one continent that was still unmarked, Africa. I knew I'd finally get my chance to remedy that situation when I walked into Orient Air's office and saw my name on the big, white planning board. I was disappointed to see Cessna 210 listed as the aircraft type, but under destination were the words Dodoma, Tanzania. The customer was a company called Mission Aviation Fellowship. They provide pilots and aircraft to missionaries all over the world. The trip to Tanzania would be the most challenging one I'd attempted so far. It included two extremely long legs that would push to the limits the range of the ferry fuel supply, my endurance and my rear end.

The Cessna 210 is one of the nicest single engine planes out there. It can carry a decent load, has good range and because of its retractable landing gear, it's reasonably fast. And this one had the bonus of having a panel mounted GPS unit, an unbelievable luxury.

The trip started off great. The first two days were fun and easy. Good weather, strong west winds and a fast plane made the St. Paul to Bangor leg quick. I even landed early enough to have my favorite dinner, fresh Maine lobster. The next day was the same, if not easier. I got to enjoy my second favorite dinner, the large seafood buffet at the St. John's Radisson. Both Maine and Newfoundland are known for their fresh seafood and I was in heaven.

Day three was more of the same. Halfway to Santa Maria I was fat, dumb and happy, thinking that if things kept going the way they were, the trip would be a breeze. It was about then that I started to get that feeling. You know, that feeling that no pilot flying a small plane ever wants to feel. That feeling that no pilot in a small plane without a bathroom ever wants to feel. That feeling that no pilot in a small plane, without a bathroom and nowhere to land for hours and hours, ever wants to feel? Yeah, that feeling.

Now I'm not talking about having to urinate. I have to do that all the time in the plane. There's no way to comfortably fly for ten hours at a time without having to relieve yourself. Especially if you like to drink coffee and diet soda to help keep you awake on those long flights. One of the very first things Pete taught me was to always bring along a piss jug. "No sense flying all day with your back teeth floating." He said. I took his advice on the first two trips, but I didn't like the jug method. Oh, it worked fine when you needed to use it. The problem I had with it was having to walk into the airport carrying a jug filled with yellow liquid. It's embarrassing.

So I came up with my own method, Ziploc baggies. They work great! Well, okay, anyway. Granted, filling them can be tricky, especially if you don't have an autopilot. (You kind of need three hands for that.) Once it's full, seal it up and you're all done! A nice, neat package. Always use two bags though. You're going to have to trust me on that one.

The Ziploc method has its advantages. Number one: You don't ever have to walk around an airport with a stinky piss jug. Full or empty everyone knows what it is. Number two: It's easy to always have some with you. I just throw a box in my flight bag once a year and never run out. That way you avoid having to do the whole, fill up an empty Coke can and hope it doesn't spill for the rest of the flight, thing. Best of all, number three: You can bomb ships with the full bags. You see, once you manage to fill a bag and get it sealed, you'll want to get rid of it before you land. All you have to do is open the window and chuck it outside. No muss. No fuss.

Unless you're a bored ferry pilot. Then you might want to save it for some juicy target. Like a ship in the middle of the ocean. Good fun. I don't think I ever hit one or even came close but I gave it my best shot.

No, that wasn't the feeling that was bothering me that day. It was the other one. So far I'd managed to avoid that particular situation. That day things were just not going to be denied. I'm pretty sure the third or fourth trip to the seafood buffet in St. John's the night before had been a bad idea. But fear not, as much as I'd been dreading that moment I'd given it lots of thought and had come prepared.

I got out two big plastic grocery bags I had along for just such an occasion and lined them with a generous amount of paper towels. Then I pushed my survival suit onto the floor, undid my pants, squatted over the bag on the seat and took care of business. It was uncomfortable, gross and I gagged a little. (It smelled way worse than any outhouse.) But I got the job done. Afterwards, I tied a knot in the top of the plastic bag, and had a neat little package. I was pretty proud of myself when it was all done. All I had left to do was get rid of it. I sure as heck wasn't going to wait for a target ship (I'm not that big of a jerk.) I just opened up the side window and carefully tossed the package out. Carefully, but not carefully enough. As I tossed the bag out it caught on the chrome window latch and tore open. Then the one hundred and fifty mile an hour airflow did the rest.

CRAP!

Crap indeed. Instead of being forever sealed in that bag and sinking to the bottom of the ocean, the contents of the bag were instead sprayed all over the side of a brand new airplane, on its way to Africa. *Great.* When I landed in Morocco the crap on the side of the plane had dried to a concrete like crust that stubbornly refused to come off. So yeah, maybe I'd skip the buffet next time.

The first long leg after crossing the Atlantic is from Agadir Morocco down to Abidjan, Ivory Coast. The leg is almost 2,000 miles across the barren and uninhabited Sahara Desert. In order to have enough fuel to cover that distance I'd have to fly the little Cessna at its max range power setting. The slow airspeed of the maximum range power setting meant the leg to Abidjan would take me almost 15 hours! And just to make things interesting, I had to fly it at night. The Ivory Coast is located right on the legendary Intertropical Convergence Zone. It's an area that runs along the Equator and spawns massive thunderstorms every afternoon. If you don't want to show up while the thunderstorms are making their daily appearance you have to takeoff just after sunset and fly all night so you arrive in the morning when the weather is usually calm.

With that in mind I scheduled my weather briefing for 8:00pm with a 9:00pm departure. When I walked into the dusty wood shack posing as the Met office, I wasn't surprised to find no one there to brief me on the weather I would encounter on my 15-hour flight over the Sahara.

Written on a dusty broken chalkboard I saw the tail number of my plane, and the current weather in Agadir,

"Some briefing," I mumbled, "I can look outside and see that."

Scribbled below was a forecast for Abidjan for early the next morning calling for scattered to broken clouds at 2000 feet and light winds.

At least it's something.

I looked around the room in a vain search for something that might tell me what winds aloft might be along my route. The one room shack had nothing of any value hidden in its shambles so I gave up and walked back outside. I wasn't very happy about the prospect of flying across half a continent with no idea of how long it might take me, or what weather I might encounter.

I was one frustrated pilot filling out my flight plan. I hesitated when I came to the box marked ETE (estimated time en route). The distance from Morocco to the Ivory Coast is almost 1800 miles. A difference of 10 knots would change my flight time by over an hour. Without a winds aloft forecast, whatever I put in that box would be nothing more than a wild guess. In the end I put down fourteen hours and ten minutes. I added the extra ten minutes to make my estimate look authentic.

While the controller looked over the fight plan I'd given him, the ancient black rotary phone sitting on his cluttered desk rang. Putting down his cigarette, the Moroccan picked up the phone and had a short conversation in french. It seemed to have something to do with me by the way he kept glancing up at me. After he hung up the phone the controller handed me my copy of the flight plan.

"This is good, but you must leave immediately." He said.

"Sure, that's not a problem, but what's the rush?" I asked.

"Sirocco coming, the airport will be closed soon."

"Sirocco?"

"Yes Sir, Sirocco . . . aaaaa . . . how you say.........
Haboob......sandstorm."

That got my attention. I'd never seen a sandstorm before, but the thought of flying into one at night one didn't appeal to me in the slightest.

"How long until it gets here?" I asked.

"Less than one hour, it's coming from the east so if you leave soon and head south you should be okay."

I wasted no time getting to the airplane and doing a quick preflight. I was disgusted to see that everything was already covered with a thick coating of fine red dust. It took one full bottle of my precious water just to get the windscreen clean enough to see through. I climbed in feeling even more uneasy about the flight I was about to take.

I contacted the tower, and quickly taxied to the runway. I'd had to deal with many different kinds of adverse weather conditions before, but being chased out of a country by a sandstorm was a new one. I did my run-up and before takeoff checklist on the fly and rolled onto the runway as the tower cleared me for immediate departure.

At 25 percent over maximum gross weight, the heavy Cessna didn't exactly leap into the muggy night air. As the final 1000 foot marker flashed by, I managed to drag the plane into the hazy, dark sky. Looking out the window I tried to see the approaching sandstorm but it was getting too dark to see very far. A heavy blanket of dust hung in the air cutting visibility down to less than three miles, making the lights of the city look fuzzy.

"November four niner four two Charlie, we show you off at two two four five zulu. You're cleared to eleven thousand feet, frequency change approved. The airport is now closed. Good night."

I looked back over my shoulder and watched the last of the city lights disappear in the gloom. "The airport is now closed." It felt like a door being slammed shut behind me.

I turned on the HF radio that was resting on top of the fuel tank loosely held in place with a few bungee cords and some duct tape. Contacting Morocco Control, I gave them my position report including my altitude, location, estimated time of my next report and endurance. My next reporting point was over two hours away.

Leveling out at 11,000 feet, I reduced power to maximum range setting and checked my ground speed. 128 knots. Oof. Painfully slow. At that speed the Ivory Coast was 14 hours away. I was able to determine my ground speed accurately because the Cessna's brand new panel mounted GPS was working perfectly. It was nice having a unit that had an antenna mounted on top of the aircraft. So far it hadn't lost the satellite signal once. The early handheld units frequently lost signal, forcing me to wave them around the cockpit trying to scoop up electrons.

When I'd started ferry flying the GPS system was just becoming operational, and none of the ferry pilots I knew had one yet. Until then we'd been flying over the ocean with nothing to guide us but a compass and a watch. With no landmarks or navigation beacons with which to confirm how fast they were actually traveling over the ocean, pilots often didn't know when they encountered strong headwinds until it was too late. The first time I used a GPS it felt like cheating.

My ground speed showed that the upper winds weren't very strong and if they didn't change I should have a solid two-hour fuel reserve when I arrived at the Ivory Coast. Things were looking good.

I trimmed up the plane, engaged the autopilot, made a few navigation notes, then took out a Tom Clancy novel and tried to get comfortable. I was feeling fat, dumb and happy. A condition that lasted for about three hours.

I was just starting to get into the groove of an all night flight when out of the corner of my eye I saw an ominous red light wink on. Curious, I leaned forward and read the words LOW VOLTAGE under the glaring red light burning on the instrument panel.

Normally when flying over the ocean my reaction to any kind of warning light coming on would be instant action. What was it? Am I going to lose my engine? Should I make a mayday call and prepare to ditch? All these thoughts would race through my head as I tried to figure out what the problem was. But for some reason that night, the red warning light just made me slightly annoyed that my quiet evening had been interrupted. A glance at the ammeter confirmed that the aircraft was using more electricity than it was producing, a LOT more. That got my attention! Immediately I began switching off everything in the cockpit that I didn't really need: radios, navigation lights, anti-collision light, overhead light and transponder.

I checked the ammeter again but the needle continued to tell its sorry tale. I was still losing power. Not as much, but still a discharge. There was no longer any question, I'd lost the alternator. *Damn, that's not good.* I thought tapping on the glass of the offending gauge. That's when it really hit me, I was in one hell of a jam. I was in a disabled airplane over the middle of the Sahara Desert, at night, and I was going to lose my lights.

"I can't turn back to Agader," I said to myself (pilots talk to themselves a lot). "Not with that sandstorm blocking the way."

I had no option except to keep heading south, deeper into the Sahara. Losing the alternator meant the only juice I had left was what was still in the battery. In my head I ticked off everything on the aircraft that ran on electricity. Emergency fuel pump, hopefully won't need that. Flaps, I can land without flaps. Landing gear, I'll need wheels. But I could pump them down manually when I needed them. I'd need at least one radio. Without a radio I wouldn't be able to pick up the navigation beacons I need to find the airport. A radio is priority. If I turned everything off that uses electricity, there just might be enough juice left in the battery to run one radio when it came time to find the airport. (Might.) And the engine? From day one of my flight training I'd been told that because the spark plugs got their power from the magnetos the engine will run even if the battery is completely dead. It looked like I was going to be putting that theory to the test.

One of the biggest users of electricity was the autopilot. Long night of hand flying the airplane, here I come. Reluctantly, I grabbed the yoke and flipped off the autopilot. There were only two things left on that were still drawing power. The instrument lights I was using to fly and navigate with, and the HF radio that kept me in touch with the various control zones I was flying across that night. I can use my flashlight to see the instruments but the HF has got to go.

Before I turned the radio off for the night I decided to give Morocco Control a quick call to inform them of my situation. I grabbed the handset and pushed the transmit button. Now, I've done some stupid things in my flying career, but pushing that button was right up there in the top five. The second I pushed that button the lights immediately went dim and stayed dim.

Oh crap. CRAP!

I knew right then I'd made a huge mistake. Too late, I realized that the HF radio used a ton of electricity and I'd just drained most of what was left in the battery.

Well that was pretty damn stupid!

I started mentally kicking myself as I quickly switched off the offending radio. There'd been no real good reason to call Morocco and tell them what happened. It wasn't like they could do anything to help me. Maybe I just wanted to talk to someone, tell them about my situation. To not be alone, if even for just a minute. My mistake was a big one.

I got out my Mini Mag flashlight, shined it at the instrument panel and turned everything off that I could find. I even unscrewed the tiny light bulb in the Low Voltage warning light that had started it all. The only thing I left on was the GPS. The manual said the unit had an internal battery, it didn't say how long it would last. The pale green display showed my ETA in Abidjan was over ten hours away. I was sure the GPS wouldn't last nearly that long.

Shortly after takeoff thick clouds had enveloped the plane, blotting out the stars and the dark desert below. I hadn't thought much about it at the time because I thought my biggest chore that night was going to be changing tapes in my Walkman. But without the autopilot to keep the plane level, holding the flashlight in one hand and flying with the other wasn't going to work very well. I looked around the cockpit trying to find a place to mount the flashlight. After several failed attempts, I finally settled on clipping it in the fabric above my head so that the pale yellow light pointed more or less at the instrument panel.

That arrangement seemed to work as well as could be expected, so I settled down to what I knew was going to be to be a very long night.

I tried not to focus on the fact that I was facing this battle alone. Letting loneliness and fear creep into the cockpit wouldn't help me survive the night. (Remember, if you have time to panic, you have time to do something more productive.)

After flying by flashlight for two hours, I approached the city of Bamako. Located in southern Mali, Bamako had literally the only airport for hundreds of miles. As luck would have it, the airport was almost directly along my route of flight. I wasn't forced to deviate much out of my way to check if I could possibly land there and get myself out of the jam I was in. I didn't have the instrument approach plates for this airport, so armed with nothing more than a quickly fading GPS and a small airport symbol on my map, I started down to have a look.

As I descended, I found myself between cloud layers eerily illuminated by the city lights below. The bright spot in the lower cloud layer reminded me of my brother reading comic books by flashlight beneath the covers when he was supposed to be sleeping. I looked longingly at the glowing clouds, desperately wanting to land and put an end to the night, but without an instrument approach to guide me down it was too risky. I had no way of knowing how low the clouds were, what the altimeter setting should be, or exactly where the airport might be. I was just as likely to find the side of a building or a radio tower as I was a runway.

I circled the light like a moth around a porch light, weighing my options. The thought of just dropping into the clouds, groping around blindly and hoping to get lucky was both tempting and terrifying.

Going down there would be pretty hairy.

Besides, Pete warned me that Bamako had no maintenance, so if I land there with a broken plane I'd probably be there for a very long time.

Probably a bad idea.

My decision made, I reluctantly turned back on course for Abidjan, still six hundred miles away. I desperately hoped I was doing the right thing as I climbed back into darkness leaving Bamako behind.

It wasn't long after leaving Bamako that the light in the cockpit started getting very dim and the artificial horizon was getting harder and harder to make out. I'd been dreading the time when the batteries in my flashlight would start to die. Even though I had spare batteries, changing them was going to be tricky. If I messed up and dropped part of the flashlight, or one of the batteries I'd be screwed. If there wasn't any light to see the instruments I would certainly lose control of the plane with no horizon to reference. The thought of desperately trying to find a dropped battery while spinning out of control, didn't make me feel very good about such a simple task.

While I was thinking about the best way to proceed I realized I should've changed the batteries when I was over Bamako.

You dummy. There'd been plenty of light reflecting off the clouds. If you'd dropped one of the batteries back there you would've been able to control the plane while you looked for it.

I kicked myself for missing such a great opportunity, but I'd gone too far to turn back. I'd never been in a situation where successfully executing such a simple act as changing the batteries in a flashlight literally meant the difference between life and death. I nervously took out a pair of fresh batteries from my flight bag and put them in my mouth. Then, very carefully, I unscrewed the end of the flashlight and dumped out the old batteries into my lap. In complete darkness I felt for the raised positive end of the fresh batteries with my tongue, slid them into the open end of the small metal tube and screwed the end back on. My heart was pounding as I turned the light back on. The bright white beam of light lit the interior of the cabin and I started breathing again. Afterwards, I felt kind of foolish for being so scared of such a simple task. But damn it, it was nerve wracking!

The rest of the night wasn't a lot of fun. Hand-flying in instrument conditions is very tiring and stressful under normal circumstances and the late night made staying awake difficult. (Fear only keeps you awake for so long.) I couldn't even listen to my Walkman because it held my last pair of fresh batteries and I thought I might need them for the flashlight. I tried to read my book, hoping it would help keep me awake, but whenever I squinted down at the page in the dim light, my heading would start to wander, and keeping a straight course was imperative.

As the night wore on my instrument scan started getting sloppy and I was having trouble concentrating. I tried pinching my legs and singing to myself, anything to stay awake. Just when I thought I might not make it much longer, I noticed a break in the clouds flash by overhead. Energized, I sat up and peered out of the windscreen and watched the clouds continue to thin until they finally disappeared completely, revealing a stunningly clear sky filled with millions of diamond-bright stars.

I turned the flashlight off and was amazed by how bright the starlight was. With no moon and no lights below the effect was magical. The milky way stretching across the sky made me forget about the situation I was in as I leaned forward to look at the majesty above me. Somehow flying by starlight seemed to rejuvenate me and realizing I could actually read the instruments, I decided to fly the rest of the night without the flashlight.

Time seemed to stand still as I was hypnotized by the breathtaking view and the steady music of the engine. My trance was broken an hour later when I finally detected a very faint glow in the east. The growing light steadily extinguished the stars one by one until a single beam of orange pierced the deep blue sky. My long night of darkness was over.

With newfound optimism I scanned the ground below. The vast Sahara desert had given way to a thick green jungle. While gawking at my first view of the African rain forest the GPS mounted in the instrument panel suddenly went dark.

Oh that's just great. Now what am I going to do?

My mood might have been briefly lightened along with the sky, but the morning sun wasn't going to help me with my next challenge, finding the airport. I was still on the last heading the GPS had given me but flying an exact course for three hours with nothing but a compass to follow was going to be extremely difficult.

I still had no way of knowing how the winds were going to affect my flight path and an error of just a few degrees one way or another would result in my being miles off course by the time I reached the coast. I sat there watching the sunrise cast long shadows through the rising jungle mist and thought about the problem. If I couldn't see the city when I reached the coast, how would I know if I was too far east or west off course? At that point I'd have no choice but to take a chance and pick a direction. Once committed I'd only have a 50-50 chance of finding the airport, because after I'd made my decision, I'd have to stick to it. I wouldn't have enough fuel to back track and search in the other direction if I guessed wrong.

What am I going to do when I hit the coast? Flip a coin? Heads or tails. Choose poorly and I'll run out of gas searching in the wrong direction.

Doubts ran through my head as I tried to figure out what to do. Just pushing on and hoping for the best didn't seem like a good idea, but I couldn't think of anything else to do.

If I only knew which way I drifted off course when I hit the coast I'd be golden. Then a thought occurred to me. What if I did know if I was left or right of course?

I sat up a little straighter, stared at my map and considered the idea of purposely altering my heading either left or right of the course that would take me to Abidjan. That way once I got to the coast I'd just have to fly in the other direction to find the city. Or so I hoped.

The idea was an appealing straw to grasp at. But as I thought it through, I came up with two very scary reasons against it. Right then I knew with reasonable accuracy, the heading and more importantly, the distance to the coast. If I took up a new course I'd have no idea when I could expect to cross the coastline. If there were clouds covering the coastline when I got there I wouldn't have a clue when I crossed the beach and started heading out to sea. It also meant that if I went down along the way, anyone searching for me would have no idea that I'd gone off course, and the odds of finding me would be slim to none.

As I tried to decide what to do, I looked down at the ground and saw the morning mist rising from the thick jungle like smoke, just hanging there. Seeing this, I realized that the wind just above the treetops was calm, a common condition first thing in the morning and maybe my salvation.

I figured that if I was flying down low, where there's little or no wind, I'd be able to hold a pretty straight course across the ground. If I did that until the wind picked up I would at least spend a little more time on the correct heading before trying my other crazy idea. So I dropped down to treetop level and continued on the last heading the GPS had given me.

For the next hour the endless green jungle passed just feet beneath my wings in a dark green blur. Finally, a legitimate reason to buzz the countryside!

As the sun rose higher in the sky it burned off the mist that had been confirming the zero wind conditions. I could see the tree tops starting to wave back and forth as the wind picked up. I couldn't tell exactly how fast the wind was blowing, but it looked like it was coming out of the west so I decided to alter my course to the right. I made a ten degree right turn, then reconsidered and made it thirty, just to be sure.

I took up the new heading and noted the time on my map, hoping I wasn't making a big mistake. As the morning wore on, the wind picked up more and more, moving the tops of the huge trees I was flying over and making my ride bumpy. I began to wonder if changing my heading thirty degrees was enough to counter the ever-increasing west wind. I worried that despite my new heading my plane might still be blown east of Abidjan. If that happened, and I turned east when (and if), I found the coastline I'd be flying away from the city instead of toward it. With a growing cloud of uncertainty hanging over my head I continued southwest, hoping to find the coast.

Three and a half hours after losing my GPS, I saw what looked like a thin white line taking shape on the horizon. As I got closer I was relieved to see that the white I was seeing were waves breaking on a sandy shoreline. I'd found the ocean.

A quick inventory of the fuel left in my wing and ferry tanks told me that I had maybe two hours of flying time left to find the airport at Abidjan.

That should be more than enough. If I look in the right direction, that is.

Before heading off to the east, I put the Cessna in a slow right turn, added power and climbed up to five thousand feet. I was trying to see if I could see a city or town, anything that might help me determine my location. I made a few orbits over the coast but the visibility was limited due to the hazy, humid air. I could see no signs of civilization. With no other ideas coming to mind I turned eastbound and began to follow the coast.

After a few miles the visibility started to get worse. I was forced to descend back down to two thousand feet in order to be able to see more than a mile or two inland. According to the map, the city of Abidjan and the airport were close to the shoreline. I hoped that if I stayed close to the ocean I would be able to at least see the city, if not the airport itself.

The first half hour was not encouraging. I'd passed only a few small shacks on the beach and nothing that looked like I was approaching a major city. I was starting to doubt my plan and began to think about turning around if I didn't see anything soon.

As I was looking at the shoreline, trying to figure out if I could land on it if I had to, I noticed a large section of jungle one mile in from the beach. It looked like it had been cleared for crops. I continued on and a few minutes later more farm fields started appearing. It wasn't long before small huts and buildings started popping up among the fields, and soon I could see taller buildings rising up ahead of me in the hazy, morning sky.

I pulled back on the yoke, climbing for a better look, and there laid out in front of me was what I'd been praying for all night, the city of Abidjan. I yelled out in joy at my luck. I'd flown 1800 miles over Africa, at night, with no electrical power and still managed to somehow find my way. The airport was easy to find. A long finger of concrete ending right at the water's edge. I'd made it.

I was ecstatic at finding the city but soon settled down and got back to work. I still had to get the disabled aircraft on the ground. I turned the master switch on and tried the radios, no luck, the battery was dead. *No big deal. I'll just get their attention and they can give me landing permission with the light gun in the control tower.*

Every control tower in the world has a light gun with red, green and white lenses for communicating with aircraft. I started circling five miles out and waited for a light signal from the tower. After a few minutes of circling with no response I assumed that they must not be able to see me, so I moved in closer. Still no light from the tower. I moved even closer. . . . Still nothing. At this point I was really starting to get pissed off. I'd been flying all night with a broken airplane, I was tired, my fuel was starting to run low, and I had to piss. I'd run out of patience.

Screw it!

I pointed the nose of the Cessna at the airport and buzzed right over the tower at about five hundred feet.

"That ought to wake them up!" I said to myself laughing. I started circling on the other side of the runway and watched the control tower for a signal. Still nothing! Well, I'd done all that could reasonably be expected, it was time to land.

First things first, I had to get the landing gear down. I moved the landing gear handle to the down position but wasn't terribly surprised when nothing happened. Without electricity to run the gear motor I was going to have to rely on the emergency extension system to get the gear down and locked. If it didn't work, I was going to have to end my long trip with a belly landing and a wrecked airplane. I grabbed the small emergency handle on the floor in between the front seats and began pumping it vigorously. The manual called for fifty-six strokes to get the landing gear fully down and locked. I looked out the window and was relieved to see the landing gear start to move. Each pump on the handle moved the wheels down about half an inch. After what seemed like hundreds of pumps, the gear moved slowly into a position that I hoped was down and locked. There was no electricity to power the three position lights so I just had to trust that I'd done everything right and the gear wouldn't collapse on landing.

With still no landing permission signal from the tower. I looked carefully for other planes in the landing pattern, lined the 210 with the runway, and got ready to land. The flaps were also inoperative so I was forced to land at a little higher speed than normal, which would really make things interesting if the landing gear collapsed.

Holding my breath, I kept the wheels off the runway as long as I could before touching down as softly as possible. I breathed a huge sigh of relief when the beautiful squeak of the tires kissing the concrete was followed by the Cessna continuing to roll down the runway straight and true. Fourteen hours and fifty-three minutes after leaving Morocco I was finally back on the ground.

Still not getting any help from anyone in the control tower, I started taxiing in the direction of the General Aviation ramp. Halfway there I was intercepted by a young black man wildly driving a battered Willys Jeep that looked like it was left over from WWII. The man was waving his free arm and shouting something I of course couldn't hear or understand. I decided to ignore him for the time being and park the plane first. I pulled into a parking spot, killed the engine and took off my headset, which by that time had started to feel like a vise on my head. Looking over, I saw my escort. He was just about beside himself frantically waving at me to hurry up and get into the jeep.

"Christ, what now?" I said wearily.

After what I'd been through the last thing I wanted to deal with was whatever my new escort wanted from me. I slowly squeezed out of the cockpit and stiffly walked up to the jeep, but before I could say anything, the driver was demanding that I get into the empty seat beside him.

"The airport manager wants to see you immediately!" the driver shouted in a thick African accent.

"Tell him I'm sorry I landed without permission. My radio was broken and I was running low on fuel." I said hoping to avoid a ride.

"The manager wants to see you immediately!" he repeated.

"Okay, fine. Can I use the restroom first? It's been a long flight."

"No, the manager wants to see you immediately!"

If I'd had more energy I would've argued with him longer, but I was just too tired. Resisting the urge to relieve myself right there on the ramp, I climbed into the front seat and we went speeding off to go see the big boss. This was exactly what I felt like doing after flying all night!

The driver delivered me to the base of the control tower and escorted me into the manager's office, without the hoped for pit stop.

Waiting for me inside was one angry Frenchman. Once a French colony, the Ivory Coast was still run by French bureaucrats, most of whom spend nine months in country and three back in France. A thin balding man jumped up from behind his desk and started berating me in French, until he figured out that I didn't speak French. He switched to heavily accented English and picked up where he'd left off. He demanded to know what I was thinking, flying all night without contacting anyone. Did I think I could just fly across half of Africa and no one would notice? Did I think just because I was American that I didn't have to respect the countries I was flying over? Did I know that four different countries had been out looking for me all night and someone was going to have to pay for all the search and rescue planes? And what did I have to say for myself?

While the manager was peppering me with nonstop questions, I reminded myself to remain calm and respectful, until he finally gave me a chance to speak. I'd learned during my short career as a ferry pilot that getting angry and arguing with airport officials in foreign countries was never a good strategy.

When he was done with his tirade, I counted to ten, then calmly explained what had happened and that I was very sorry but there was nothing else I could've done. That didn't seem to make much difference to him. He went on to explain that if he wasn't leaving for France that afternoon he would be throwing me in jail, but he didn't have the time to do the paperwork it would require. The manager stomped around his office, waving his cigarette around as he went on, and on.

Eventually he put a piece of paper in front of me and made me write out a statement describing the events of the night. As I was writing, I really needed to use the restroom.

And I almost asked him for a cigarette but figured that'd be pushing it. When I was done, the manager grabbed the paper from my hand and told me to get the hell out of his office, which I was glad to do. It had been a very long night. And I really needed to pee.

210 TO DODOMA

"In reference to flying through thunderstorms; "A pilot may earn his full pay for that year in less than two minutes. At the time of incident he would gladly return the entire amount for the privilege of being elsewhere."
- Ernest K. Gann

It took two days for the local mechanics to fix the alternator on the 210. I spent the time cooling my heels in the hotel swimming pool. I don't know if it was the break from flying, or the beautiful scenery, but I was feeling refreshed when I finally took off for Libreville, Gabon.

As the landing gear retracted with a thump, I looked down and was sobered by what I saw. Spread out just off the end of the runway was a massive shanty town that stretched out for miles on either side of me. The shacks were made out of corrugated tin, scrap lumber and anything else the residents of the shanty town had found. The homes were crammed together in a massive, jumbled warren of narrow alleys and sewage filled streets. Huge mounds of smoldering garbage added to the smoke from thousands of cooking fires and cigarettes that rose from the packed sea of humanity. I couldn't help but be humbled by the stark contrast of my life and the people I was flying over. I hadn't seen any of this on the short drive to the hotel from the airport. And I hadn't wandered far from the beautiful upscale hotel on the beach during my short stay in Abidjan. This exposure to abject poverty was something completely foreign to me. There aren't a lot of shanty towns or slums in the suburbs of Minneapolis. I grabbed my camera and took a quick picture of the shanty town before passing over the shoreline and heading out to sea again. I left the Ivory Coast, but not a slight nagging guilt, behind.

The ocean leg over the Gulf of Guinea to Gabon is a short 980 mile flight. Compared to the 1700 mile Atlantic stretch you would think it would be a lot safer, but it's not. If you ditch in the Atlantic, there's a good chance someone is at least going to come look for you. Canada, the US or Portugal, will send out search planes if you get out a mayday in time. They're probably not going to find you, but they'll make the effort. Off the coast of Africa? Not so much.

Half way to Gabon I noticed the GPS wasn't receiving a signal. This immediately got my attention. Aside from shutting down when its battery ran out, the GPS had worked perfectly the whole trip. I tried turning it off and on (the extent of my troubleshooting ability), but was unable to bring the magic box back to life.

I wasn't very worried. I didn't have far to go that day and would be able to pick up the standard VOR navigation beacon in Gabon as I approached the coast. On the other hand, I was a little concerned about the next day's 2000 mile leg from Gabon to Tanzania. Even though I'd logged tens of thousands of miles all over the world without a GPS, the thought of flying across the entire continent of Africa with just a compass wasn't something I was looking forward to. I guess I'd gotten spoiled.

I arrived in Libreville rather late due to lazy pilot syndrome and the time zone changes. After shutting the plane down on the dark and deserted ramp, I grabbed my bags and walked over to the nearest building looking for a ride or directions to the nearest hotel.

Finding the doors locked, another issue jumped to the head of the line in importance, getting rid of the three cans of soda and two cups of coffee I'd consumed that day. Looking around I decided the bushes next to the main door were the best cover for my defueling activity. I set my briefcase on the steps in front of the door and ducked behind the bushes to take care of business.

Feeling much lighter and less stressed I stepped back into the light of the doorway. There I found a young man going through the unattended flight case I'd left sitting on the concrete steps. As if coming face to face with a thief, late at night, while all alone in a foreign country wasn't exciting enough, the sawed-off shotgun he was holding just made things more interesting.

"WHAT IN THE HELL ARE YOU DOING!!?" I yelled as I shoved him away from my briefcase and slammed it shut. Or maybe I just said, "Excuse me, can I help you?" I can't quite remember which.

Either way, the man jumped back and claimed he was an airport security guard, and was just trying to figure out whose case it was. I couldn't help but notice that he was "accidentally" pointing the shotgun at me as he explained himself.

I didn't believe him for a second. But he was the one with the gun, so I decided that discretion was indeed the better part of valor and casually asked my new "friend" for directions to the nearest hotel. Smiling, he told me that there was a very nice hotel within walking distance. He also said he would be happy to escort me there because it would be dangerous for a white man to walk alone in that part of town late at night. I tried to tell him that I would be fine going alone, but he insisted on going with me. In the end, the shotgun got the final vote. So off we went down the dark road, me carrying my suitcase and briefcase, and my guide carrying his shotgun . . . wonderful. By the way, I thought, wasn't he supposed to be guarding the airport?

The farther down the road we walked, the darker it got and the more nervous I became. Halfway to the hotel it was so dark that I could hardly make out the man walking next to me. If he was going to rob me that was the time. I tried to keep an eye on him and got ready for action, but nothing happened. He probably knew that even with a shotgun he didn't stand a chance against a skinny, American ferry pilot from Minnesota. Yep, I'm sure that was it.

The roadway got brighter as the lights of the hotel drew near and soon we arrived at the entrance. Under the watchful and disapproving eye of the bellhop, I gave the guard a five dollar tip which produced a toothy white smile that literally glowed in the dark. With some relief and a little guilt I watched my guide disappear back into the night. I don't know why I gave him such a generous tip. I think it was a combination of not robbing me, walking me to the hotel, looking after my airplane and giving me a good story. All I knew was that I was glad to arrive at the hotel in one piece and that five dollar tip was going on my expense report.

I had dinner in the hotel's old dining room that at one time must have been amazing but was now a dingy shadow of its former opulent grandness. After dinner, I wandered onto the patio bar for a drink. The location was right out of a 1940s Humphrey Bogart movie. Mysterious strangers discussing secret business in dark corners, sweaty native bartenders mixing drinks under slow moving ceiling fans and a group of fat businessmen playing cards in the back corner. I got a drink from the bar and struck up a conversation with two English pilots who flew an old DC-3 for a local freight company. The three of us sat around doing what pilots everywhere do when the day's flying is done, drink weak gin and tonics and swap flying stories.

Nigel and Biggles (my names for them, I don't remember their real names) were a wealth of information about flying in Africa. They told me that they'd been flying the 45 year old relic up and down the west coast of the continent for over two years. Mostly hauling legitimate cargo to and from small cities and villages that didn't have any other reliable transportation. They didn't go into any details about what other types of cargo they hauled, and I didn't ask.

The stories they told me about flying in Africa were extremely helpful. I got a priceless amount of information for the three rounds of gin and tonics I bought. I told them that my final destination was Nairobi, but that I'd been requested to make a stop in Tanzania first. Before I left, Pete told me that this route would be safest. It would keep me from over flying the war torn country of Rwanda. Nigel and Biggles both agreed that ever since civil war broke out between the Hutus and the Tutsis the previous year, it had been a good idea to avoid Rwanda, if at all possible. The warnings turned out to be justified because less than a year later over 800,000 people would be killed in the Rwandan genocide.

They also told me that Rwanda wasn't the only country on my route to be concerned about.

"The Congo's a country that you really want to avoid these days," Biggles said, "if you talk to the air traffic controllers over there they'll make you land at Brazzaville even if you have an overflight permit."

"You do have an overflight permit don't you?" asked Nigel.

"Well . . . not exactly." I replied sheepishly. "My boss told me that he'd been trying for over a month to get the necessary permits but the government in Zaire hasn't replied."

"They'll force you to land for sure," Biggles said sagely, "then they'll confiscate your money, throw you in jail and force your company to pay a huge ransom, I mean fine," he corrected with a smile, "for your release."

"As a parting gift they'll steal the radios in your plane before letting you go," Nigel added, taking a drink of the third gin and tonic I'd bought him, "happened to a colleague of ours just last month."

"What do you suggest I do?"

"If I were you I'd just turn off your transponder, fly low and avoid any cities or airports." Said Nigel.

"I don't think they would waste an expensive missile on you," Biggles added cheerily, "but they might send a fighter after you. If they have one that still flies that is."

"Sounds wonderful," I said.

"Welcome to Africa." Biggles replied.

We ordered another round of drinks, and the two pilots told me more tales about flying in the Dark Continent. The more we drank, the crazier their stories got.

One thing that they told me that really got my attention was that I'd timed my arrival in Gabon just right. The week before there'd been some sort of strike in Gabon. The airline workers had shut down the airport by blocking the runway with the fuel trucks for three days. The situation was better for the moment, but they didn't suggest hanging around for too long.

After another round or two worth of stories, we decided to call it a night. The boys wished me luck on my trip and I went back up to my room to study my maps and decide on a plan of attack that would get the Cessna (and me) to Tanzania in one piece.

The next morning I went to the MET office at the airport to find out what kind of conditions I could expect on my trip across Africa. The leg that day was a long one. I'd be flying almost directly along the equator from the west coast of Africa all the way to the east coast. For a trip of that distance, I was hoping for a very detailed forecast of the weather and winds aloft that I would encounter along the way. Hoping for, not expecting.

The MET office was like a time capsule. Ancient teletype machines and typewriters sat on crowded counters, and faded maps covered the dingy walls. I was greeted by the "meteorologist". A young man from Gabon, who got up from his squeaky office chair, tore a piece of paper off an old drum style printer and came over to me. The paper was a glossy black infrared satellite picture of the whole continent of Africa. There were two large white blobs on the picture, one over Kenya and the other over Tanzania.

I stared at the photocopy for a few seconds, trying to make sense of it, then looked up at the young man for help. The briefer leaned over the counter and pointed to the first white blob on the map, "You see dis? Vedy, vedy bad." He pointed to the second white blob, "You see dis? Vedy, vedy bad." He handed the paper to me, "Have a nice flight." The briefing was over. At least it was quick.

I shook my head while I made my way across the ramp to the 210. "Nice briefing." I muttered to myself staring at the satellite picture. All I knew about the weather ahead of me was that there were two big thunderstorm systems in eastern Africa. I had no idea what direction they were moving, no forecast of cloud cover or visibility along my route and worst of all, no winds aloft forecast (again). The lack of a winds aloft forecast bothered me the most. On a trip of almost 2000 miles, not knowing if I had a ten knot headwind or a fifteen knot crosswind could mean coming up over one hundred miles short of Dodoma, or missing it completely and flying out over the Indian Ocean. It was like the night without power all over again. I sure wished the GPS in the 210 was still working.

The bright morning sun was already cooking the runway when I lifted off for Tanzania. I was hoping the weather would stay nice for most of the trip. If I could somehow get an accurate fix on my position later in the flight, I'd be able to determine my ground speed, which would help my navigation problem immensely. I'd decided to fly at one thousand feet because the Congo would be coming up soon, and I planned to take the English pilot's advice and fly low over that country.

My hopes for clear skies were soon dashed as an almost solid wall of moisture greeted me when I left the coast and flew inland and over the jungle. Visibility dropped to just a few miles and the cloud deck was down around 1,500 feet. I briefly considered turning back and waiting for better conditions, but after dealing with Gabon's top-notch weather service, I figured I might as well keep going. At least with the mist hanging above the trees, I could tell that there wasn't much wind to push me off course. This was important because the last navigational aid along my course was in western Zaire. When that was out of range, I'd have only my compass to rely on for about five hours before picking up the next VOR.

Approaching Gabon's border, the controller told me to contact the Congo's air traffic control center and wished me a good day. "Here we go," I said to myself as I switched off the transponder and dropped down to tree top level over the thick green jungle. I didn't bother switching to Congo's frequency because it would have just made me more nervous if they started yelling at me or threatening to shoot me down.

I'm not sure why I kept going. I had a crappy weather briefing, low clouds, a broken GPS and unknown winds along the route. Add a little low level flight to avoid getting shot down and any sane pilot would abort. Then there was the fact that if I did have a problem and went down in the jungle, no one would come and look for me because I hadn't checked in with Congo's ATC. Officially, I wasn't even there. Yep, I was really hanging it out.

But I was only mildly concerned about the situation because I was having too much fun. I love flying low. If given a choice between flying at 10,000 feet on a beautiful sunny day or scud running under a 400 foot ceiling, I'll take the low road every time. As long as the visibility is good and the air is smooth, flying low doesn't scare me. It might be because I spent so much time riding in the back of Army helicopters flying NOE (nap of the earth) or doing buzz jobs at the dropzone. Whatever the reason, I loved it.

The dark green tree tops flashed by in a never ending blur as the 210 raced over the jungle at one hundred forty knots. After a few miles, I got more and more comfortable, and started dropping down under the tree line when the terrain allowed. I guided the Cessna up and down the gently rolling hills. Dropping down low over small grassy fields, gently banking around any trees, then pulling up just enough to clear the wall of trees on the far side. The frustrated military pilot in me was coming out and I finally had a good reason to fly down in the weeds. With the threat of being forced to land by a hostile nation, costing my employer and his client thousands of dollars doing anything but flying as low as possible would've been irresponsible. Right? Of course it wasn't that I was really worried about getting picked up on radar, I wasn't penetrating Soviet airspace after all. I was just testing myself to see if I could fly as low and as well as the Army helicopter pilots I'd trained with for so many years. And anyway, I was in Africa! I could do whatever I wanted!

A lot of the pilots I flew with in the National Guard had learned to fly and fight during the Vietnam war. They flew low, fast and aggressive. That meant that I'd been given a first class course on low level flying. As soon as I got my license (or possibly even sooner) I flew low and fast whenever I got the chance.

An hour and a half later my calculations told me that I'd left Congo's airspace safely behind and had entered Zaire. I considered trying to contact someone on the radio, but after all I had been through in Africa so far, there didn't seem to be much point.

With the threat of heat-seeking missiles behind me, I regretfully climbed back up to 1,000 feet and looked at the map.

Navigational aids in Africa are spread much thinner than in Europe or the United States. In 1991, there were still large areas of the African continent that weren't covered. One such area was Zaire. With just two VORs and one NDB navigation beacon on the western border of the country, I estimated I would be relying on dead reckoning for five hours before I'd be able to pick up the next VOR in Burundi.

Flying over central Africa on a gray and hazy day, with less than two miles of visibility was like flying in a never ending Tarzan themed snow globe. Miles and miles of triple canopy jungle passed beneath my wings with just the occasional jet black river snaking its way through dense forest to break up the monotony. It was mesmerizing, and eventually, boring. But that would change.

After four and a half hours of compass work I tuned in the radio to the next VOR beacon. I spun the dial 360 degrees hoping to get the needle to move but was disappointed when the radio failed to pick up the VOR. It was disappointing, but not terribly surprising. I hadn't really expected to pick up the weak signal that far out but I was getting a little anxious after flying for so long without getting an accurate fix on my position and wanted some reassurance.

Fifteen minutes passed and I thought that maybe I wasn't picking up the signal because I was flying so low. Fifteen minutes after that I was tapping the glass of the dial (because that always works) and double checking my math.

I should've been able to pick up that VOR by now. . . . *Damn.*

I checked the map for the tenth time, and was at a loss as to what the problem was. If I was on course, I should have flown just twenty miles south of the VOR. Even at the low altitude of 1,000 feet I should've been able to pick up the station over forty miles away. Possible explanations ran through my head. The VOR wasn't working, unlikely. Both receivers on the plane were broken, very unlikely. Or most likely, I was over forty miles off course. That's what I was worried about most. I'd flown over 800 miles without any navigational aids or landmarks. With nothing but a compass and no winds aloft forecast, I could easily be miles off course.

I thought about what I should do. It didn't make sense to go looking for the VOR. With no other information, changing course to randomly search for the missing beacon would be foolish. All it would accomplish would be to throw my original nav plot completely out the window. I could try climbing up into the clouds to a higher altitude to try and get better reception. But that would mean that eventually I'd have to blindly descend back down through the clouds to try and find the ground again. Not an inviting prospect, especially with a mountain range out there somewhere. I had to face the fact that I was lost over the vast jungles of central Africa. Well, not exactly lost. I just didn't know precisely where I was. With no other option I just kept going on my original heading and hoped I would pick up the next VOR that was a little over two hundred miles away.

When I approached what I hoped was the eastern border of Zaire, the weather conditions started to show signs of improvement. I was able to climb up to almost 1,500 feet over the tree tops and the visibility had increased some. It still wasn't great, but I hoped the extra altitude would help me pick up the next VOR I was approaching.

The time I expected to start receiving the next VOR came and went with the same result, no reception. The needle on the receiver never quivered once. Now I was really starting to get worried. One VOR out of service wasn't unheard of (this was Africa after all), but two of them being out at the same time was just too much of a coincidence to swallow. I had to face the fact that I was lost. Lost over Africa.

Wonderful.

I started kicking myself for some of the decisions I'd made earlier that day. I should've insisted on getting a better weather briefing, one that at least had some sort of winds aloft forecast. Barring that, when I ran into the low clouds and visibility, maybe I should have turned back and waited for better weather that would allow me to see some landmarks and fix my position. But no, I'd just thrown caution to the winds and took off across Africa without a care in the world. What was that saying about old and bold pilots?

After I was done kicking myself, I decided it was time to get back to work and figure a way out of the mess I'd gotten myself into. (Remember, if you have time to panic, you have time to do something more productive.) Staring at the map, I saw that if I was anywhere near where I thought I was, I still had about 600 miles to go before reaching Dodoma. If I couldn't find the city it was another 250 miles to Dar es Salaam on the coast of the Indian Ocean. The situation was almost exactly like the one I'd been in just a few days ago over the Sahara. This time however, sunset was just an hour away. If I couldn't find an airport before my fuel ran out I'd be forced to find a place to set down, at night, in the bush.

The more I thought about the possible ways my night might end, the less happy I became. If I missed Dodoma and Dar es Salaam, hopefully there would be lights on the shore marking the coastline. Otherwise, I might end up flying out over the Indian Ocean. I was pretty sure I didn't have enough fuel to make it to the other side.

In the United States a coastline would be easy to define. The lights of vacation homes would line the shoreline like a string of pearls because everybody wants to live on the beach. In Tanzania, on the other hand, there was no electricity except around a few of the larger cities, so the odds of me identifying the coastline at night were slim.

With the heavy cloud cover, and the fact that I was flying east, it seemed to get dark in the blink of an eye. One minute everything was hazy gray, the next, everything was pitch black. It was like someone switched off the lights.

There was no sense flying low anymore since I couldn't see the ground anyway. And according to the map, there was a small mountain range I had to cross before entering Tanzania. Calling it a mountain range was being generous. The map told me the tallest peaks were only 7,000 feet high but it was enough to force me to climb into the clouds with only a vague idea of my position. I hoped I would be able to find a way down at some point but that problem was still hours away.

Climbing through 6,000 feet, I suddenly burst through the cloud tops and into a beautiful starry sky. After so many stressful hours of scud running in the haze, my relief at being able to see the sky again was almost physical. Even though I wasn't even remotely out of the woods yet my mood brightened considerably.

I continued to climb up to ten thousand feet to try and pick up any navigation aids. I wasn't surprised when nothing came up. If I was even close to where I thought I was, I wouldn't be able to receive anything before the weak beacon at Dodoma.

Leveling off at 11,000 feet, I put the 210 on autopilot and spread out the map to consider my options. There weren't many. I could continue on my original course and hope to pick up the beacon at Dodoma, or I could head northeast and try to find the city lights of Nairobi. Not knowing exactly where I was made taking off on some new random course unwise. Nairobi might be big, but Africa was bigger.

In the end I decided if I couldn't pick up Dodoma or Dar es Salaam, I would head north and when I hit the coast line and try to find Nairobi. It was a big city, and even if my radios were broken, a remote possibility to be sure, I should still be able to see the lights of the city many miles away. All I had to do is find the coastline before I wandered out over the Indian Ocean.

Another hour slipped by before I noticed huge cloud buildups ahead. After a few minutes I saw the first flash of lightning. "Vedy, Vedy Bad." Echoed in my head. With all the other problems I had that day I'd forgotten the briefer's warning about storms.

Like the Great Wall of China, the towering wall of cold gray clouds barred my way over the mountains. A series of castles, battlements and walls stood in my way as if to say "Thou shall not pass!" At least that's how someone with poetry in his soul might describe what lay stretched out before me. All I saw was a line of thunderstorms I was going to have to plow through. I wondered what else I was going to have to do to get that damn plane to Dodoma.

I'd grown up flying in the Midwest and was very familiar with thunderstorms. America's Tornado Alley was home to the biggest and baddest thunderstorms in the world. But the storms along Africa's Intertropical Convergence Zone were nothing to sneeze at. As one of Orient Air's pilots found out a few years prior.

The ferry pilot had apparently gotten caught in a violent updraft while trying to fly through a thunderstorm over northern Kenya. His small plane was flipped inverted and lifted up at over 2,000 feet per minute. The plane rose so fast that the glass on a few of the instruments blew out before the pilot regained control at 22,000 feet. When he told me the story I had a little trouble believing the part about the shattered instruments, but seeing the towering thunderheads before me, I had no doubt. It made me think twice about challenging them.

My mood darkened as I stared out at the impressive light show laid out in front of me. I didn't bother looking at the map for an escape path. I needed to go east and the storms were in my way. As I approached the storm wall I felt tiny and insignificant, like an ant at the base of a skyscraper. The boiling mass of dark gray towered above me, topping out at 40,000 . . . feet? . . . 50? . . . higher? The tops didn't matter to me. I was heading for the middle. Tightening my seat belt I studied the flashing clouds, looking for a weakness. Not seeing any breaks in the wall I picked an area with the least amount of flashes, kicked off the autopilot and dove in.

Strong turbulence slammed into the plane as soon as I penetrated the cloud wall, tossing me around like a rag doll. A strong downdraft made it feel like a trapdoor had opened beneath me. The little Cessna lost a thousand feet of altitude in just seconds. Loose items floated around the cockpit as I shoved the throttle to the stops and hauled back on the yoke, trying to arrest the uncontrolled descent. In spite of my efforts I was still going down at fifteen hundred feet per minute. Then just as suddenly, an updraft grabbed the plane and pushed me down in the seat as the altimeter spun back the other way. This cycle repeated several times while lightning flashed around me like a crazy strobe light show. The sound in the cockpit was deafening as heavy rain pelted the windshield and airframe. I slowed my airspeed down as much as possible to prevent structural damage. (The words "in-flight breakup" echoed in my mind.) Holding a heading was impossible.

Suddenly, I burst out of the clouds and found myself in clear air with massive thunderheads towered above me on all sides. The difference was incredible. One minute I was desperately fighting for control of the plane in severe turbulence, the next minute the air was smooth as glass. Flying between the huge pillars of flashing clouds, set against a background of a crystal clear, starry sky, left me feeling awestruck and insignificant. Illuminated by a bright full moon, the storm clouds were almost glowing and very easy to navigate around. After twisting and turning between three or four large cells, I left the storms behind and flew into a clear black sky. The clouds were gone and I'd caught my first lucky break of the day.

The eastern side of the mountains were clear of the low clouds and soupy haze I'd been fighting all day. I could even see a few precious jewels of light scattered across the valley floor. My mind eased some. The outside world still existed. As I flew over one of the lights below, I looked down and saw that it was a small brush fire. The further east I went the more fires I saw. I guessed that the locals were clearing the land for farming or grazing livestock, but I really had no idea. It was another mystery that I left behind me at 140 knots.

I flew through the smooth night air until my watch told me that if my dead reckoning was even remotely close, I should be approaching Dodoma. I turned on the NDB receiver and tuned in the beacon on the airport. I wasn't surprised when the needle swung lazily around the dial. By this point I was past expecting anything to go my way.

With nothing else to do I put a tape in my Walkman and listened to some Pink Floyd while I waited for the night to play itself out. It wasn't that I was unconcerned about my situation, you could say scared shitless, but with a few hours still to go before my fuel ran out, there wasn't anything else to do but sit back and relax. What was going to happen was going to happen.

I love flying at night while listening to music. With the instrument lights turned down low and a mellow song on my headphones, an airplane becomes a magic carpet and my mind usually wanders as I glide through the night. It can be very hypnotic.

I'm not sure what I was daydreaming about when I noticed the NDB needle had stopped wandering and was pointed straight ahead. I jumped up in my seat. I was receiving Dodoma! The needle was only a few degrees to the left of center indicating that I was almost perfectly on course.

"YES!"

I turned up the volume on the NDB receiver and listened to the Morse Code signal that identified the beacon. It matched. I'd picked up Dodoma!

"YES! YES! YES!"

To say that I was happy about that development would be a huge understatement. The rest of the flight was a piece of cake. I followed the comforting needle to a small cluster of lights that slowly appeared in the distance. When the lights got closer I made a call on the airport frequency and was rewarded by a double row of dim runway lights winking on in the darkness. A more beautiful sight I've never seen. After a really long and exhausting day of flying the wheels of the Cessna plonked down onto the dimly lit runway.

A large group of people, including the chief pilot for Mission Aviation Fellowship, greeted me on the ramp.

"Welcome to Dodoma Captain McCauley! How was your trip?"

"Just fine sir. Just fine. Piece of cake."

After putting the plane to bed, he took me to his home for a late night dinner with a few of his fellow bush pilots. Dinner with a bunch of missionary pilots is exactly like eating with any other group of pilots, except for the unfortunate lack of alcohol. After the day I'd just had I really could have used a cold beer.

They wanted to hear all about my trip from the United States. They shared stories of their trips into the African bush, hauling missionaries to remote villages to do the Lord's work. I told them about my trip from Libreville that day. When I got to the part about not being able to pick up the VORs in eastern Zaire, the pilots stopped eating and looked at each other.

"What?" I asked, seeing their reaction.

The chief pilot spoke up, looking slightly guilty. "Didn't anyone tell you?"

"Tell me what?"

"Those VORs are almost never in operation."

"What? Why not?"

"Because they're powered by generators and the local warlords steal the gas that runs them almost as soon as it gets delivered."

"We never count on those VORs working," another pilot chimed in, "that's why we had that new GPS installed in the 210 before it left the U.S. Someone should've told you."

I heartily agreed that I could have used that information just a little earlier in the day.

Then came the bombshell.

"So tell me Kerry, why did you stop here in Dodoma instead of flying direct to Nairobi?" Asked the chief pilot.

I stopped with the fork halfway to my mouth. "What do you mean? This was where I was told you wanted the 210 delivered to."

"Oh no, we need it at our base in Nairobi. There must have been some misunderstanding. If you wouldn't mind, could you fly it there tomorrow?"

I couldn't believe it. Not only was I not in the right city, I wasn't even in the right country! Thanks Pete! The big international airport in Nairobi would have been only 25 miles farther to fly and would have been WAY easier to find in the dark than the tiny little dirt strip in the middle of Tanzania.

The next day I left Dodoma for Nairobi. The final flight was a short one compared to the long legs I'd flown on that trip, it was also the most enjoyable. I started out by making a slight detour to see Mt. Kilimanjaro. The top was a little too high to fly over, so I took a quick picture and descended to the next area of interest, the Amboseli National Park, just south of Nairobi.

The MAF pilots told me not to miss flying over the park because it was filled with all kinds of wildlife. I dropped down to tree top level over the broken, brush-filled savanna. I was almost immediately rewarded by seeing a herd of impalas, running from the sound of the 210. I spent the next hour buzzing over the acacia bushes and deep rocky valleys looking for wildlife. I saw a lot of giraffes, elephants and herds of assorted animals. It was amazing. The park ended abruptly. One minute I was over completely wild and uninhabited savanna, the next I was pulling up to avoid a block of apartment buildings. You gotta love Africa.

Ten hours later I was sipping champagne in the first class section of a DC-10. My captain epaulets had again worked their magic and I was leaving Africa in far more style than I had arrived in. As I reflected on my first trip to the dark continent I couldn't believe that every single day had presented me with some of the craziest challenges I'd ever run into. It had been a constant battle from start to finish.

I smiled as I sunk back into the plush leather seat. At least this flight wouldn't be filled with an endless series of maintenance and navigation problems. Then I remembered I was flying on Air Kenya. The smile left my face as I reached down and tightened my seat belt.

THE SOUND OF SILENCE

"Always keep an 'out' in your hip pocket."
- Bevo Howard

Things were really starting to get busy for me in the summer of 1992. Pete was sending me to the four corners of the world delivering planes, and I was taking a more active role in managing the skydiving school in Wisconsin. All over the country skydiving was going through a metamorphosis, and our little club was no exception. Teaching people how to skydive, and taking them on tandem jumps, was starting to become a profitable business. Now, instead of paying to jump out of perfectly good airplanes, I was getting paid! Taking people on the ride of their lives was the best job ever. But it didn't pay enough to live on so I was once again sitting in a single engine plane on my way to Europe. The plane was a nice shiny Mooney that needed to go to Ricardo in Italy.

My first challenge of the trip was a large line of thunderstorms over the Adirondack Mountains in New York State. If God was trying to make me feel small and insignificant the wall of clouds he had laid out in front of me would do the trick. From 19,000 feet the billowing white mass towered five miles above me and stretched 100 miles to either side.

I'd been talking to the professional weather guessers at Flight Services on the radio for the previous half hour and I was presented with two choices. I could land, and wait for the storms to work their way across New Hampshire and Maine, which would mean spending the night somewhere. Or I could find a way to push through the storms. The thought of stopping two hours short of Bangor didn't appeal to me very much. If I stopped, not only would it mean an extra two hours of flying time tacked onto the next day, but I'd still have to stop in Bangor to clear customs. The extra flight time and paperwork would delay my arrival in St. John's until well after dark.

I liked to get to St. John's early so I could get the plane fueled and ready for the next day's trip and make an appointment with the weather briefers the next morning. Then get to the hotel in time to have a good dinner and relax a bit before the long transatlantic crossing. A late arrival in St. John's would cut everything short and probably cost me a few hours of sleep. Stopping short of Bangor would have cascade effect I'd feel for the rest of the trip.

Of course I chose trying to punch through the storms. I pushed my oxygen mask aside and called Center to ask them to help me find a crack in the wall. The controller thought there might be a break to the south and suggested I fly that direction and see what I could find.

As I flew in the clear sky along the trailing edge of the storm, I monitored the storm on the strike finder that was installed in the plane. The dozens of green dots on the screen made it clear that I had my work cut out for me. I flew forty miles south before I found a gap between two groups of green dots that I thought I could sneak through. The controller consulted his crystal ball(radar), agreed that I stood a remote chance of not dying and wished me luck. I tightened my seat belt, cleaned up all loose objects in the cockpit and turned east into the dark wall of clouds.

The turbulence started immediately and was stronger than I expected. But it was tolerable, even fun. Once again I was pushing my limits, in my element, on the edge of control. The clouds got darker and I entered an area of heavy rain, but the strike finder showed the way clear of lightning. Suddenly (bad things always happen suddenly), I heard a loud beeping sound coming from somewhere. I turned down my Walkman, (Yes, I was listening to music while flying in thunderstorms, don't judge me. Epic battles always have a great soundtrack.) and tried to figure out what was making the noise. Maybe the GPS I'd duct taped to the glare shield was the source of the beeping. It was too quiet in the cockpit to be that. I could tell it was coming from the instrument panel.

Wait . . . . WHAT?? . . . why was it quiet? It's not supposed to be quiet! Crap!! The engine's out!

A quick glance out the windscreen confirmed it. The propeller was windmilling, not making power. Frantically, my eyes shot around the cockpit looking for an explanation. The Magneto switch was still on both, the fuel mixture was unchanged and the fuel selector was on a full wing tank. I knew I hadn't bumped anything. *What the hell?*

When I scanned the engine instruments I spotted the culprit. The needle of the fuel pressure gauge was resting on zero! I stabbed the fuel boost pump switch and the offending needle twitched once before falling back down. While I was doing all of that I was still getting kicked around quite a bit. Just keeping the plane on an even keel was proving to be quite a challenge. I pulled back on the yoke and slowed to the best glide speed. That would give me more time to work on the problem while I continued killing snakes in the cockpit. *What the hell was wrong?* The rain seemed to be getting stronger and the sky darker. I decided it was time to get pointed toward the nearest airport in case I couldn't get the engine back. I put the plane into a shallow left bank and tried to find an airport on the map. This was easier said than done. I was forty miles, or more, off my original course. While I'd been looking for a break in the storm front, I'd made the big mistake of not keeping a real close track of my position. I made an effort to find my location by tuning in the NAV radios. I quickly found that holding a map, tuning in frequencies and controlling the dead stick Mooney in severe turbulence made that impossible. It was time to stop screwing around and call for help.

"Boston Center, six eight Quebec has an engine out. Request vectors to the nearest airport." I said. I tried to sound calm and cool, because that's how a pilot with the "Right Stuff" handles an emergency situation. Plus, sounding calm helped keep me from panicking.

"Roger six eight Quebec, I can give you a steer to the nearest airport, but the weather is a lot better at Smith Falls, forty-five miles west of you."

Maybe I'd sounded a little too calm. "Boston, I've lost an engine, and I'm flying a single engine Mooney. By my count that leaves me with none. I don't think I can make forty-five miles."

"Roger, Potsdam airport is ten miles southwest, and is reporting seven hundred overcast, can you make that?"

I was still holding the Mooney in a more or less continuous left bank, going through 16,000 and descending at about 400 feet per minute. I figured I could glide ten miles easily and told Center. The controller read off the latitude and longitude coordinates and I copied them on the back of my map. But it was almost impossible to punch in the numbers on my GPS while I was getting bounced around like that. I hit the "GO TO" button and squinted at the results. The airport was fourteen hundred miles west, ETA, ten hours and thirty-five minutes. I'd obviously done something wrong and was in no mood to try again.

"Boston, I'm having trouble entering the coordinates on my GPS, could you just give me vectors instead, please?"

"Roger six eight Quebec. Fly heading two four zero."

Finally pointed toward someplace to land, I turned my attention back to getting the engine going again. The only thing I could think of trying was to turn the ferry tank valve off and isolate the original fuel system. I wasn't optimistic, the mechanic who'd briefed me on the ferry system in St. Paul told me that it didn't matter if I left the valve open after the tank went dry. I turned the valve off and double checked that the boost pump was still on. No change, the only sound was the air flowing over the wings. That, and my pounding heart.

I got ready for a dead-stick landing. The controller, who'd become my new best friend, informed me that I was only three miles from the airport and had me adjust course slightly. The ceilings were still around 800 feet and the visibility was two miles, not great, but not bad. At least I wouldn't have to make a low instrument approach to the airport.

I wasn't looking forward to my third dead stick landing. The first one was the Cessna full of skydivers. The second was in a beat up Piper cub whose engine just stopped when a head gasket blew out. Both times I was close enough to the airport to make the runway. I was hoping for a hat trick. With this in mind, I concentrated on flying the Mooney and getting ready to land. Passing through 800 feet the thick clouds slowly changed to a gray, misty haze and I was able to see farmland and trees passing below. The controller gave me a slight correction and to my great relief, a runway appeared out of the haze right in front of me.

Sweet!

Then, as I was about to sweat out my third dead stick landing, the engine coughed a few times, then started up with a roar. I had the engine back! I wasn't sure that the engine would keep running, so I stayed high and aimed to touch down on the first third of the runway.

But the engine continued to run and the landing was anticlimactic. As I taxied to the ramp I saw a sheriff's squad car with its lights flashing, speeding toward me. "What the hell is this?" I said to myself.

The squad car turned in front of me and stopped. It was blocking my way and forced me to hit the toe brakes and come to a halt. I sat there with my engine running as an overweight Sheriff's deputy struggled out of the car and motioned me to cut the engine. Frustrated and annoyed at this impromptu road block, I pulled the mixture control and shut the engine down.

With his police utility belt bouncing up and down he clumsily ran around to the right side of the plane. I opened the door and stuck my head over the ferry tank to talk to him.

"You need to clear the area! There's an airplane in trouble coming in!" He said breathlessly, after his long run. Apparently Boston Center had alerted the local fire department and the deputy had been dispatched to help out.

Kind of hard to do with your damn squad car in my way. Wasn't I doing just that when you stopped me?

I had a hard time keeping my mouth shut, but he was there to help after all, so I cut him some slack. I explained that this was the plane that was in trouble and I didn't need any help. He didn't understand at first, or didn't believe me, and he looked genuinely disappointed that he didn't get to see an airplane crash. I had to tell him the whole story before he would move his car and let me taxi to parking. When I got to the ramp, the local volunteer fire department came roaring onto the airport, sirens blaring and lights flashing. I think they took the last corner on two wheels. Then an ambulance arrived, followed closely by two more cars. As each vehicle skidded to a stop its occupants would pile out and come rushing up to my plane hoping to be of assistance of some kind.

Having squeezed over the ferry tank and out the door, I stood on the wing and watched in amazement as cars continued to pull into the airport and onto the ramp. I'm pretty sure a minivan full of Boy Scouts showed up, each hoping to get his "Saw an airplane crash and poked a dead body," merit badge.

As each group of rescuers found out that I had made it, they all showed obvious signs of disappointment. I almost felt like setting the plane on fire, just to make them feel better. The first responders milled about congratulating each other on their quick response time. I'm sure they were wondering if they still had to go back to work, or could they head to the local bar and celebrate a successful rescue. One by one, the crowd got back in their vehicles and went back to whatever they'd been doing before I disturbed their sleepy, little town.

As I was pulling the cowl off the Mooney to check the engine for damage, an attractive young woman walked up with a small notebook and pen in hand. Eagerly, she identified herself as a local reporter and asked for an interview. I answered her questions as best I could, while looking to see if anything was obviously wrong with the engine.

The reporter thanked me and drove off with her scoop. I then walked to the pay phone to call the mechanic who installed the ferry tanks, hoping he would have an idea why my afternoon was so exciting. The mechanic thought that maybe when the ferry tank ran dry, the air pressure flushed the fuel out of the system and prevented the fuel in the wing tanks from getting to the engine. By the time I shut off the ferry tank valve, the fuel lines and boost pump were full of air and it took a few minutes for the fuel to reach them. At least that was his theory.

Great, a theory. I'm only flying this plane to Italy. And you have a theory. Wonderful.

With the mystery hopefully solved I buttoned the Mooney back up and took off again, hoping the mechanic's theory was correct. I headed northeast to try and punch through the line of storms once again, but it was getting dark and the storms seemed to have gained strength. Or maybe I'd lost some nerve. Either way, I decided to admit defeat and call it a night.

I landed at a nearby airport only fifty miles past Potsdam and taxied to the ramp. Before shutting the Mooney down a fuel boy walked up and offered to lead me to the tie downs in a grassy area next to the fuel pumps. My taxi light illuminated the man making "keep coming forward" motions as he walked backwards in the grass. Suddenly, the nose wheel of the Mooney dipped down sharply. I winced as I heard and felt the propeller hit the turf.

"CRAP!" I yelled as I realized what'd happened."GOD DAMN IT!!"

I shut the plane down and got out, royally pissed. My flashlight told the story. One of the propeller blades had a small ding near its tip. Definitely not something the new owner was going to miss. My ground guide was apologizing over and over, claiming that he never knew about the hole in the grass the Mooney's nose wheel had dropped into. I kept my mouth shut, there was no sense yelling at him. It was my problem now. The perfect end to a perfect day.

I bought a metal file on the way to the airport the next morning and then spent two hours filing the ding out of the damaged propeller blade. I took, what I hoped was the same amount of metal, off of the other blade to balance them. When I was done the propeller looked good enough to pass a casual inspection. I hoped.

After I topped off the Mooney's tanks, I went inside to pay for the fuel and saw the airport manager sitting with his feet up on his desk reading a newspaper. Looking closer, I was surprised to see a picture of me working on the Mooney on the front page. The caption "Close Call" was under it.

"You want my autograph?" I asked laughing.

He was slightly confused until I told him my story, then he laughed as well and gave me the newspaper as a souvenir. I still have that paper in my scrapbook. Who said that job wouldn't make me famous?

PRESSURE

"The emergencies you train for almost never happen. It's the one you can't train for that kills you."
- Ernest K. Gann, advice from the 'old pelican'

Millions of stars glittered coldly in the pitch black sky while a solid layer of silvery clouds slid beneath my wings. I was sitting in the cockpit of a brand new Beechcraft Bonanza high above the Atlantic Ocean, retracing the same path Charles Lindbergh made from North America to Paris 65 years before.

I glanced at the handheld GPS propped up on the glare shield and smiled. It registered that I was racing eastbound above the cold dark waters of the Atlantic at a sweet 195 knots. In 11 hours I would arrive in Paris, right on schedule.

Having a GPS for navigating was only one of the advantages I had over "Lucky Lindy" that night, but probably the most important one. Without it I'd be forced to use good old fashioned "dead reckoning," as I took the long way across the Atlantic.

I was cruising at fifteen thousand feet, where an unusually strong tail wind was allowing me to skip the normal 1,700 mile leg to the Azores and fly nonstop to Paris. Going direct to Paris from St. John's was a butt numbing 2,487 miles and was usually an impossible crossing option when heading to Europe. But I'd seen the forecast for strong tailwinds when I'd received my weather packet and calculated that the Bonanza could make it. I had a smaller fuel reserve than usual, but I could live with that if it meant cutting a full day off my trip. Not flying all the way down to Santa Maria before heading back up to Paris would also save Pete almost one thousand dollars in fuel and landing fees. Enjoying an extra day in the City of Lights before catching my flight home didn't hurt either.

Sitting in a soft leather seat was another important advantage over the stiff wicker chair used in the Spirit of St. Louis. The technology in the brand new 1994 Beechcraft F-33 Bonanza was light years ahead of what the Ryan Aeronautical Company used when it built Lindbergh's plane in 1927. The Bonanza had a more reliable and efficient engine, a more aerodynamic airframe, retractable landing gear, cabin heat and state-of-the-art avionics. It even had that new plane smell. I still had one thing in common with Charles Lindberg. If my single engine stopped turning avgas into noise, I'd be in trouble.

The stress and apprehension of taking off from St. John's on another solo transatlantic flight had worn off hours before. Once aloft, with the engine running smoothly, and no weather demons to contend with, I settled into the pilot's seat like it was an old familiar easy chair, comfortable, but alert.

Four hours into the flight, it was time to transfer some fuel from the ninety gallon ferry tank installed in the cabin to the wing tanks. I turned the valve on the bottom of the steel tank mounted behind my seat. That would allow the fuel in the ferry tank to flow into the wings tanks. I then went back to the book I was reading.

When I checked the progress ten minutes later, I was perplexed to see that the wing tanks had made only a modest gain, if any. This got my attention. Although I hadn't really timed the transfer rate when I'd tested the fuel system the last time I used it, I was sure that it had gone much faster than that. Hoping it was my imagination, I took out a pencil, marked the fuel level on the steel ferry tank and sat back to see how fast it went down. It didn't take long for the devastating reality to hit me. The fuel wasn't moving at all! *Damn.* The news hit me like a thunderbolt. It only took a few seconds to realize what a terrible position I was in. A quick glance at the fuel gauges told me what I already knew. The fuel remaining in the wing tanks was not nearly enough to reach Europe or to get me back to Canada. If I couldn't use the fuel in the ferry tank, I was screwed.

It was then that I realized just how truly alone I was. My course from St. John's to Paris took me far south of the normal routes the airlines took when crossing the pond and I knew for a fact that there weren't any other ferry flights out there. It's not an exaggeration to say that there probably wasn't another human being anywhere within five hundred miles of me. At that moment I was literally the loneliest man in the world. I might as well have been halfway to the moon. And *Houston, we have a problem.*

Denial was the first emotion to poke its head into the cockpit. *I must have not opened the valve all the way . . . nope, it's good.* The valve was open as far as it would go and moved back and forth easily. I double checked the aircraft's fuel selector and found that it was indeed where it should be to allow the fuel to transfer.

Amazingly, I didn't allow panic to join the party. But the seed had been planted, and it took all the self-control I could muster to keep it from growing. *Okay Kerry, stay calm. Think. What's the problem and what's the solution?* I took a deep breath, sat back and tried to work out what might be wrong with the fuel system. I pictured the fuel system in my mind, trying to determine where the problem might lie. The fuel level of the ferry tank wasn't going down so it's not a leak. I looked down at the outflow valve located at the bottom of the big metal tank. There might be something blocking the valve hole inside the ferry tank. I thought about the possibility for a few seconds. *Maybe I can shake it loose.*

I turned back around in my seat, buckled my seat belt and secured any loose items in the cockpit. Then I grabbed the yoke, flipped off the autopilot and proceeded to put the Bonanza through a series of aggressive maneuvers. I was hoping to dislodge anything that might be blocking the fuel from flowing. Random items I hadn't been able to reach and secure floated around the cockpit in zero gravity as I nosed the Bonanza over again and again. When I finished my impromptu aerobatic routine, I twisted around in my seat and stared hopefully at the plastic fuel gauge. The fuel level remained stubbornly fixed.

Disappointed that just shaking the plane up and down hadn't fixed the problem, it was time to start taking things apart to try and find an answer. First I unscrewed the rubber filler cap on top of the ferry tank to make sure there was enough outside air pressure to force the fuel into the wing tanks. Bingo, I'd found the problem, or at least "A" problem.

With the cap off, I should've been rewarded with a blast of cold Atlantic air and gasoline fumes. Instead there was nothing. The ferry tanks we used were designed to be pressurized by ram air collected from a L-shaped tube. That tube was mounted on the belly of the aircraft and routed through a half inch rubber hose which went into the top of the metal tank.

Normally, the L-tube is mounted to the aircraft by drilling a hole in the belly, sticking the fitting through it and screwing it in place with a lock washer and nut. This method of fixing the ram air tube in place had worked well in past flights and kept it perfectly aligned into the slipstream, and very secure. When I delivered the plane to its destination and took the ferry tank system out, I'd just stick a metal plug into the hole we'd drilled in the belly. It was a small plug that we painted the same color as the plane. No one ever noticed.

But the L-tube wasn't mounted like that on this plane. Before I left on the trip, Pete had shown me the difference.

"Take a look at this, McCauley," Pete said kneeling down on the hangar floor and pointing under the Bonanza.

"We loosened the screws on an access panel, stuck the L-tube through it sideways and taped it in place."

I squatted down on my heels, looked under the plane and saw the L-tube sticking out of the belly at an angle and what looked like a half a roll of silver duct tape holding it in place. "Why the hell did you do it like that?" I asked, not liking what I'd seen.

"Do you know how much this plane is worth? I'm sure as hell not gonna drill a hole in the belly of a four hundred eighty thousand dollar airplane."

"Okay fine, but don't you think you could have found a better way to mount the tube?"

"Don't worry McCauley, it's not going anywhere. Feel it, it's solid. Just make sure you check it when you get to St. John's."

I grabbed the tube and tried to move it back and forth. It seemed secure but not nearly as solid as it normally was. *If it's so damn secure, why the warning to check it after I'd flown the plane to Newfoundland?*

I grabbed a wrench out of the tool kit I always flew with, and unscrewed a coupling in the ram air supply hose that ran from the L-tube in the belly of the aircraft to the ferry tank. The high pressure jet of cold air, essential for the system to work, was AWOL. Nothing, not breath of air was coming out of the hose. I blamed the duct tape. The airstream must have turned the L-tube, which in turn disabled the ferry fuel system. I also blamed myself and my willingness to go against my better judgment. I looked at the fuel remaining in the wing tanks and did some quick calculations. I didn't have enough gas to turn around and fight the headwinds back to St. John's, or to stretch my fuel and make it to Ireland. I really needed that gas.

I spent a few more minutes kicking myself for being such a moron. If I'd checked to see if the ferry tank was working after the first two hours, I would have had enough fuel in the wing tanks to get me back to St. John's. But I'd been using the ferry system for two full days, and had gotten complacent. *Stop beating yourself up dumb ass, you'll have plenty of time for that in the raft if you can't figure this out.* I sat there holding the silent rubber hose, my eyes glazed over in thought as the challenge glared at me. How to pressurize the ferry tank and force the fuel into the wing tanks where it could be used. Then from the dark recesses of my mind I remembered a conversation with Jim Bell.

"If your ram air tube is ever iced over and you need to move some fuel, what you can do is descend to sea level, open the ferry tank to equalize the pressure then seal the tank," Jim said. "Then you climb back up to altitude, open the valve and the high pressure air in the tank will force some of the fuel out."

"How much fuel will transfer?" I asked.

"I'm not really sure. I've never really had to do it myself, but I imagine you should be able to move five or six gallons each time you go up and down."

"That sounds like a pain in the ass."

"I suppose, but so is trying to get into your life raft wearing a survival suit."

The procedure sounded like it would work in theory, but I could see a few problems in my situation: Number one, the only reason I'd chosen the long route straight across the Atlantic instead of stopping in the Azores was because of the unusually strong tailwinds. But they were only strong above fifteen thousand feet. If I spent all night repeatedly descending to sea level and back, I wouldn't spend enough time in those strong tailwinds to make it across the pond. Number two, just the act of climbing and descending multiple times was going to eat up a ton of fuel. Fuel that I needed, even if I could get it all moved, which I doubted. And number three: Dropping through fifteen thousand feet of clouds and darkness without a current altimeter setting, before hopefully pulling up in time to avoid crashing into the cold black ocean, was, in a word, scary. I needed to find another way of pressurizing the ferry tank.

Sitting there holding the two ends of the hose I looked at the tank and wondered just how much pressure would be required to move the fuel. The air space in the tank was not very big due to it being almost full. I thought to myself, If I can blow up an air mattress with lung power why not a ferry tank?

Not really expecting success, I put the end of the black rubber hose in my mouth and got started. After a number of deep breaths, the back pressure in the hose began to increase. A positive sign that encouraged me to blow harder.

I worked as long as I could, then slapped some duct tape over the end of the hose to seal it and waited to see if my labors would produce any results. Less than a minute later the bubble on the sight gauge slowly moved past the mark I had made on the side of the tank.

"YES! It works! All right!" I yelled, pumping my fist in excitement. My mad scientist experiment was a success! I was able to pressurize the 90 gallon steel tank by lung power alone.

I was feeling pretty full of myself for being so damn smart as I watched the fuel level drop. After the bubble dropped about an inch and a half it stopped going down. With a few calculations and some sloppy guesswork, I determined it took me ten minutes to move less than five gallons of gas to the wing tanks.

Hmm, not too bad. Let's see what that gets me.

Grabbing the manual for the Bonanza, I went to the performance charts and saw that at my current power settings, five gallons would keep me in the air for nineteen minutes.

"Okay, let's see, if I have eight hours and thirty-five minutes left to go," I said, looking at the GPS and grabbing my calculator, "and moving five gallons gives me nineteen minutes of flight time . . . ." My fingers banged away on the buttons as I tried to figure out how many times I would have to blow into the ferry tank to make it to Paris. *Nineteen times sixty is . . . no that's not right. Must be nineteen divided by sixty . . . . Okay. Point three one hours. Divided by eight point three five . . . no . . . wait.* I was confused.

I couldn't figure out why I was having such a hard time doing a simple flight time vs. fuel burn calculation. I did those all the time. The lack of oxygen at high altitude was starting to have an effect on me. After a few failed attempts I finally concluded that I would need to pressurize the tank at least 27 times to reach Paris. It sounded like a lot, but it was doable.

I was also hoping that the weather in Shannon, Ireland would be better than forecasted. They were calling for dense fog at the airport, but if I could somehow land there, all my troubles would be over. But even Ireland was still hours away. Resigned to the fact that it was going to be a long night either way, I took the tape off the end of the hose and got to work.

The rest of the night became a marathon session of hyperventilation, and 100 octane gasoline fumes. As the fuel level dropped it became harder and harder to pressurize the growing air space in the ferry tanks. The longer I worked the worse I felt. Normally, I could fly at fifteen thousand feet all day without becoming hypoxic due to the lack of oxygen. If I sat still and didn't exert myself, I could fly as high as eighteen thousand feet with little effect.

What I was doing in the cockpit that night was the exact opposite of taking it easy. Forcing my breath into the hose again and again started to make my head swim. I found that I was starting to have trouble focusing on the engine instruments and GPS. I sat there holding the hose in my mouth with my eyes closed, breathing in through my nose and exhaling into the hose, over, and over, and over. The dry, high altitude air immediately dried out my nostrils and made my throat burn.

After the second hour of exhausting work, I found myself nodding off after I capped the hose with tape, waiting for the fuel to transfer. I was used to fighting sleep on ferry trips. But that night in the Bonanza was the worst. As the hours wore on, staying awake became like a form of torture. I tried all my old tricks; pinching my inner thigh, shadow boxing, drumming on the dash and singing along to the music I was listening to. Anything I could think of to get me a few minutes and a few miles further along. But it was a losing battle and despite the blinding headache I'd developed, the seductive call of sleep led me to close my eyes, for what I told myself would only be a minute. *Just a quick cat nap to recharge the batteries.* I promised myself. Five minutes later I jerked awake, alarmed that I'd allowed myself to sleep for so long. I knew if I slept long enough to run the wing tanks dry I'd never get enough fuel moved in time to start the engine before I crashed into the ocean.

One thing I was trying not to think about was what Pete Jr. told me about what had happened to one of Orient Air's young pilots just a few months before I'd been hired. The rookie ferry pilot was on one of his first few trips when he ran into icing trouble halfway between St. John's and Shannon. He was almost exactly in the middle of the Atlantic when he made a May Day call before ditching in the ocean. Pete said that he made it into his raft and even made brief radio contact with one of the rescue planes sent to find him. But that was it. Rescue planes from both Canada and Ireland scoured the area for two days but they could find no sign of the lost pilot. I couldn't help but think about the fact that I was flying over the exact point on the exact route that the young pilot went down.

After another grueling session on the black rubber hose, I decided to try eating something to hopefully keep my energy up. I broke into my goody bag and ate some Cheese Wiz on Ritz crackers and downed a can of soda. The food and caffeine picked me up a little, but I wasn't optimistic about it helping for long. The fuel gauges on the wing tanks were bouncing on empty as I picked up the rubber hose again and got back to work.

As time wore on, my mental condition worsened. It took forever to do the math required to estimate my arrival time for my next position report and my voice on the radio was slurred. When I'd finally transferred enough fuel to make it to Shannon, I was just about done in. From the beginning of my ordeal I'd been praying that the weather in

Ireland would improve enough to allow me to land and end that horrible night. But the forecast had called for dense fog until late the next morning so I wasn't too optimistic. I could have called Shannon control earlier that night, but I'd been afraid that if I heard bad news I might just give up. I just didn't know if I had the stamina to keep going all the way to Paris. But I couldn't put it off forever so I radioed Shannon for a weather update.

"Shannon control, Fox, Golf, India, Fox, Mike."

"Go ahead Fox Mike."

"Yes sir, could you give me the current conditions at Shannon please?"

"Roger, stand by."

The short wait was unbearable.

Please, please, please be good! I thought, hoping for the best.

"Current conditions at Shannon; sky obscured, fog, runway visual range fifty meters. The airport is closed at this time."

My head sank into my chest as I listened to the controller confirm my worst fears. The large area of fog that was forecast was not only still covering the coast of Ireland, but was worse than they predicted.

"Roger Shannon. Are conditions any better further east? In the London area perhaps?"

"Negative Fox Mike, conditions don't improve until you cross the channel. Le' Bourget Airport is currently four hundred overcast with one mile visibility and light rain showers."

God, I thought, *I don't know if I can do this for another four hours.* But my options were few. I could declare an emergency, and attempt a landing at Shannon, or push on to Paris. My thumb hovered over the push-to-talk button. It would be so easy, just push down on the button, declare an emergency and land at Shannon.

Do it! the little devil on my shoulder said, *Just declare an emergency and this will all be over. You won't have to blow into that damn hose ever again!* God it was tempting. I was so tired. With a possible end to my flight only forty-five minutes away I was sorely tempted to give it a try. But attempting a landing in zero visibility conditions was something that I just wasn't equipped to do. For me to try it in my current mental state would be pure suicide. Resigned to my fate, I thanked Shannon for the update and continued on into the night.

The last three hours to Paris were the worst. As the ferry tanks got close to empty, the transfer rate was down to a point that barely kept up with the demands of the engine and I was forced to blow into the hose almost continuously. I was getting so tired that I knew why they used sleep deprivation as a form of torture. I was also flying through the multiple airspaces that surround London, and then Paris. Answering the radio calls from ATC was interfering with my work so much that I almost turned the damn thing off.

As I crossed the English Channel, I encountered heavy rain showers, but my fatigued numbed brain hardly noticed. The trip was almost over, but the most challenging part was still ahead; a night approach to minimums in the rain. I was concerned because even simple tasks were starting to become difficult. When I finally had the wing tanks full enough to make it to Paris I capped the pressure line for what I hoped was the last time and got ready for the approach.

Paris ATC cleared me to descend out of fifteen thousand feet, and as I passed ten thousand, the thicker air started to clear my head, like I was coming out of a dream. It was then that I realized I should have dropped down and started flying at a lower altitude as soon as I didn't need the strong tailwinds to reach Paris anymore. The lower altitude would have made pressurizing the tank a whole lot easier. It would've helped me think more clearly as well. Unfortunately, I would've needed to think more clearly to realize that flying lower would help me think more clearly.

Starting the approach to Le Bourget I felt better and better as the increased oxygen and adrenaline of the approach cleared my head. The ceilings were reported to be at four hundred feet and the runway lights appeared out of the gloom right on schedule.

Twelve hours and fifty minutes and over 2400 miles after leaving Newfoundland, the wheels of the Bonanza thumped down at Le Bourget Airport. I taxied to the ramp, stopped the plane and pulled the mixture knob to shut the engine down.

As the gyros spun down, silence descended on the cockpit. I looked out at the deserted rain soaked ramp and realized I was utterly spent. My whole body ached, my chest hurt, my throat was sore and dry, and I had one hell of a headache. The events of the long night seemed like a hazy dream that I was already having trouble remembering.

I climbed out of the Bonanza like an old man, swung my backpack over my shoulder, grabbed my flight bag and headed to the only lit doorway in the terminal. As I walked across the deserted ramp I wondered where everybody was. After all I had been through that night, I felt I deserved there to be a cheering crowd, eager to see the pilot who just pulled off one of the greatest feats in aviation history. Lindbergh had a huge crowd waiting when he landed, and all he had to do was sit there all night. I'd had to work. Instead, all I found was a sleepy customs agent inside who stamped my passport and went back to watching his portable TV without saying a word. He didn't seem impressed at all.

ILLUSTRATIONS

Leading Pete to safety.

Santa Maria, Azores

Kerry with the Aerostar on his last flight with Orient Air.

Pete Demos

402 in the ditch. Oops!

Ferry tanks in the 402.

Jim Bell's wreck.

High altitude flying with oxygen.

Narsarsuaq, Greenland

Kerry and Lee with the Twin Comanche.

Buzzing the pyramids.

Goal posts!

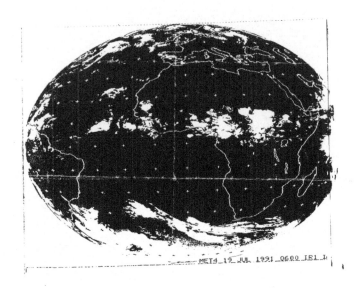

Entire weather briefing received for crossing Africa.

Front page in Potsdam!

Crammed in!

Icing on the spinner of the Aerostar over the Alps.

I SUPPOSE THAT WAS YOU

"Mistakes are inevitable in aviation, especially when one is still learning new things.
The trick is to not make the mistake that will kill you."
- Stephen Coonts

There is an old saying in aviation, "Learn from the mistakes of others. You'll never live long enough to make them all yourself."

That saying is certainly true in the business of ferrying small aircraft over big water. Ever since New York hotel owner Raymond Orteig offered a prize of $25,000 to the first man to fly across the Atlantic in 1919, men have been making mistakes over that big, cold ocean. Mistakes that other pilots could learn from. Mistakes that often cost them their lives.

Whenever ferry pilots run into each other on the road, the first question might be "Where are you headed?" or "How was the weather?" but it's always followed by "Did you hear what happened to so and so?" The story of some brother ferry pilot's misfortune would then be brought forth and examined. Not just for its entertainment value, but for any lesson it might contain. Ferry pilots are dedicated students of other's mistakes. They have to be.

All pilots hold to the belief that they are masters of their own destiny, but ferry pilots even more so. No sane man would willingly strap himself into a strange plane and fly it around the world if he didn't think he was the one in charge, not dumb luck.

Every ferry pilot's attitude about someone else's accident is that he would've done things differently, and survived. That is, of course, if the pilot was killed, which was not always the case. You could learn a lot from the things that happened to pilots that didn't kill them. Mostly because the pilot is around to talk about it and give us all the gory details.

Shiv Chutani was a ferry pilot from Pakistan who was a never ending source of entertainment, great stories and lessons. It seemed like every time I landed in Greenland or Iceland, I'd be treated to another story of how Shiv managed to get himself into some crazy predicament or other.

Like the time Shiv developed engine trouble over the Greenland icecap. Unable to clear the 10,000 foot dome of ice barring his way, Shiv was forced to set down on the remote ice sheet. Luckily, before he went down, he managed to get an answer to his mayday call. So he knew help was on the way.

Owing to the fact that helicopters aren't very fast, and Greenland is very big, Shiv was expecting a wait of a few hours before he could expect to be rescued. With nothing much to do until help arrived, Shiv decided to go for a short walk to check out the ice cap while he waited. Unfortunately, he only got about 100 yards from the plane before he broke through a thin snow bridge and fell into a deep crevasse.

Now falling into a crevasse on top of the Greenland ice cap, hundreds of miles from anywhere, would usually be the end of anyone's story. Not Shiv. The lucky son of a gun somehow managed to land on a ledge thirty feet below, uninjured, but trapped like a rat in an ice cage.

A few hours later, a Danish search and rescue helicopter arrived at the downed aircraft. The Crew Chief got out and ran through the snow to Shiv's plane, only to find it empty. He looked around but there was no sign of the pilot. Which he found surprising because that section of the Greenland icecap is as smooth as a billiard ball.

Then the Crew Chief saw tracks in the snow leading away from the plane and followed them to a pilot-sized hole in the snow. Carefully lying down on his belly, the crewman inched up to the hole, peered into the crevasse and saw the missing pilot staring back up at him, cold but alive.

Shiv was half frozen because he hadn't planned on being out of the plane for more than a few minutes. He was wearing only dress shoes, slacks and a light windbreaker. It wasn't long before the helicopter winched Shiv to safety and into ferry pilot history.

Lesson learned: When you crash, stay with the airplane. And dress for crevasse.

Another legendary Shiv story took place when he was flying from the Faroe Islands, off the northern coast of Scotland, en route to Iceland. Shiv was flying under a low cloud deck in hazy conditions in order to avoid serious icing in the clouds when he temporarily lost track of his exact position. In other words, he was lost.

He was in contact with Reykjavik ATC at the time, but was flying too low to be picked up on radar. The controller told him that all he had to do once he found the coastline was turn left and follow it all the way to Reykjavik.

Flying in and out of the clouds, he only caught occasional glimpses of the wind swept ocean. Then Shiv finally saw a shoreline through a small hole in the haze. He dove down through the hole, banked left and started following the shoreline like he'd been instructed. After an hour, Shiv called Reykjavik wondering how far it was to the airport because he hadn't even seen anything that looked like a city yet, and shouldn't he be there by now?

The controller was familiar with the area and asked Shiv to describe what he was seeing. Shiv told him that he only saw a few homes on the shoreline, and a lot of small white churches. When the controller asked him what he meant by a "lot of small white churches" Shiv told him that he was passing a white church every five miles or so. The controller was confused because he was unaware of any churches on the southern coast of Iceland. He asked Shiv to describe the next church he flew by. When Shiv described the church, the controller thought he might have figured out where he was and asked Shiv if the next church was built exactly like the last one. The next church came into view and sure enough it looked exactly like the previous one. Shiv asked the controller how he knew what the church was going to look like before he got there. The controller told him that was because he wasn't really following the coast of Iceland at all, but was instead flying around an inland lake just east of Reykjavik and was passing the same church, over and over.

Lesson learned: I'm not really sure what the lesson was there. Don't get lost in a lake I suppose.

* * *

Most of the lessons that ferry pilots passed on to one another were written in blood, sweat and tears. So it's frustrating to run into a rookie pilot who doesn't want to listen to the wisdom of older, more experienced pilots.

Pete and I ran into such a pilot one winter while stuck in St. John's. Pete was taking a turbine Cessna 206 to a skydiving school in Switzerland while I was flying a beautiful twin-engine Piper Seneca III to Ricardo in Rome.

Flying another plane on this trip was Peter Bourberg, Orient Air's oldest pilot. Peter was a cheerful old German who'd served as a Luftwaffe mechanic in World War II. He was now delivering planes for Pete on a part-time basis. I think the crazy old kraut was flying small planes over the ocean just for kicks. That, and to get away from his wife for a week or two.

The three of us had been stuck in St. John's for two days due to strong headwinds over the Atlantic. I was also waiting for a new ADF antenna for my plane. The antenna broke on the way to St. John's and even though I had a handheld GPS with me, I wasn't leaving North America without a working ADF.

The introduction of the GPS was having a dramatic effect on the ferry business at the time, and not all in a good way. Before GPS, ferry pilots had nothing but a compass and a winds aloft report to navigate with. Now we had a newfangled contraption that would tell us exactly where we were, how fast we were going, and when we would get there, usually. We'd been using the GPS system for about a year at that time, and although it was a great tool, it was still new, and not one hundred percent reliable. That was the reason none of the pilots at Orient Air would attempt a crossing without a trusty old ADF in the instrument panel.

It took three days for the winds to change, but finally the two Petes and I were at the airport getting ready to make the fifteen hundred mile leg to Santa Maria. While I was waiting for the two old guys to finish using the restroom for the umpteenth time, I wandered over to a small Cessna 172 sitting on the ice covered ramp next to me. The plane was being ferried to France by a young pilot we'd just met the night before at the hotel bar. When I looked inside the cockpit I noticed that there wasn't an ADF receiver in the plane. Concerned, I went back inside the pilots' lounge and asked him about it.

"Do you have an ADF in that 172 out there?" I asked, pointing my thumb over my shoulder out at the flight line.

"Nope, the plane didn't come with one." The young pilot replied, "No big deal though, I got this new GPS last month, and it's been working great!" he said holding up the new handheld unit.

Pete looked up from across the plotting table covered with maps, computer printouts, coffee cups and overflowing ashtray. "Okay, smart guy, what are you going to do when your fancy new GPS craps out on you?"

"Not a problem, I haven't had any trouble with it so far." He replied rather smugly, "The only time it doesn't work real well is in clouds and rain."

Pete and I looked at each other in dumbfounded astonishment.

"Didn't you get the same route forecast as we did?" I asked, reaching for one of the blue weather packets each of us had received less than an hour before. "The whole second half of the trip is going to be in clouds and rain!"

"I'm not worried, I've always managed to get it working again, every time it's crapped out on me."

Pete and I spent the next fifteen minutes trying to convince the young pilot that he was making a mistake. I pointed out that I was flying a much more capable aircraft than he was, and there was NO WAY I would fly to the Azores without an ADF. But try as we might, the headstrong young pilot just wouldn't listen. In his opinion, having flown the Atlantic once before made him an expert and nothing a bunch of washed up old farts had to say seemed to matter. A typical cocky, young know-it-all who didn't want to listen to the advice of more experienced pilots. He reminded me of someone, but I couldn't put my finger on it. As he gathered up his maps and walked out to his plane Pete and I shrugged our shoulders and told each other that at least we'd tried.

Five or six hours later I was sitting sideways in the Seneca's cockpit, reading a book and munching on bridge mix, when a desperate voice came in over the radio. It was the young, upstart pilot in the 172. His GPS had lost the signal and he couldn't get it to come up again.

I slapped my head. This was exactly what Pete and I were talking about! Without a working GPS or an ADF he was screwed! Pete got on the radio and told him to maintain his course and speed while we tried to think of something.

Finding Santa Maria visually in the daytime is unlikely. Finding it in bad weather, at night, is almost impossible. He might get close using his compass and the winds aloft forecast, but close just wasn't going to cut it.

At the time of his first mayday transmission the pilot of the 172 was approximately fifteen or twenty minutes ahead of Peter Borberg. Pete and I were further back, but catching up. But what could we do? We could talk to him on the radio until his fuel ran out and not do him any good. The only way the lost pilot was going to be able to find Santa Maria was for one of us to spot his plane and guide him in. That was easier said than done. Spotting another plane in flight is hard to do, even if you know where to look. What we needed was a landmark to meet him at. Unfortunately, landmarks are few and far between over the Atlantic Ocean. On my first trip Pete and I had met up over Flores Island when he'd lost his vacuum pump. Unfortunately it didn't look like that would be an option today. We were currently flying in clear skies, but were approaching a thick area of clouds that would cover all the Azores islands, including Flores.

I was looking at the various cloud buildups trying to see if one of them was distinct enough to use as a landmark, when I had an idea. What if he held his course until he reached the limit of the clear area and waited for us there? We were all on the same course and altitude and should hit the area of overcast at approximately the same point. When each of us reached the limit of clear sky, we could start flying back and forth along the face of the clouds and try to spot the little 172. If nothing else, we would all be buzzing around the same general chunk of sky. Maybe we'd get lucky. I got on the radio and outlined my plan to everybody and they said it was worth a shot.

A little while later the 172 pilot called and said he'd reached the end of the clear sky and was starting to circle at the edge of the clouds. I noted the time on my knee board and estimated that I'd be in his area in under an hour. Peter Bourberg, who was flying a Piper Cherokee far ahead of me, would arrive first. I sure hoped my plan would work. Fifteen minutes later Peter radioed that he'd reached the clouds and was going to head south for five minutes before turning back north. Pete reminded everyone to make sure all of their lights were turned on to help us see each other. The minutes ticked by as Peter searched south of his course. Then just before the five minutes were up, an excited voice blared out in my headset.

"I SEE YOU! I SEE YOU!" The 172 pilot yelled over the radio. "Rock your wings so I can tell that it's you!" he said.

I shook my head at that one, who in the hell else would he be seeing in the middle of the Atlantic?

The lucky young man formed up on Peter's plane and followed him all the way to Santa Maria.

Lesson learned: If you're going to try and find a small island in a big ocean at night. Have a backup plan, hell, have two.

* * *

There are a number of airports around the world where ferry pilots cross paths; Goose Bay, Shannon, Wick, Santa Maria, Narsarsuaq, Reykjavik, and of course, St. John's, Newfoundland.

If two or more pilots happen to be at the same airport when flight planning an ocean crossing they will often check each other's navigation, thoughts on the weather and possible routes. It's also a great opportunity to catch up on the latest gossip.

Sitting at the flight planning table in St. John's one morning, I watched snow swirling on the icy ramp without really seeing it. My mind was miles away, thinking about the hundred little details involved in my flight to Santa Maria that morning. My thoughts were interrupted when a rookie ferry pilot walked up and asked if I was taking one of the northern routes.

The routes he was talking about were the legs from Goose Bay Labrador, to Narsarsuaq, Greenland and Reykjavik, Iceland. They are relatively short, 750 mile legs instead of the long 1700 mile stretch from St. John's to Santa Maria. If you're heading to northern Europe that route can save you both time and money.

But one of the first things Pete taught me when I started flying for Orient Air was to stay away from the northern routes in the winter. The brutal cold found above the Arctic Circle made flight operations extremely difficult and dangerous. On the ground oil congealed, engines were difficult to start, throttle and mixture cables froze and broke, batteries ran down, and maintenance was expensive. Need to have the plane de-iced in the morning? That bill will look great on your expense report. And the flying conditions are crazy dangerous. Blizzards and icing conditions have killed more ferry pilots than all other factors combined. As bad as the flying was, it was nothing compared to the hostile terrain you were flying over. Crashing in northern Canada or Greenland means losing a few toes to frostbite or freezing to death. Going down in the Arctic Ocean was worse. If you found yourself in your life raft at that time of year it was unlikely you could survive the frigid temperatures long enough for a ship to reach you, even if you were wearing a survival suit.

Just weeks before, I'd heard about a pilot who'd been rescued after going down midway between St. John's and Iceland. He was one lucky son of a bitch and I didn't hesitate to add my opinion of him to my answer.

"No, I'm not taking the northern route. Not like that moron who went down last month did." The tone of my voice made my opinion crystal clear.

Then a new voice spoke up from behind me, "And what moron would that be?"

I turned around in my seat and looked at the man standing there.

"I suppose that was you," I said, a little embarrassed.

"Yep, that was me."

Crap.

"Sorry," I said, sheepishly trying to get my foot out of my mouth, "what happened?"

The ferry pilot brushed off my insult, and sat down on the edge of the table I was working on and told me his story.

He'd been flying a Mooney to England with the new owner along as co-pilot. The two men were about three hours out from St. John's on the way up to Iceland when they noticed the oil pressure starting to drop. Almost immediately, rising engine oil temperature confirmed the ferry pilot's worst nightmare. They were losing oil and losing it fast. The pilot immediately put out a mayday and headed back toward St. John's. But it wasn't long before the engine started making a loud squealing noise, followed by wisps of smoke coiling into the cockpit.

The pilot told me his biggest mistake was leaving the engine running as long as he did because flames started flickering under the cowling before they'd gone very far. They shut the engine down and shut off the fuel, but the fire continued to burn as the Mooney made its long, shallow descent through a thick cloud deck. Luckily by the time the engine fire really got going they were less than a thousand feet over the frozen, wind whipped sea. It was time to get wet.

Every ferry pilot has his own opinion of ditching in the ocean. We've all seen the diagrams that depict your two options when it comes to landing in the water. According to the experts you're either supposed to land parallel to the swells, or on the back side of a swell. Of course, it's a little more difficult when you're on fire.

When the Mooney broke out of the clouds at four hundred feet, the pilot saw that he was already set up parallel to what appeared to be eight to ten foot swells. He held the flaming aircraft in the air as long as he could before the plane hit the water. The plane skipped once on its belly before it nosed in hard. It was a violent impact, but luckily the Mooney came to a rest right side up.

The men grabbed their survival gear and scrambled out onto the wing as the plane bobbed in the waves. The pilot pulled the activation lanyard and the raft and it blossomed into a beautiful orange rubber boat. The inflated raft was sitting on top of the wing and the pilots were able to step right into the raft without even getting their feet wet.

Once in the raft, the pilots-turned-sailors got the old, good news, bad news, routine.

Good news: The raft they were counting on to save their lives was a good one. It was large enough for both of them and had the most important feature you could have in the North Atlantic, a cover. A cover gives stranded pilots protection from the wind and waves. A very important feature in December. The cover also helps the pilots stay inside the raft when it gets tossed ass over teakettle by one of the notoriously huge waves of the North Atlantic.

Bad news: Their survival suits were junk, and completely inadequate for the job they were designed for. While comfortable to fly in, the suits they had were thin and cheap. Made of a thin layer of rubber and nylon, their suits kept them dry but offered no insulation. By contrast, the thick neoprene "Gumby" suits that all of Orient Air's pilots wore had excellent insulation properties. They were uncomfortably hot to fly in, but would keep you nice and warm in even the coldest waters. Which was the whole point of wearing them afterall. Unfortunately, after being worn by dozens of sweaty pilots over the years, the Gumby suits smelled terrible.

Another weak point of the lightweight suits was they just had rubber cuffs around the wrists, ankles and neck.

The Gumby suits had built in boots, gloves and a hood that only left your face exposed.

Really bad news: Their ELT was dead. An emergency locator transmitter (ELT) is a small radio transmitter that broadcasts an emergency signal for search planes to home in on. After the raft, the ELT is THE most important survival item to have with you in the event of a ditching.

When the pilot pulled the ELT out of its case, he noticed the battery cover was cracked and leaking battery acid. He opened the cover and was dismayed to find the insides were corroded and ruined. The ELT was useless. With nothing else to do, the two men huddled together for warmth and waited for rescue while their raft rode up and down the swells. But they didn't have long to wait. After less than three hours in the water the castaways heard engine noises approaching. They unzipped the raft cover and were overjoyed to see a big, gray Canadian Air Force C-130 rescue plane heading almost right at them. The pilot quickly grabbed his flare gun, fired into the air and was rewarded by seeing the rescue plane bank its wings and head for the raft. The two men yelled for joy and waved their arms as the big four engine turboprop overflew them and banked steeply to circle back. On the second pass the C-130 came back lower and dropped a line of flares into the water to mark the raft's position. The rescue plane was so accurate on the drop that the pilots had to use one of the raft's oars to fend off one of the floating flares that got a little too close.

The C-130 circled a few more times. It then made another low pass, dropping what appeared to be a torpedo. Not knowing what it was, the pilots didn't bother to try and retrieve it. They later came to regret that decision when they found out that it was a well stocked, fifteen man life raft that had everything in it but a mini bar and a hot tub.

The two pilots continued to watch the circling rescue plane until the cold ocean spray reminded them that a C-130 is not a seaplane. Although they'd been found, actual rescue was still some time away. When the men tried to put the cover back up they discovered that they'd made a huge mistake by leaving it down for so long. The zipper for the cover was coated with frozen sea spray, and their bare hands were too cold and numb to clear it. The cover was useless, and the pilots were now exposed to the elements. Pretty dumb move.

Reduced to wrapping themselves up in one flimsy, silver space blanket the two men huddled together and waited for rescue. The pilots knew they were over five hundred miles from land, and far beyond the range of any rescue helicopter. Their only chance of being picked up was by ship. Unfortunately, ships are much slower than planes, and even the fastest Coast Guard vessel launched from Newfoundland would take well over forty hours to reach them. With the cover on the raft stuck open, the pilots doubted they could last long. The crew of the C-130 put out a call on the maritime emergency frequency asking for assistance from any ships in the area. Miraculously, a fishing vessel responded. They were in the area, and could be there in eight hours. In terms of ocean speed and distance, they were practically next door. True to their word, eight hours later the crew of the fishing boat hauled aboard their latest catch, two miserable pilots, cold but alive.

The two of us talked for a few minutes more, both agreeing that he was extremely lucky to be alive. Before we parted ways, I tried to get as much information from him as I could about the ditching and time spent in the raft. Any information I could get about surviving in the North Atlantic could only help if I ever found myself in that situation.

After leaving St. John's for the Azores, I spent a lot of time staring down at the waves far below, imagining myself sitting in a small raft, waiting for rescue. I'd been told by the airport manager in Wick, Scotland that on average, three ferry pilots a year die crossing the Atlantic. That figure sent shivers up my spine. Three dead pilots a year was a lot and Orient Air wasn't an exception. Pete lost two pilots in the Atlantic just before I started flying for him. One went down halfway between St. John's and Ireland and the other off the east coast of Greenland. They both had rafts and survival suits and they both died in them. I tried not to think about it but I couldn't shake the image of being in a raft, at night, slowly freezing to death as the waves tossed me about like a toy. It wasn't one of my more enjoyable flights.

Lesson learned: Avoid the North Atlantic in the winter. Or always make sure your zipper's up.

* * *

At sixty-five, Jim Bell was Orient Air's second oldest pilot. He had over one hundred crossings under his belt and wasn't showing any signs of slowing down. Jim had been with me on part my first trip, and listening to him swap stories with Pete every night was like taking a master's course in ferry flying. They laughed so hard they cried, telling stories about the early days. Not having many stories of my own, I sat and listened to two of the pioneers of the business, soaking up the information like a sponge.

Jim's career ended one night in 1997 while trying to get into St. John's. The conditions were terrible with low clouds, strong winds and turbulence. As he approached the airport the St. John's control tower radioed to him the conditions at the field, and current altimeter setting.

Unfortunately, the controller manning the tower was tired and made a mistake in the altimeter setting. As mistakes go, it was a big one. The setting Jim received was off by exactly one thousand feet, and it wasn't on the high side. Jim accepted the change and started his arrival procedure using the incorrect altimeter setting. As he set up on the instrument approach, Jim might have questioned his decision to try and land in those conditions but he never questioned the altimeter setting. Jim died when his plane struck a hillside three miles short of the runway.

Two weeks after the accident Pete and I stopped in St. John's on the way to deliver two planes to Europe. We were taken to the hangar where they'd moved what was left of Jim's plane. Tears welled up in my eyes as I stood there looking at the crumpled mess. It was the second time in two years that I had lost a good friend in a plane crash and I was getting sick of it. I looked inside what was left of the cockpit, and couldn't help but picture Jim in the pilot's seat, fighting the wind and turbulence and wondering why the glideslope needle wasn't where it should have been. What was he thinking those last few moments of his life?

Did he question what the control tower told him? Did he think about abandoning the approach and trying again? It's difficult for a pilot to even consider the possibility of the control tower giving you a wrong altimeter setting.

When flying on instruments, your altimeter is your Holy Grail, your Bible, your Rock of Gibraltar. You know that as long as you don't fly below the safe altitude shown on the charts, you'll be okay. Not being able to trust the altimeter setting, could shake a pilot's faith in the system to the core. A pilot's confidence depends on his ability to tell himself that he's too good to make the same mistakes that kill other pilots. That he will get down safely if he just follows the rules and doesn't screw up. But when we hear about a crash like Jim's, it makes you question your faith in everything you've been taught. And when things are going bad up there, you need all the faith you can get to make it through. Because even though deep down we know it's true, we still don't like to be reminded that sometimes even if you do everything right, it might not be enough.

As Pete and I walked away from the, hangar and symbolically from Jim, we were both quiet and thinking our own thoughts. I couldn't get the image of Jim's crumpled plane out of my mind. I kept thinking about what I might have done differently. It was a difficult conclusion, but I was forced to admit to myself that if it had been me, the outcome would have likely been the same.

Lesson learned; even if you do everything right, you can still die. I think that lesson was the hardest one to accept.

402 DOWN

*"Just remember, if you crash because of weather,
your funeral will be held on a sunny day."*
- Layton A. Bennett

The number of ocean crossings in my logbook continued to mount as the years passed. I was absolutely loving the swashbuckling adventure of being told to fly a plane to the other side of the world with nothing more than a credit card, ten thousand dollars in cash and a handful of old maps. I was the king of the world, having the adventure of a lifetime and it was starting to go to my head. In my not very humble opinion I was Indiana Jones, Lewis and Clark, Charles Lindbergh and Han Solo all rolled into one. My ego was growing by leaps and bounds and I'd lost some of the natural caution a ferry pilot needs if he's going to count on something other than luck to survive. But I was too young and cocky to think about that. All I cared about was where I was going next and what kind of plane I'd be flying there. The trips I tried to sweet talk Pete into giving me were based on two things; where it was headded and how many engines the plane had.

The groan a ferry pilot makes when he hears what type of aircraft he is going to fly next is directly proportional to the size and speed of the plane. The vast majority of the airplanes ferry pilots are hired to fly across the ocean are small single engine aircraft. Small, cramped, tiny little planes with-out-of date avionics. Interiors that are twenty years past their prime. Paint jobs so scratched and faded they look like a bunch of kindergartners painted it during nap time. And top speed? Well, I don't have a clever analogy for just how slow most single engine planes are but trust me, they're slow. A small plane, like a Cessna 172, can take up to eleven hours to fly from St. John's to Santa Maria. Ugh.

Of course when you're flying over the ocean having all your eggs in a single engine basket isn't much of a selling point either. But in the ferry business single engine planes are your bread and butter. They are the planes that only a crazy ferry pilot would fly over the ocean. It's why we get the big bucks. Once in a while though, you get a treat. Not only a nice, shiny plane that's a joy to fly, but one with two engines! The added safety margin of having two engines makes me feel a whole lot better when flying over hostile terrain, especially at night, or over the ocean. Plus, the difference in speed and comfort make a ferry trip in a twin feel like a vacation compared to a single.

In the winter of 1995, Pete hired me to ferry a Cessna 402 to my old friends at Mission Aviation Fellowship in Dodoma, Tanzania. The plane was a beautiful, nine passenger twin that cruised at over 200 knots, and a cabin that was large enough to walk around in (an unheard of luxury). The sleek twin also had a brand new set of radios, a solid autopilot, and another luxury, onboard radar. Having radar meant I could dodge the worst thunderstorms at night, when I couldn't see them. I was really looking forward to this trip. A feeling that lasted about two hours into the first leg.

I was on the way to Bangor when I encountered icing conditions in between St. Paul and the Canadian border. I turned on the de-ice systems and was pleased with how well they worked. The electrically heated windshield and propellers worked just fine and every time I pushed the button to activate the de-ice boots on the wings the ice flew off in satisfying chunks. The de-ice boots on the wings worked by using air pressure from the vacuum pumps to inflate the rubber bladders on the leading edge of the wings, and break up the ice that accumulates there.

I was happy until I saw a small red warning light come on indicating a vacuum pump failure. Normally this would be considered an emergency situation. If you lose your vacuum pump you lose your de-ice boots and most of your flight instruments. But if you're flying a twin it's no big deal because you've got a backup pump on the other engine. Not a problem. Until the other warning light comes on indicating the loss of the second vacuum pump. *Oh, come on, you've got to be kidding me.* I watched as the artificial horizon slowly fell off to the left and remained on its side like a dead soldier while the DG just froze in place. *Great.*

Flying in instrument conditions without a working artificial horizon can be extremely challenging. Correction. "IS" extremely challenging. First of all, you lose the autopilot. It runs off the vacuum driven instruments. No vacuum pump, no autopilot. That means hand flying. And hand flying without the artificial horizon is a bitch. Especially if you haven't practiced it in a while, like Pete hadn't, or me, for that matter. Because it takes a few minutes to get the hang of it again. A precious few minutes you might not have to spare. And God help you if you get even a little bit out of control, it can be damn near impossible to get back under control. Completely impossible, if you get a good case of vertigo.

If that happens a pilot might find himself in what's known as the "death spiral" which occurs when the pilot thinks he is correcting the turn but is actually making it worse. As the pilot continues to pull back on the yoke in hopes of regaining his quickly dwindling altitude, the bank increases and the nose drops as the disoriented pilot frantically and incorrectly tries to get the plane back into level flight. However, since he is heavily banked, he merely tightens the turn. The aircraft continues descending all the way to the ground, or breaks up in the air as the load limits on the aircraft are exceeded. This is widely considered to be the cause of the crash that killed John Kennedy, Jr.

This reality weighed heavily on my mind as I started the dreaded "needle, ball, airspeed," instrument scan used when your vacuum system fails. It's a technique that has a pilot using a crude instrument called a turn and bank indicator (basically nothing more than a small vertical needle tells you if your wings are banked left or right), and his airspeed indicator to tell if he's climbing or diving. A pilot is supposed to focus on one instrument at a time and make small corrections before moving on to the next one, never spending too much time on any one instrument. And this goes on until the pilot gets out of the clouds or loses control and crashes.

I was sweating there for a while, but I soon got the hang of things and my heading and altitude control became only poor instead of downright crappy. The fact that ice was building up on the wings wasn't helping. I called ATC and asked to land at the nearest airport, which turned out to be Sault Ste. Marie. Fortunately, the instrument approach went smoothly, and I was back on the ground before I picked up too much ice.

Not a great way to start the trip. Completing only 400 miles of the eighteen hundred miles I'd hoped to cover that day was a major set back. I got Pete on the phone and he wanted to know how soon I could make it back to St. Paul so he could get the plane fixed.

"It's five hundred overcast from here down to Michigan, with two to three miles visibility and scattered snow showers," I answered. "It gets a little better after that. From Iron Mountain on it's supposed to improve to 700 feet."

"What do you think? Are you going to try it, or spend the night in Sault Ste. Marie?" He asked.

The tone of his voice told me that he wanted me to try and fly under the weather and get the plane back to St. Paul where he'd be able to get it fixed quickly. He'd also avoid having to put me up in a hotel, waiting for the weather to improve. I have to admit it was tempting to try scud running under the clouds back to Minnesota. I didn't want to spend two or three days stuck in a hotel with nothing to do. The problem with that strategy is if the weather closes in on you, things can get rather interesting. Flying under the 500 foot cloud deck didn't bother me as much as the visibility. It was about two miles and the trend was worsening. To make matters worse, it was snowing, making it likely conditions would deteriorate further. So, to recap, bad weather, inoperative instruments, icing conditions and no de-ice equipment. Great . . . let's go flying.

I'm no stranger to scud running. In fact I actually enjoy flying low under the clouds in poor visibility. I like the challenge of picking my way around the hills and TV antennas that invariably pop up, and the view is always better when you are down low. At 500 feet you really get the sensation of speed as the ground rushes by underneath. The difference was that I usually had the option of climbing up into the clouds and flying on instruments if needed. That option wasn't very appealing in a plane without a working vacuum system. Cooling my heels in some crummy Sault Ste. Marie hotel really didn't appeal to me either. In the end my ego got the best of me. After all, what could possibly go wrong?

"I might as well go for it now, it's not supposed to be any better tomorrow. I'll see you in about three hours." I said.

"Okay McCauley, I'll meet you at the hangar, and hey, BE CAREFUL!" he demanded.

"Don't worry Pete, you know me!"

"That's what I'm worried about!" he said as he hung up the phone.

I flew at 500 feet for two and a half hours, dodging scattered snow showers and low hills along the route. It was a blast, but after a whole day's flying I wasn't any closer to Africa than when I'd started.

One week later, I was cruising over the Atlantic at nineteen thousand feet with two new vacuum pumps and a song in my heart. I was in a great mood due to two things. The first reason for my good mood was that it was just a great day for flying. The sun was shining, I was in a beautiful fast plane, and a strong tailwind was making up for a late departure. The second reason for my good mood was that I was experiencing the early stages of hypoxia. I was flying at nineteen thousand feet and only taking occasional sips of precious oxygen from my portable tank. I was trying to make the O2 last as long as possible, in case I really needed it later on the trip. It wasn't really all that dangerous because I'd been flying and skydiving so much lately that my altitude tolerance was at an all time high. It was actually kind of fun to see how well I could function at high altitude without oxygen. I would occasionally dig out my signal mirror and check to see if my lips were turning blue. Blue lips are a sure sign that you're suffering from hypoxia. Another is a strong feeling of well being and euphoria, which isn't entirely a bad thing. After a few years of ferry flying I found that I could function just fine at nineteen thousand as long as I sat relatively still. If I had to move around, even a little, such as getting a map or going back into the cabin to check on the ferry tanks, I would get short of breath and feel a little woozy. If that happened I'd take a few short hits off my portable oxygen tank and feel right as rain again.

It was well after sunset when I checked in with Santa Maria approach. The controller told me the weather was really lousy, with low clouds and thick fog hanging over the airport. The wind was out of the north at fifteen knots favoring runway 36, and the tower cleared me to start the instrument approach to that runway. The problem was that the approach to runway 36 was a non-precision NDB approach. That meant there was no glideslope or localizer beacon to precisely help me find the runway. Just a needle on a dial that points in the general area of the airport. This navigation system was state of the art, in 1930. That kind of approach also had a missed approach altitude of six hundred feet. This meant if I got down to six hundred feet and didn't see the runway lights I'd have to add power and climb back up into the night to go around and try it again. With the forecast conditions at Santa Maria well below the decision height, trying to land on runway 36 would be next to impossible and a complete waste of time. Plus, the thought of trying to shoot the NDB approach in the horrible conditions that were being reported didn't make me very happy. I really didn't want to screw up and run into the volcano that lurked just south of the airport. The wreckage of an unlucky American bomber crew that made that mistake during WWII was still scattered all over the lava fields.

My other option was to shoot the approach from the opposite end of the runway. Landing in that direction would allow me to use the precision ILS (instrument landing system) approach. The ILS had a very accurate localizer and glideslope to follow all the way down to the end of the runway. It also had a lower missed approach point of 200 feet which was much better. The only problem was if I landed to the south I'd be landing with a tailwind and would use up a lot more runway getting the big twin stopped. But the runway at Santa Maria is a nice, long

10,000 foot strip of asphalt so even with a stiff wind at my back I should have no problem getting stopped in time.

I called Santa Maria tower and requested the ILS approach to the south runway. There was a long pause. I imagine they were trying to figure out if I knew that I would be landing downwind with that approach. I repeated my request, and told them I knew it would be a downwind landing, but wanted to try it anyway. They granted my request, and I set up for the approach. As I slipped the approach plate into the holder and strapped it to my leg, I shook my head at the guys in the tower. All the pilots at Orient air had the same mixed opinion of the air traffic controllers in Santa Maria. They tried hard, but were nowhere near as good as their American counterparts. It sometimes seemed like they had the janitor up in the tower instead of trained controllers.

I got set up on the final approach course, and things were going well. Both the glideslope and localizer needles were centered. About halfway down the glideslope, a white light appeared ahead of me. I glanced up, a little confused. *What the hell?* When I started the approach, the controller reported the cloud base at 200 feet and the visibility at 1/8 mile. I was passing through 800 feet and shouldn't have been able to see the runway lights, or anything, yet. I wondered what that white light could be. My first thought was that the guys in the control tower had forgotten about me and let a plane takeoff while I was flying the approach. I was landing downwind and anyone taking off would do it into the wind, heading right at me. But on the other hand, I was tuned into the control tower's frequency and would have heard the tower give anyone permission to takeoff. I couldn't figure it out.

As I watched, the light climbed above and to my right before disappearing completely. Convinced that I wasn't about to smash into some random plane in the dark, I looked back at the instruments and was horrified by what I saw. Instead of being perfectly centered (where I'd left them), the glideslope and localizer needles were both WAY off center! I was well below the glideslope and left of course and was headed right for the cliffs at the end of the runway! I shoved the throttles to the stops and pulled hard on the yoke in a frantic attempt to bring the 402 back into the groove of the approach.

The light I'd seen must have been a runway marker that was somehow visible through a freak break in the clouds. I'd broken the cardinal rule of flying an instrument approach. Never allow yourself to get distracted. Taking my eyes off the instruments and staring at the light outside the cockpit had been a major mistake. Focusing on the light I had allowed the plane to drift off course, making the light appear to be moving.

I cursed as I completed the aggressive correction back to the approach course, pushing the vision of the cliffs rushing up to meet me out of my mind. I was really pissed at myself, but didn't have time to deal with that right then. I still had to finish the approach and land in the lowest conditions I'd ever attempted. I concentrated on the instruments and I slowly guided the plane back into the groove. The altimeter wound down and as I approached the two hundred foot missed approach point. If I didn't see the runway lights by then I was supposed to go around and try it all over again. That was what I was supposed to do. But what was the point? It wasn't like I had anywhere else to go. The weather wasn't going to get any better and my fuel wouldn't last forever. I decided if I was flying a good, stable approach I was going to continue down until I found the runway. One way or another.

At 200 feet, I still couldn't see anything but the twin beams from my landing lights. At 100 feet, I caught a glimpse of pale glow below me. Then, just as my nerve was slipping, two rows of fuzzy lights appeared out of the gloom. The engine noise decreased as I pulled the throttles back to idle, raised the nose and let the plane settle on the runway. As the aircraft slowed down, the runway lights in front of me started to disappear. Halfway down the runway the visibility dropped to less than fifty feet and I had hard time finding a taxiway leading off the runway. I couldn't believe how lucky I'd been. If the fog had been that thick at the approach end of the runway I would've had to abort my landing and gone through the entire process again. I wasn't sure my nerves could've handled another approach. The tower called and asked if I'd landed. They couldn't see anything past the glass in the control tower. I acknowledged that I was indeed safely on the ground, and would be at the ramp as soon as I could find it. The fog on the ramp was so thick that I got lost, and was forced to taxi very slowly and use my compass to help me find the lights of the terminal.

After shutting the plane down I just sat in the darkness replaying the events of the last few minutes. I couldn't believe how badly I'd screwed up. I couldn't get the picture of those cliffs suddenly appearing in front of me out of my mind. But I had to accept my mistake and learn from it. I couldn't let almost killing myself affect my confidence because I still had a long way to go and if I started to doubt myself I'd never make it. There was nothing I could do but accept the fact that I'd just made another withdrawal from my luck bag. Luckily it was turning out to be a pretty deep bag.

Early the next morning Lou Victorino picked me up at the hotel and brought me back to the airport. As usual, he followed me around like a little puppy while I did the preflight inspection ready to spring into action in the event I needed anything. *Not this time, Lou.* The plane was in good shape. I thanked him for his help, and promised to bring him more eight track tapes next time I came through Santa Maria. I always felt bad for not spending more time with Lou. He seemed so lonely, but on those eastbound trips we just didn't have any time to spare. It was just land, eat, sleep and takeoff again.

Leaving the Azores behind, I pointed the nose of the 402 at northern Africa. Next stop, Agider, Morocco. I'd spend the night and most of the next day there, before setting off for another night crossing of the Sahara Desert.

After landing in Agider I taxied behind the yellow FOLLOW ME car to the general aviation ramp, shut the plane down and caught a ride to the terminal. Inside, I ran into a small snag at airport customs. I'd forgotten that Morocco is a Muslim country and therefore, didn't approve of alcohol of any sort. That included the bottle of rum I had in my overnight bag. The customs agents didn't speak any English. Interpreting their sign language, I understood they either wanted to throw me in jail, confiscate the bottle or have me give it to them as baksheesh (the Arab word for tip or bribe). I really didn't want to part with my rum this early in the trip, so I pretended not to understand and finally wore them down. The five dollar bill I gave them might have helped a bit.

That evening, as I was having dinner at a seaside restaurant, a well-dressed young man in his mid twenties walked up and asked if I was an American. When I acknowledged the fact, he asked if he could join me for dinner and practice his English. He seemed like a nice enough fellow, so I invited him to sit down. This wasn't the first time strangers had joined me while dining alone. Apparently I look so pathetic eating by myself that people feel sorry for me. I always enjoy the company and have had some great conversations over the years.

My new dinner companion asked a steady stream of questions and seemed fascinated about my job of delivering airplanes around the world. He told me a little about himself, but the conversation was mostly him asking questions and me answering. As we finished our meal, he looked me in the eye and suggested we go back to my hotel room. I was confused for a second or two, then, CLICK! I got it. He was trying to pick me up! A second look at his fancy clothes, perfect hair and smooth skin confirmed it. I don't know how I could've missed it. Even though I'd welcomed the company for dinner I'd still been wary about what his angle might be.

Being an American abroad makes you a target for all kinds of beggars, con men and thieves, especially when traveling alone. I learned over the years to keep my hand on my wallet when dealing with strangers who approached me, both figuratively and literally. I'd learned the literal lesson while in Rome, watching some street performers put on a juggling show for a small crowd. As I stood there watching the show, I noticed a wrinkled old gypsy woman moving among the crowd with one withered hand out, begging for money. Her other hand was holding a small baby in a cloth sling around her neck. I was trying to avoid eye contact as she shuffled up to me, mumbling something in Italian. Suddenly, she grabbed my bare arm with a gnarled old hand and dug her dirty fingernails into my skin. As I yelped and pulled back, I felt a light touch digging into my right front pocket. The pocket that just happened to have six hundred dollars worth of Italian Lira in it. She was distracting me with one hand, while picking my pocket with the other!

I grabbed for my pocket and came up with the old Gypsy's free hand (the one she was supposed to be holding the baby with).

It was like I'd grabbed a monkey with its ass on fire. She started squirming and screaming, pulling, kicking, cursing and twisting. Trying anything, to break free of my grip. I held on tight because she had something clenched in her hand and I wasn't letting go until I got back what she'd stolen. It was quite a fight. She was pretty strong for such an old lady. But I was mostly concerned about her dropping the baby in the scuffle. A couple of other spectators finally came to my aid. They held her still while I pried her fingers apart. But I found nothing in her hand but my ATM receipt. I double checked my pockets and found nothing missing except the receipt. My assistants asked me if I wanted to find a policeman to press charges, but I just let her go after yelling at her for risking a baby like that (in English, of course).

The situation in Morocco was a little less dramatic than that. I suppressed a chuckle as I politely turned him down. I suppose I should have been flattered.

Two hours after sunset I took off for the overnight trip over the Sahara to the Ivory Coast. The trip was, for the most part, fairly easy, just really long and boring. When I finally arrived at Abidjan twelve hours later, I was greeted by a beautiful sunny morning. Everywhere that is, except over the airport. Covering the airport was one single low cloud bank, about five miles in diameter and parked right smack dab over the runway. I received permission from the control tower to fly the approach, and started my descent. Passing through 1000 feet, I was still quite a ways above the top of the cloud bank. I was having a hard time wrapping my head around the situation. Then I realized what was so strange about it. On a normal instrument approach you usually are flying in the clouds for a few minutes before you hit the decision point. But that morning I was going through 500 feet still in bright sunshine, very strange. At 300 feet above the ground the sun disappeared as the 402 entered the clouds, just seconds from decision height. It seemed like I'd just entered the clouds when the needle on the altimeter hit the critical 200 foot mark. I shoved the throttles to the stops and pulled up. As I brought the landing gear up and blasted back into the bright morning sunshine I called the tower and told them that I had performed a missed approach. Their reply was both confused and frantic.

"Missed approach?" The man in the control tower asked, in a bit of a tizzy, "Why missed approach? We have DC-10 departing at this time!"

There was a long pause on the radio as they tried to pull their heads out their asses. Meanwhile, I was busy banking the plane steeply left and right, trying desperately to see the departing airliner that was about to blot me out of the sky. Why in the hell did they have me flying an approach when there was another aircraft departing at the same time? God damn! I missed the controllers in the United States!

Suddenly, a large white twin engine jet burst from the low cloud deck like a killer whale. I threw the yoke over hard desperately banking away from the approaching jet. *That was a close one!* I replayed the radio transmissions leading up to the near miss in my head, trying to think if I'd done or said anything wrong that led to me almost buying the farm in such a spectacular fashion. I think they just plain forgot about me.

That evening, I sat out on the balcony watching the sunset and wondering if I could ever stand to have a normal, boring day job. I knew there wasn't a flying job, or any job for that matter, that could touch ferry flying in terms of adventure and excitement. And despite the dangers, I couldn't imagine myself doing anything else. Or something at least as exciting as ferry flying. Unfortunately, that kind of attitude was going to severely limit my career options.

Two days later I was lifting off the runway in Gabon, bound for Tanzania. And once again, I was about to fly across the entire continent of Africa without a clue as to what the weather was going to be along the way. Not getting a proper (or any) weather briefing was annoying, but becoming par for the course. I figured I could deal with whatever I encountered, especially in the big twin. My biggest concern was again the lack of a winds aloft report. The 402 wasn't nearly as fuel efficient as the Cessna 210 I'd flown on this route previously and with almost 2000 miles of thick jungle to cover before the next airport, a strong headwind could really ruin my day.

With that in mind, I had two plastic fuel containers stowed in the aft cargo area. My plan was to put the plane on autopilot and transfer the fuel from the containers to the ferry tanks if I needed it. The only flaw I saw was I had no idea how I was going to transfer that fuel into the ferry tanks. The only containers I'd been able to scrounge up were tall and skinny and held around twenty gallons each. The airport worker who found them for me, was also able to come up with three feet of rubber hose to use as a siphon. I'd never siphoned fuel before, but figured How hard could it be? With that flawless plan in my back pocket I took off for Dodoma.

Halfway to Tanzania my GPS gave me the bad news. A strong headwind was really affecting my ground speed. And that meant that the fuel I had in the ferry tanks was going to get me almost all the way to my destination. Close, but no cigar. I was going to need the gas in those two plastic containers.

Without much of a choice, I set the autopilot, unbuckled my seat belt, and climbed into the rear cabin. It was weird looking up at the cockpit with no one at the controls. With the occasional glance up front to make sure George, the autopilot, was doing his job, I got to work moving some fuel. Twenty minutes later, and a half a gallon of fuel swallowed, I gave up trying the siphon method. I just couldn't get the plastic container high enough to make the fuel flow. Either that, or I sucked at siphoning, or didn't suck enough at siphoning . . . or, well, you get the idea.

Next, I tried to make a funnel out of a one liter plastic water bottle. I didn't get much gas into the ferry tank, but I did manage to spill a fair amount in the cabin. In the end I was forced to cut up a second water bottle and pour the fuel into the ferry tank one liter at a time. It was time consuming, but it worked.

Later that afternoon it looked like I had the trip in the bag. I'd dodged a few thunderstorms in the early afternoon, but the sky had cleared and if my calculations were correct I would arrive in Dodoma with well over an hour's worth of fuel still in the tanks. Feeling good (cocky), I decided to drop down and do some low level sightseeing over the African savanna.

The huge expanse of jungle had given way to wide open grasslands. As I approached a small shallow lake, I noticed that the far end was bright pink. Curious, I dropped down to one hundred feet and grabbed my camera. When I crossed the shoreline, I could see that the lake was filled with thousands of bright, pink flamingos! Terrified of the big white predator bearing down on them, the sea of Barbie colored birds took flight in a huge wave that would do any sports stadium proud. The flamingos skimmed the surface of the water in front of me, eventually falling behind only to be replaced by their brothers and sisters getting up ahead of them. Laughing out loud, I buzzed three more pink lakes, snapping pictures and generally having a blast! When I left the last of the flamingo lakes behind I decided to stay low for a while and enjoy the scenery. Because why wouldn't you?

The rest of the flight was like being on a high-speed safari. Herds of animals roamed the grasslands underneath my wings. I even passed a column of brightly dressed natives walking along a trail, each balancing a load of some kind on their head. As I approached Dodoma, I still had some gas left in the tanks. I couldn't think of any reason to land with the fuel I'd worked so hard for still in my tanks. So I spent about an hour zigzagging back and forth, buzzing whatever looked interesting, putting the big twin in steep banks and generally goofing off. I was having the time of my life. I figured I'd earned it! Unfortunately, every trip must come to an end, even a trip as thoroughly enjoyable as that one. With my fuel gauges bouncing around empty, I regretfully brought what I had grown to think of as "my" aircraft, in for a smooth landing at the dusty, red dirt runway of Dodoma Tanzania.

When I walked down the stairs in the back of the plane, I was greeted by the chief mechanic from Mission Aviation Fellowship and his two young daughters. He was extremely happy to see his new airplane. He told me that after clearing customs we would taxi the plane to the other end of the field to their hangar and main base of operations. He asked me if it would be all right for his two daughters to ride in the plane on the short trip to the hangar. I told him that it would be no problem, and after the usual passport stamps and fees, we boarded the 402 and started rolling down the taxi way for the last thousand feet of the trip.

Halfway to the MAF hangar, the 402's left wing started dragging through some tall weeds that had grown up alongside the taxiway. This was making me nervous, the grass was so thick that it might hide something like a fence post or other object that could possibly damage the wing. That would be a shitty way to end the trip.

The grass on the right side of the taxiway looked like it had been recently mowed so I asked the mechanic if it was okay to taxi on that side. He assured me that it was, so I eased over to the right and slowed the plane down to a fast walk. With only 100 yards to go on my 7,000 mile journey I wasn't taking any chances.

Suddenly, the right wing began to droop! I stomped on the left rudder and brake while giving the right engine full throttle to try and get back on firm ground and stop the slide. But it was no use. The right wing continued to drop, while the madly spinning propeller got closer and closer to striking the ground. With disaster imminent I frantically pulled the throttle and mixture controls, shutting the engine down. The plane continued its slow motioned slide to destruction as the propeller slowed to a stop.

After the engines shut down, I was momentarily confused because it was still very loud in the plane. I took off my headset, and realized the shrieking sound was coming from the mechanic's daughters in the back, screaming their bloody heads off.

We all piled out of the plane, which was now sitting at quite an angle. Reluctantly, I ducked under the nose to survey the damage. I was dreading what I was going to see. I couldn't believe what I'd done. After flying almost halfway around the world I'd screwed the pooch in the last 100 yards.

As soon as I stepped around the nose of the 402, I could see the trap I'd fallen into. Hidden in the short grass right next to the taxiway was a shallow concrete drainage culvert filled with tall weeds. As I bent down to survey the damage, I turned to the chief mechanic behind me and shifted responsibility.

"I thought you said it was okay to taxi here?"

I was trying not to be too much of a jerk about it, but I was pretty pissed off and looking for somebody besides myself to blame. Highly embarrassed, he quickly apologized, saying that in the three years he'd worked in Dodoma, he never knew the culvert even existed. I felt bad about blaming the poor guy as I crawled down into the thick grass and took a look. Amazingly, there was no damage at all! One of the propeller tips had left a small scratch on the top of the concrete drainage ditch and that was it. I'd shut the engine down just in time. Luck bag -1. Experience bag +1.

Greatly relieved, we summoned an army of natives, armed with large planks and manpower and eased the plane back onto the taxiway. Then I started up and taxied the final 100 yards as carefully as I could before shutting the trusty Cessna 402 down for the last time. And just like every time I finished a ferry trip I sat in the plane for a few moments, reflecting on the trip as a whole and taking in what I'd just accomplished.

That was the end of my fourth year as a ferry pilot, and although I'd become extremely confident in my skills (cocky again), the close calls had given me a reality check that I'd apparently been needing. I thought about the odds involved and what a thin wire I was walking every time I took off. But as I sat in the 402, I couldn't help but feel happy and proud of myself for my latest accomplishment, despite some of the truly boneheaded mistakes I'd made along the way.

The next day the missionaries dropped me off at the bus that would take me on a 10 hour ride to Nairobi. Why wasn't I getting a nice, fast, safe ride to Nairobi in one of MAF's aircraft? Because, apparently, the hours on their aircraft engines are far more valuable than a lowly ferry pilot's time. Just for the record, I disagree.

I was dreading the bus ride. I was told it was over ten hours long, and when I saw the huge crowd pushing and cramming their way into the bus, my mood darkened even more. I managed to shove my way onto the crowded bus. I was met by a very large native woman, who was apparently in charge of telling everyone where they should sit. She took one look at me and directed me to the back seat of the bus. My seatmates were two young boys, both about six or seven years old, who looked up at me with big scared eyes, as I pushed my way down the aisle. I sat down, not sure if I'd gotten lucky having such small bodies to share the seat with or if they were going to be a pain like young boys can be. My money was not on lucky.

As the bus got more and more crowded, the heat became almost unbearable, and I was glad that I was sitting next to two young boys who really didn't need deodorant yet. Then the woman who was in charge, pushed her way back to us and asked the boys if they wanted to sit up front with their mother. (Why weren't they sitting with their mother in the first place?) The boys sheepishly nodded yes, got up and pushed past me. The head woman then waved to someone at the front of the bus and pointed back at me.

Great, now I'm probably going to have to share my seat with a family of six and their goat! I watched the crowded aisle intently, trying to see who I was going to be stuck with for the next ten hours. Then a small patch of blonde hair appeared in the middle of the packed bus full of Africans as a beautiful young woman elbowed her way through the crowd. When she looked up and saw me sitting in the back of the bus with an empty seat next to the window, her face broke into a huge grin that matched my own. I couldn't believe my luck! Instead of being stuck next to a farm animal, or a family of 6, I had a gorgeous young blonde walking down the aisle instead. We grinned at each other like idiots as she sat down next to me. And just like that the trip went from painful, to fantastic. Her name was Astrid, and she was a twenty-three year old university student from Augsburg on her way back home after a month-long safari. Her German accent and sky blue eyes were intoxicating and we fell into one of those conversations that lasts for hours, blocking out everything else.

We told each other our life stories as majestic views of the African Savanna filled with elephants, zebras and giraffes, passed by the windows. As wonderful as the company was, the bus ride was still very long, and soon after crossing into Kenya, Astrid fell asleep with her head on my shoulder. I stayed awake for a while wondering how I could be so lucky. I got to fly a cool plane halfway around the world on an amazingly exciting adventure to an exotic

African location, only to end up with a beautiful foreign woman asleep on my shoulder. I still couldn't believe they paid me to do this.

PYRAMID SCHEME

"Flying is done largely with the imagination."
- Wolfgang Langewiesche

When I was growing up I read a lot of books about WWII pilots and the amazing adventures they had. I spent countless hours in the room I shared with my brother, mesmerized by tales about swirling dogfights over Europe and the Pacific. In one there was a picture of a flight of P-38 Lightning fighters, flying in formation over the pyramids in Egypt. The image stuck with me over the years and fired my imagination of flying over exotic lands and having adventures all over the world. So when Pete called and asked if I wanted to deliver a plane to Cairo, I jumped at the chance.

The plane I'd be flying was a single engine Piper with fixed landing gear called the Cherokee Six. Like the name suggests, this midsized, low wing aircraft has room for six passengers, and an engine almost powerful enough to carry them. Pete told me that the new owner wanted something with big enough cargo doors to fit a jet ski inside for when he flies to the Red Sea on weekends.

"It sounds like the guy has a little bit of money." I said, impressed.

"Probably more than a little bit, his name is Jabri Sadat." Pete replied over the phone.

"Sadat, you mean, like, Anwar Sadat? The president of Egypt who just got himself assassinated?"

"Yep, it's his son. Now don't screw this one up! He and his buddies have a lot of cash, and if we make a good impression, we might end up flying some corporate jets for them."

I promised to be a good boy and hung up feeling ecstatic. I was going to Egypt! I went home and told Cathy the news. She was excited for me until I told her when I was supposed to leave. The date was just three weeks before the rehearsal dinner for our upcoming wedding. But Cathy had been around aviation long enough to know that delays are the norm, not the exception.

Cathy and I had been dating exclusively for years and had recently decided to tie the knot and make it official. That decision, while wonderful, started the clock ticking toward the end of my career as a ferry pilot. I wanted a family, and I'd accepted the fact that I could be a good father or a ferry pilot, not both. Because the hectic and unpredictable schedule of a ferry pilot would mean missing many important events in my kids' lives. Plus, the dangerous nature of the job meant a good chance of leaving my children without a father at all. The end was coming and the only thing to do was grab all the adventure I could. So I was off to the land of the Pharaohs.

The first part of the trip to Egypt had been routine. Bad weather over the Atlantic, bad food in the Azores and smuggling aircraft parts into Spain. Same old boring stuff. After a ten hour flight over the Mediterranean, the coast of Egypt materialized out of the sand-colored haze. My first stop was the coastal city of Alexandria. Mr. Sadat would meet me there and together we would fly to Cairo. After landing on the long and dusty runway (everything in Egypt is dusty) I taxied to the ramp and climbed out.

Waiting for me were four of the grumpiest looking customs officials I'd ever seen. Without any of the normal small talk, they escorted me into the terminal building and sat me down with a pile of papers to fill out while they inspected my passport. The men jabbered away as they handed my passport back and forth, like they'd never seen one before. When I finished the paperwork the man who I assumed was the head honcho came over and inspected the forms. With a disapproving look on his face he handed me the forms back and in heavily accented English told me there was something missing. I was a little confused. I looked over the forms, trying to figure out what I'd done wrong. Not seeing anything missing, I held up the forms and asked for help.

"What did I do wrong?" I asked.

"We need more!" Honcho said, pointing at the forms and my passport.

"Just show me what else I need to fill out and I'll do it." I replied.

"NO! NO! MORE!" He shouted as the three other dusty customs agents, or airport guards, or whatever they were, stood over me.

"Look, sir, I'm trying to do what you want, but you have to show me what that is. I have more paperwork in the plane, if that might help." I told them, starting to get frustrated.

"NO! WE NEED MORE! MORE!" He said as they looked at me expectantly.

Honcho put my passport on the table in front of me and then he and the other guys left the room. Then I figured it out. (Sometimes I'm slow.) They were waiting for their bribe. They obviously thought I just forgot to put some cash in my passport, and they were giving me a chance to rectify my mistake. Almost every time I dealt with airport officials in Africa, they expected a little something extra, you know, for the effort.

Whenever I was confronted with one of these guys who wanted a little Baksheesh, I liked to mess with them by putting on my "Stupid American" act. No matter how obvious they were in wanting some cash, I played dumb and pretended that I just couldn't understand what is was that they wanted. It was great fun. They would hint, I would shake my head and pretend not to understand, they would make stronger hints, I would just get dumber. None of these guys would ever just come right out and ask for money, so finally they would shake their heads in exasperation and send me on my way, muttering "stupid American" under their breath. I didn't do it because I was cheap, Pete covered all trip expenses, including tips and bribes. Nor out of principle; I didn't have any scruples about paying, it was simply for the sport of it.

Because Mr. Sadat still hadn't shown up yet, I decided to see if the stupid-American trick would work with these guys. The next fifteen minutes were tough, with lot's more yelling and carrying on. I was just about to cough up twenty bucks when an extremely handsome middle-aged Egyptian man walked through the door. Mr. Sadat had arrived.

"Mr. McCauley! Welcome! It is so good to meet you!" He said cheerfully as he walked up to me and shook my hand. "How was your trip? Did everything go well? How is my new plane?"

"It's nice to meet you Mr. Sadat, the trip went well. The plane is in great shape, it was a joy to fly." I responded shaking his hand.

"Excellent! Excellent! I'm glad everything went well. Are you all done here?" Mr. Sadat asked, looking at the paperwork in front of me, and the customs officials standing around. He was clearly in a hurry to see his new plane.

"Well, sir, there seems to be some sort of problem with the way I filled out these forms or my passport or something." I replied trying to sound innocent. "I'm not really sure what I did wrong." I said, shrugging my shoulders and looking at Honcho in mock confusion.

What followed was great theater. Mr. Sadat asked Honcho a question in Arabic, presumably about what the holdup was. Honcho looked around at his co-workers for support, but they had all suddenly found something very interesting on the floor that needed staring at. His weak and mumbled answer obviously didn't satisfy Mr. Sadat at all because he started yelling at Honcho, and wildly gesturing with his hands. Then he grabbed the paperwork and thrust it at him, apparently demanding that it be approved and completed. Honcho took the papers and handed them to one of his stooges with a quick word that sent him scurrying off. While waiting for the forms to be stamped fifteen times (the Egyptians love their official stamps as much as anyone), Mr. Sadat pointed at me, while continuing to yell at Honcho. I think he was not only angry about the delay, but also how I had been treated.

It was apparent that the son of Anwar Sadat had a lot of clout, and was considered a very important person in Egypt. In no time we were given our paperwork, more apologies and were on our way out to the plane. As we were walking out I resisted gloating over my victory when I passed Honcho. In fact, I sort of felt bad for the guy. I hadn't meant to get him in that much trouble.

Jabri and I climbed into the Cherokee and took off for Cairo. During the flight I checked him out in his new plane. It was soon apparent that even with only 300 hours of flight time, Jabri was my kind of pilot. After covering the boring stuff; stalls, slow flight, steep turns and such, the excited little kid wanted to know if he could play with his new toy.

"Do you think it would be acceptable if we did some mild acrobatics?" Jabri asked, with a look of eager anticipation.

I smiled in response, "Sure thing, Jabri! It's your plane, have fun!"

For the next half an hour or so we did wingovers, hammerheads, zero-G dives, and steep turns. Basically, just screwing around. When we approached Cairo, Jabri had a treat in store for me.

"Have you ever seen the pyramids of Giza before?" He asked.

"I've never even been to Egypt before," I replied, hoping he would show them to me.

"I think you should see them. Let's fly over and take a look."

"Sounds good to me."

SWEET!

Jabri turned the controls over to me and before long the distinct triangular shapes of the pyramids came into view. To say I was excited would be the understatement of the year. My childhood dream had come true: I was flying over the pyramids!

"How close can we fly?" I asked, not looking at the map but thinking the restricted area must be pretty big.

"Oh, I think we can get pretty close," he said with a grin.

As I flew closer, and closer, I kept glancing at Jabri, waiting for him to tell me that we were close enough, but he just sat there and smiled. Finally I couldn't stand it anymore.

"How close are we going to get?"

Then he hit me with the bombshell. "Do you want to buzz them?" he asked with a mischievous grin.

I was incredulous "Are you serious? Isn't that, I don't know, highly illegal?"

"Yes, but I have a certain amount of privilege with the authorities. I can get away with a lot."

"Okay, well in that case, you bet! I would LOVE to buzz the pyramids!"

I couldn't believe my luck! I was going to get to buzz the pyramids! I flew us off to one side, and started a diving turn to pick up speed and pointed the nose of the Cherokee at the most famous landmark in the world. As the pyramids got bigger and bigger in the windscreen, the grin on my face grew accordingly. Doing one hundred sixty knots I dropped us down to one hundred feet, and split the uprights built by slaves (or aliens), thousands of years ago. Passing the pyramids I got another surprise, the Sphinx was just off to our left. I had no idea they were so close together, I couldn't believe it.

We made two more passes, taking pictures and giggling like school girls, before Jabri suggested we get out of there.

"Even I can't do much more than this," he explained. "I'll have some explaining to do tomorrow, but it will be okay."

I banked away from the pyramids and headed towards Cairo thinking that the excitement for the day was over. I was wrong.

Jabri gave me a heading to Imbaba airport, our final destination. Our course took us right over the heart of Cairo. I was immediately impressed with the sheer size of the city, it was huge! The city has almost eight million people, and covers one hundred seventy-five square miles. The closely packed buildings seemed to go on forever with thousands of minarets poking up all over the place. It was a truly exotic scene, dusty, but exotic.

Jabri was handling the radios while I flew the little Cherokee Six over the massive city. He was speaking Arabic so I had no clue what was being said. I just followed his directions and went where he pointed. When he told me to start my descent because we were cleared for landing I looked ahead and thought he must be wrong. There was nothing ahead of us but buildings, thousands of buildings. The sea of concrete structures were packed together like dominoes, waiting for us to crash into them and knock them all down. Where was the airport?

Then I saw it, a void in the endless sea of dusty buildings. It was unlike any airport I'd ever seen.

Surrounding the runway, hangars and control tower, was an unbroken wall of tall apartment buildings. There would be no shallow approaches into Imbaba airport.

I set up for a steep final to clear the tall buildings when I noticed some colored dots in the air above the approach end of the runway. As we got closer I could see what they were, KITES! Kids were flying kites on top of the apartment buildings in front of the runway. I banked the Cherokee back and forth to miss the closest kites (though it was tempting to just dive in for a few quick "kills"), and dropped down over the last building. After clearing the tissue paper barrage balloons, I looked at the runway and got my next shock. There were hundreds of kids playing soccer on the runway! *Holy crap this place is weird!*

"Jabri, there are kids all over the runway".

"Don't worry, they will move." He replied calmly.

As instructed, I pointed the nose of the Cherokee at the end of the runway. I was ready to apply full power if I needed to. But, as advertised, the kids stepped to the edge of the runway as we approached, then filled in behind us as we passed by. It reminded me of American kids playing street hockey and shouting "CAR!" whenever some suburban mom invaded their asphalt arena with her minivan. It was definitely weird rolling down the runway with hundreds of dirty kids peeling off to either side like the parting of the Red Sea.

At Jabri's hangar we were greeted by a few of his buddies who, like all pilots everywhere, did the classic walk around. They did the whole, nod their heads approvingly and point at his new plane routine, while a group of mechanics began removing the ferry tanks and HF radio.

I removed my bags and survival gear then cleaned out any left over trash from the plane. Making doubly sure I hadn't left a Ziploc bag full of piss under the seat. Then I sat down with Jabri and his friends on some folding chairs in front of the hangar. We drank orange soda and tea, while I told them about the trip. As the ruddy sun dipped below the horizon, a lonesome loudspeaker calling the faithful to prayer, began echoing through the apartment buildings. Jabri gestured to the city outside the airport and told me in a hushed voice to listen. I wasn't sure what I was supposed to listen for. but then I heard it. It started out as a barely discernible murmur, then slowly built to a low undulating roar, as the millions of Muslims in Cairo stopped what they were doing, got down on their knees and prayed aloud to Allah. The eerie sound made the hair on the back of my neck stand up as I sat there in the fading light.

That night, I sat on my hotel balcony watching the brightly colored party boats and Egyptian Dhows cruise up and down the Nile. Arabian music drifting up from the patio below, completed the scene. Slightly buzzed from 6 days of nonstop flying, and the mellow satisfaction of another completed trip, I was struck by just how foreign and exotic Egypt really was. It had been one hell of a day.

The next morning Jabri's big, burly driver/bodyguard picked me up and brought me to his office. The two of us shared coffee and sweets, while discussing the sights I would see that day. His office was expensively decorated. His father's Nobel Peace Prize was on display on one wall, along with pictures of him signing the Camp David peace accords with Menachen Begin and President Jimmy Carter.

Jabri wasn't what I was expecting when I thought of a president's son. Even though he was an extremely important man in Egypt, he was also very personable, and easy to talk to. The fact that he took time out of his busy day to take care of me showed what a great host he was.

Jabri told me he would give me his personal car and driver to use each day as I took in the sights of Egypt. He not only told me that he would pay for everything, he also gave me about three hundred dollars worth of Egyptian currency for walking around money. I have to say I was thoroughly impressed by his hospitality.

The next four days were a blast. The president of the United States couldn't have received better treatment. First stop was a tour of the pyramids. I'd be seeing them at a lower altitude than the day before (though not by much). Having Jabri's driver with me was great. When confronted by a long line of tourists waiting to get inside one of the pyramids he just escorted me to the head of the line, went up to the grizzled old Arab in charge and slipped him some cash to let me cut in. There was some grumbling from the people I cut in front of but hey, what's a guy to do?

The next night Jabri and his friends took me on an incredible dinner cruise down the Nile. It reminded me of scenes from *One Thousand and One Arabian Nights*. Brightly dressed waiters with platters of exotic food weaved among us as belly dancers circled doing the Dance of A Thousand Veils.

On my last day before heading home, I was taken to the world famous Cairo Museum. As I walked in I noticed a sign saying there was a small fee for taking pictures inside the museum. I had my camera in my jacket pocket, but figured that there wouldn't be anything really worth taking pictures of so I didn't bother paying.

The Cairo Museum is so big, and has so many great pieces, that they stuffed artifacts into back corners that would be the featured exhibit at most other museums. One of the exhibits that wasn't hidden away was the treasure of King Tutankhamen's tomb.

I loved the exhibit and decided to sneak a picture of King Tut's famous mask. I'd gotten away with taking pictures in the museum all day, and with a room full of tourists, I figured I could get away with one more. I pulled the camera out of my pocket, held it above the crowd and quickly snapped a picture. But before I could get the camera back into my jacket pocket a strong hand grabbed my wrist. A stern looking security guard that I hadn't seen, took the camera out of my hand, and started scolding me in Arabic. At least I think he was scolding me. This was a serious situation because I had all the pictures from my trip in that camera and losing it would be a disaster. Suddenly an Egyptian man intervened in the situation. He calmly talked to the guard while gesturing toward me. He seemed to be saying "Hey give the guy a break, he's just another stupid American." He took the camera from the guard, gave it back to me, patted me on the shoulder and smiled. The guard suspiciously gave in very quickly and walked away. My savior smiled and patted me on the shoulder again. He then turned his back to me and put his hands behind his back. I looked down and saw he was rubbing his thumb and forefinger together in the age old manner that's impossible to misinterpret. Then I got it, these guys were working together. I had to admire them, they had a pretty good scam going. Bust a tourist, save his camera, and split the tip. Not a bad gig. I laughed to myself as I took out a couple of bucks and slipped it into his hand. It was totally worth it.

Egypt was everything I'd hoped for. A far away exotic land as unlike Minnesota as anywhere I could imagine. Once again, I couldn't believe I actually got paid to have adventures like this. I hoped it would last.

RING OF FIRE

*over every"More than anything else,
the sensation of flying is one of perfect peace mingled with
an excitement that strains every nerve to the utmost ~ if
you can conceive of such a combination."*
- Wilbur Wright

It's been said that flying is hours and hours of boredom, punctuated by moments of stark terror. This is usually true for most pilots, but for a ferry pilot the boredom is more like a wary truce with terror. Flying over the Atlantic in a single engine aircraft means many long and boring hours with nothing much to do. Set your course, adjust the power, check the engine instruments and make a position report. After that, it will probably be two or three hours before the next heading change or position report. Not much to do then, except keep a wary eye on the engine instruments, and wait. To the casual observer a ferry pilot would look bored after a few hours in the cockpit, and in a sense he is. The thought or fear that something might go wrong at any minute, can only keep him on the edge of his seat for so long. But the underlying worry that something might go wrong, that something in the engine might choose that day of all days to fail, never truly goes away. You hear the slightest change in engine noise, feel strange vibrations and imagine bad weather over every horizon. For some pilots the stress is too much. They turn around before the point of no return, leave the plane on the ramp and go home in shame. Or they actually finish the trip but say, "Never again."

But a lot of the time, it's just plain boring. Ferry pilots do many things to pass the time. Some read, some chain smoke, some guys check and recheck their navigation. I read paperback novels and listen to music. And when that isn't enough, I get creative. Once in a while I'd tune into the common frequency airline pilots use to chat with each other, put the earbuds of my Walkman to my headset microphone and broadcast a song over the air. At the end of the song I would get on the air and play DJ. "THAT WAS, I WANT A NEW DRUG, BY HUEY LEWIS AND THE NEWS! YOU ARE LISTENING TO W.O.O.O.SHIT I'M LOST. ROCKING THE NORTH ATLANTIC! THE REQUEST LINES ARE NOW OPEN!" Sometimes an airline pilot would bitch about me being unprofessional (true), but most of the time the guys had funny comments. My favorite was, "Hey do you have Dead Skunk In The Middle Of the Road?"

I laughed and responded, "Okay, that must be a first officer! This one goes out to all the captains out there!"

Whatever a ferry pilot does to pass the time, he's really just waiting for a problem to pop up, and it usually does. Most of the time a major problem will creep up on you. The weather will start getting worse, your next navigational aid won't come in or you start running low on fuel. Problems like that give a pilot time to analyze the situation, work on a solution, make choices and come up with an answer. Other times a problem hits you suddenly, sending a jolt of adrenaline through your body as a moment of stark terror is dropped in your lap.

Over the years I've had my share of heart stoppers. Usually it's an engine that, for no apparent reason, starts running rough for a few seconds then smooths out again. I hate that. Or the mysterious vibration that you start to feel in the plane. "Was that vibration there before? Is something in the engine about to go?" I hate that, too.

Then there's the engine instruments that suddenly start acting up. Your engine instruments monitor the heartbeat of the aircraft you're flying and can give you a heads up when things are turning sour. Of course just like the things they are supposed to monitor, engine instruments can break too. There's been more than one time that I've looked at some instrument that showed a reading that just didn't make any sense at all.

Is it the gauge, or is the engine really about to come apart?

Like the time a Mooney gave me a heart attack on the way to Santa Maria. I didn't have a care in the world when for the hundredth time that day, my eyes lazily roamed over the engine instruments, looking for trouble. I just happened to be looking directly at the fuel pressure gauge when the needle innocently twitched twice. Frowning, I leaned close and reached out my hand to tap the glass at the exact moment the needle suddenly dropped all the way down to zero.

My heart stopped. Zero fuel pressure . . . . The engine will quit in just a few seconds . . . . I'll be in the water in minutes!

I hit the boost pump, held my breath and waited for the engine to quit. But the fuel pressure needle stayed stubbornly at zero. I flew into action. Calculating my latitude longitude and scribbling it down on my map, getting ready to make the May Day call I'd been dreading ever since I started flying over the ocean. And the engine kept running. I had a few more precious seconds of time. I cleared the soda cans and remnants of lunch off the life raft while reaching for the radio transmit button. And the engine kept running. Shaking with adrenaline and fear my thumb hesitated over the transmit button, a May Day call poised on my lips. And the engine kept running. Fuel pump failure, or a faulty gauge? I could literally feel my chest unclench as the engine continued its steady hum. A false alarm...Just the gauge...Jesus.

As the engine continued to run, I looked down at my shaking hands. Nothing like a massive shot of adrenaline to spice up an otherwise boring day over the Atlantic. That was a minor scare. I've had worse.

On September 10, 1992 I was 600 miles off the coast of Portugal, cruising along with just five hours left to fly before reaching the sunny island of Mallorca. I was in a Cessna 206 turbine conversion that was, as usual, converted into a flying fuel truck (bomb) with two 60-gallon ferry tanks filled with Jet-A shoehorned in the cabin behind my seat. The tanks were there to give me the range to cross the Atlantic. They would also help the search and rescue folks find me in case I crashed by making a REALLY big fireball. I have a love hate relationship with ferry tanks. I really love the extra range they give me. The ability to fly for many hours can come in really handy. On the other hand, if you develop any kind of a fuel leak in the cabin it would only take one small spark to turn the plane into a roman candle.

I looked up from the book I was reading and saw a cloud bank up ahead. It wasn't a big cloud bank, or a dark cloud bank, or even a very thick cloud bank. Just a flat, wide cloud maybe five hundred feet thick and a dozen miles across. I didn't think much about it. I didn't even consider changing course or altitude. Why bother? It didn't pose any danger to me. I was slightly annoyed though because I'd have to divide my attention between reading and hand flying the plane on instruments because it didn't have an autopilot.

I lazily began my instrument scan, keeping my heading and altitude within reasonable parameters. When you literally have an ocean of sky all to yourself, there's no need to be super precise in your flying. I mean, what are you going to hit?

I'd been in the cloud for less than a minute when, KABOOM! A bolt of lightning appeared out of nowhere and hit the propeller! For a split second bright white electricity followed the tips of the propeller turning it into a brilliant ring of fire. The noise was incredible. I shot bolt upright in my seat. I couldn't tell if I had been shocked by the gazillion volts of electricity shooting through the plane, or by the gazillion cc's of adrenaline shooting through my body. My mind had a hard time grasping the enormity of what just happened, and the fact that I was still there. I winced, remembering the fuel tanks behind my back, and waited for them to explode.

I sat there, stunned for a second before whipping my head back and forth trying to look at everything at once. Fuel tanks on fire? Nope. Engine instruments showing any sign of impending doom? Not yet. Radios and GPS still working? Unknown. I pushed my headset off my ears and listened intently to the engine. But the ringing in my ears made this impossible. Lightning is LOUD I made a more careful and detailed examination of the aircraft's systems and fuel tanks, and found nothing wrong. I couldn't believe it! Out of nowhere I had been hit by lightning, and apparently, not only survived but suffered no ill effects to my body or my plane. A few minutes later I burst from the back side of the cloud that had just ambushed me, and bright sunlight filled the cabin. As the minutes wore on, and I didn't fall out of the sky, my heart rate settled down. With many hours of flying ahead of me, and nothing else to do, I shrugged my shoulders, picked up my book and started a new chapter.

When I landed in Palma de Mallorca I was met by my friend Onofre. I told him what had happened and together we inspected the 206. There was a chunk of metal the size of a paperclip melted off where the lightning struck one of the propeller blades. We also found a hole the size of a quarter burned into the wing root. And one of the aluminum tire rims was melted as if by a blow torch. I have no idea why the rubber tire didn't blow when the lightning left the plane. Thank God for small favors.

Once again, I found myself working on a customer's new propeller with a large, metal file. When someone gives me an airplane to deliver, I feel it's my responsibility to get it to its destination in the same shape as it was when I started the trip. Or as close to it as possible. Any damage that happens along the way is my fault, period. But this wasn't my fault! The lightning strike was a freak incident. Pilots fly through thousands of similar clouds every day and not once have I ever heard of someone being hit by lightning. I mean, just what am I expected to do? Fly around every little cloud in the sky? Impossible. But that thought didn't make me feel any better. The plane was damaged and I felt like crap.

Two days later I landed at a cool, little Swiss airport cut into the side of a mountain. And standing there, waiting for me, was the Cessna's new owner Mr. Eichenberg. Tall and thin with perfectly combed silver hair, Mr Eichenburg was a classic example of a proper Swiss businessman. He was all smiles and congratulations as he stood there admiring his new plane. He even gave me a brand new Swiss Army knife with his company's logo on it, as a reward for a job well done.

But his mood changed dramatically when I finally found the courage to tell him about the lightning strike and showed him the damage. I told him about the little nothing cloud that was responsible, but he didn't believe me. He accused me of purposely flying in thunderstorms. No matter how much I protested my innocence he was unconvinced. In the end there was nothing he could do about it. I still felt like crap delivering him a damaged plane.

I found out later that the engine of the 206 seized up 50 hours after I dropped it off. The pilot managed to land safely, but the engine needed a complete, and very expensive, overhaul. Apparently the lightning strike had damaged one or more or the engine bearings, causing the failure. Shocking.

THE BANK JOB

"Do not let yourself be forced into doing anything
before you are ready."
-Wilbur Wright

The ferry business is unlike any other business in the world. It involves some of the most dangerous and challenging flying a pilot can face, while at the same time taking him on incredible adventures to some of the most beautiful places on the planet. It also presents the pilot with some unique challenges. From flying a plane filled with five gallon gas cans because the next airport was out of aviation fuel, to bribing airport officials to keep the aircraft from being impounded. But I never thought it would lead me to robbing a bank.

After getting married I knew my days of being a full time ferry pilot were numbered. I began to take a few less trips in the summer in order to pursue a possible career in skydiving. I got all my freefall instructor ratings and started working at the skydiving school in Wisconsin more or less full time. I still managed to make a ferry trip every month or so but I started to spend more time jumping out of planes, rather than flying them. Cathy liked the change because I got to spend more time at home and less on the road. I liked it because I love teaching people how to fly their bodies in freefall. It was also a whole lot safer to jump out of planes than it was to fly them over the ocean.

One day, while preparing a student for his next jump, I got a call from Pete's wife Barb. She told me that a letter had been delivered to Orient Air with my name on it. The return address was from Mallorca, and it looked official. That was odd. I hadn't been to Mallorca in almost a year, and couldn't imagine what the letter might be about. When I got to the office the next day, Pete had faxed it to his friend Onofre for translation. He told us that the letter was a bank examiner's audit statement, confirming that the amount in my checking account was twenty-eight thousand dollars. That was all well and good, except for the fact that I didn't have a bank account in Mallorca, much less one with twenty-eight thousand dollars in it.

Onofre knew that it was unlikely that a poor, starving ferry pilot would've deposited twenty-eight thousand dollars in a Spanish bank and then forgotten about it. So he'd started a little investigation. His best guess was that some criminals, possibly the Mafia, had somehow gotten my personal information from one of the many forms I filled out when I visited Mallorca, and used it to open a fake bank account. That made sense because whenever I filled out any form relating to a ferry flight, I used my name but Orient Air's address.

After he got off the phone with Onofre, Pete asked me what I wanted to do.

"What do you mean, what do I want to do?" I replied.

"It seems to me that if the account is in your name there's nothing stopping you from just going into the bank and making a withdrawal,"

"Except for the fact that whoever put the money in there will be mighty pissed off when they find out it's gone."

"So what? What can they do about it?"

"Oh, I don't know, Pete, maybe come over here looking for it. They have my name and they have your address you know."

"Don't worry about it," Pete said reassuringly, "they wouldn't go to all that trouble over a measly twenty-eight grand."

"That's very reassuring," I said sarcastically, "and just how am I supposed to get the money out of the bank?"

"Piece of cake. I'll fly us to Palma, all you have to do is walk into the bank, withdraw the money, and close your account. Then we fly home and split the money, fifty-fifty, nothing to it." Pete smiled.

I thought, Fifty-fifty? How does he rate half the money? I'd be taking all the risk. Still, the thought of marching into a Spanish bank and taking that money scared the hell out of me.

I told Pete I'd think about it and went home to mull it over. The money would be nice but I couldn't help imagining mob goons breaking into Pete's house some night looking for their money. That, plus the fact that I might get caught, made me hesitate. I really didn't feel like finding out if Spanish prisons were anything like in the movie *Midnight Express*.

In the end I couldn't do it. The risk of something going wrong just seemed too great, even for all that money. Pete tried to talk me into it but my mind was made up, and I was scared. I'll stick to ferry flying and skydiving, thank you very much.

One year later, I received another letter from the bank. We faxed it to Onofre who looked it over, and said it was the same form as last year confirming my account balance. The only difference was this year there was forty-six thousand dollars in the account. Pete and I had the same conversation as the year before, but this time we were talking real money.

I was tempted, with money like that I could have a nice down payment on a house. It wasn't life changing money, but it was close.

But I was a married man with a wife to answer to and Cathy was dead set against it. She reasoned that the reward didn't justify the risk. The fact that more money was now involved, really made things more dangerous. The more money that was involved increased the odds that something would go wrong at the bank, or whoever put the money there, would come looking for it. So once again, I told Pete thanks, but no thanks.

The thought of all that money just sitting there was still on my mind when Pete called me a few weeks later. He'd just gotten off the phone with Onofre who had some news on the mysterious bank account. It seemed that Onofre and his partners in the flight school they owned had been suspecting their manager of embezzling funds for some time. They'd had an accountant audit their books, and found that the manager had indeed been skimming money from the business. The accountant told them that over the past three years he had taken about forty-six thousand dollars from them, the exact amount of money in the bank account.

Armed with that information, Onofre did some digging and found out that the manager's brother worked in that very same bank that had the mystery account in it. It didn't take Sherlock Holmes to figure out that the manager had gotten hold of my information, and had his brother open a phony account in my name. This information solved the big mystery of the bank account, but I wasn't really ready for what Pete said next.

"Kerry, Onofre wants you to go to Palma and get the money out before his manager can move it."

I was taken aback. "I don't know about that, Pete. Just because it isn't a mob account, doesn't make it any less dangerous. I can still get into trouble if I get caught."

"Caught doing what? It's your account, it's in your name," he said as if it was simply a matter of fact.

"Yeah, but it's not my money. If you take money out of a bank that doesn't belong to you, it's called a bank robbery!"

"Don't be so dramatic McCauley, it's not a bank robbery. It's not like you're using a gun in a stick up, you're just closing your account,"

"And taking out money that I didn't put in. What if they check or ask for an ID? I don't even speak Spanish! How in the world could I have opened the account in the first place?" I said, desperately digging up excuses that might get me out the crazy situation I suddenly found myself in.

"I don't know, just call Onofre and see what he has in mind."

My reservations hadn't just occurred to me on the spot. I'd been thinking about what could go wrong ever since getting the first notice from the bank. I really wanted that money, but the thought of just walking into the bank and closing the account sent shivers up my spine. I mean, come on, what bank manager would believe that a young American pilot would have forty-six thousand dollars in a bank in Mallorca? But Onofre was a good friend of mine and if I could help him out I would. I figured I should at least find out what he had in mind. So I called him to find out exactly what he wanted me to do. I should have known better. He told me that he'd hired a lawyer to help him get his money back but that he needed me there because it was my name that was on the account. Onofre said he and his partners would fly me to Palma where we would meet with his lawyer and discuss what to do from there. His plan to use a lawyer to help get his money back made me feel a little better about the whole plan, but I was still scared as hell. In desperation I played my last card.

"I don't know Onofre, I've been telling Cathy all summer that I'm too broke to take her on a honeymoon. If I try to tell her that I'm going to take a week off work to go and visit you in the Mediterranean, she'll kill me."

"No problem," Onofre said. "We'll pay for her ticket as well, and you two can have a nice honeymoon! I'm sure your wife would love to see Palma. You'll be a hero!"

Crap. That didn't work very well.

When I got home and told Cathy about the plan she was less than pleased, to say the least. I tried to reassure her that everything would be handled through the lawyer, and that all that I was needed for was to sign a few documents to make everything official. That seemed to put her mind at ease, but I could tell that she was still nervous about the entire affair. I know I was.

A few weeks later we flew to Palma and Onofre picked Cathy and me up at the Palma airport. He loaded us into his small Mercedes, and took off towards his apartment in the heart of the city. He was very glad to see us and was waiving his hands around and talking a mile a minute about what a nice hotel we would be staying at and the dinner plans for that evening. Onofre was so distracted by our conversation that he never saw the red light. The resulting crash totaled two cars but miraculously left everyone unhurt. Not a great start to "THE BANK JOB" as I had come to call it.

The next morning Onofre picked me up at our hotel in a borrowed car, I told Cathy that we were going to meet his lawyer to discuss our plans, and would be back soon. We drove downtown and met the lawyer at an outdoor café. The three of us sat down for espresso while the lawyer explained what we were going to do. The plan was for the three of us to go into the bank, close out the account and take the money. Then, the lawyer would take us to a notary public where he would draw up a power of attorney, so I could legally give Onofre the money.

"THAT'S your plan?" I asked incredulously. "Go into the bank, close the account, and take the money? What kind of a plan is that? I thought the reason we had a lawyer with us was to tell the bank manager what happened and somehow transfer the money to you legally."

"If you admit that you didn't open the account, the bank will seal it. It will take the courts years to sort it out and give Onofre the money, if ever," the lawyer replied.

I didn't like the way this was going. I thought the plan was to go in with lawyers blazing, declare that my name had been used against my will and demand justice. But no, I was supposed to just waltz in and ask for my forty-six thousand dollars, please. If I wanted to do that I could have done it by myself a year ago, and kept the money.

Onofre and his lawyer looked at me expectantly, waiting for my decision. I tried to think of another way to get the money, another argument, another . . . something, anything.

A sense of dread came over me. "Okay, I suppose I could give it a try." I said, immediately regretting it. *Why can't I ever say no?*

Onofre smiled and clapped me on the shoulder, "Wonderful! Thank you very much! Don't worry, everything will go smoothly."

He paid the check and stood up, "Okay, let's go."

I was a little surprised at the abrupt departure. Europeans, especially the Spanish, usually linger over coffee. *Why aren't we lingering? I like lingering.*

"Where are we going?" I asked, getting to my feet.

"The bank," Onofre replied, "it's right over there," he said, pointing to a set of glass doors just fifty feet down the sidewalk. We'd been having coffee and discussing our plans right next to the bank!

"Wait, we're doing it now?"

"Yes, when did you think we would do it?"

"I don't know. Later. Tomorrow. Never." I said, thinking that I would have time to go back to the hotel, talk it over with Cathy and think about it some more. Maybe come to my senses and fly home. The two Spaniards stood there looking at me expectantly, waiting for me to make up my mind. Damn it, I wanted more time. Everything was happening too fast!

"Okay, let's do it," I said, resigned to my fate. We walked up to the glass doors of the bank and pushed a buzzer on the side. A voice over a speaker asked something in Spanish, Onofre answered, and the doors slid open. *Oh great. If anything goes wrong, I'll be trapped!* Unlike banks in the United States, the doors in Spanish banks remain locked at all times and an employee has to buzz you in and out. No running out the door for me, now that I was in, I was committed.

Onofre walked up to a smiling man behind a long marble counter. When he asked how he could help us, Onofre launched into a long reply that I didn't understand. Then Onofre gestured to me and when the teller looked at me his face went white. The shocked teller behind the counter was none other than the flight school manager's brother. And by the look on his face, he obviously knew who I was. The man regained his composure, came out from behind the counter and ushered us over to what I assumed was the bank manager's desk. A middle-aged man with slicked back, gray hair and an expensive looking suit rose to greet us. After introductions, and a short conversation in Spanish, the manager gestured for me to have a seat.

My heart was pounding so hard as I sat down in the overstuffed chair that I thought I might pass out. I tried to control my breathing and remain calm as Onofre's lawyer and the manager chatted back and forth. As the teller walked up behind the desk and handed the manager a large file, our eyes met, and he looked visibly upset. The manager put on a pair of reading glasses and began looking over the file in front of him. After what seemed like an eternity, he looked up at me over the tops of his reading glasses and studied me intently. The moment dragged on forever. He finally asked me a question in Spanish and Onofre translated for me, saying that the manager asked if I wanted to close my account. Playing along, and hoping I was doing the right thing, I nodded my head and said yes. Without taking his eyes off me the manager turned the file around, laid it in front of me and asked me another question.

"He wants to know if that is you and if that's your signature," Onofre said.

I looked down at the file and the first thing I saw was a photocopy of my passport with my picture on it. I scanned the file further and saw Orient Air's address on it and at the bottom was my signature, which, to me at least, was an obvious forgery. I wondered how they got a copy of my passport. Then I remembered something odd that happened the last time I delivered a plane to the flight school in Palma. The manager had asked for my passport saying that he needed it to fill out some paperwork. I remember waiting in his office for an awfully long time before he came back with my passport. Looking back, I realized he must have been making copies of it to use in opening the fake account.

On the verge of panic I looked at the file and wondered what to do. *This is it. If I say yes I'll be lying and committing a crime. If I tell the truth, and call the signature a forgery, I'll be calling whoever opened the account a criminal and then who knows what would happen.* I didn't know what to do, so I stalled for time. Desperately, I looked up at Onofre and the lawyer trying to get some guidance and asked, "What?" *Wow, quick thinking, Kerry. Way to go. That'll sure buy you a lot of time.*

"He wants to know if that is your signature." Onofre repeated. I looked up at the manager then back at my companions, but they only stared back at me, stone faced, offering no help. I pretended to not understand one more time, stalling again, but just delaying the inevitable. No one was going to help me. I felt very alone at that moment. The blood was roaring in my ears as I sat there wondering what the hell to do. When I could stall no longer, I made a decision I hoped was right. I Looked back at the bank manager and answered in what I hoped was a confident voice.

"Yes, that's my signature."

No one moved, no one said a word. The bank manager stared at me with penetrating eyes that said, "You're lying!" He held my gaze for a few moments longer, then sighed and motioned to his assistant. After my declaration the four Spaniards surrounding me launched into a long discussion that I couldn't follow. I just sat there waiting for either a pile of money or the police to show up. I wasn't sure which one was more likely.

A few minutes later, Onofre explained to me that the bank didn't have enough cash on hand to cover the account, and they would have to write us a check for half of the balance. I told him that would be fine. *Whatever! Who cares? Let's just get the hell out of here!*

Onofre conferred with the manager and said, "They say it will take an hour or so to get everything in order. We can wait, but I think we should use the time to go to the notary public and get the power of attorney finalized."

I couldn't believe what I was hearing. I was so nervous, it was all I could do not to panic and make a break for it. Now they were telling me that I was going to have to leave and come back, and do it all over again! I tried to look calm as I told Onofre that would be fine. The teller opened the sliding glass doors, and as we walked out of the bank I could feel his eyes burning two holes in the back of my head.

We hailed a cab to take us to the notary public's office. I collapsed into the back seat greatly relieved to be out of the bank. In the taxi we talked about how things had gone in the bank and what we should do next. Both Onofre and his lawyer thought things were going well, but I wasn't convinced. I couldn't help thinking that the delay in getting the money together was just an excuse to give the bank time to check on my story and call the police. I only knew one thing for sure; I REALLY didn't want to go back into that bank.

There were less than twenty in the entire country, so getting to meet one is a very big deal. The notary's office and he took his time looking over the power of attorney contract. I didn't mind one bit. Anything that delayed us going back to the bank was fine with me. All too soon, the notary was signing his name across the entire front page before giving it the usual fifty stamps.

The ride back to the bank was not a fun one for me. I kept thinking about what, or should I say who, would be waiting for me. Did the bank manager call the police? Was there a SWAT team staking the bank out, just waiting for me to leave with the money before arresting me? I had no way of knowing and the closer we got, the more nervous I became. The cab dropped us off in front of the bank. As we walked up to the bank I saw a man sitting in a car right in front of the doors, reading a newspaper. Sitting in a car reading a newspaper? How stupid did these cops think I was?

We were let back into the small bank lobby. I immediately noticed a man about thirty years old, fit, short haircut, dressed in cheap slacks, polo shirt, and sport coat. He was holding a folded newspaper under his arm and seemed to be just hanging around, obviously not a bank employee. I tried not to stare at him as the bank manager walked up to greet us again, but I thought I could detect a slight bulge under his jacket. *Yep,* I thought to myself, *another cop. I'm screwed. Oh well, I might as well play this through to the end.* The manager had the teller/accomplice bring out a metal box that he opened on the marble counter. He reached inside and started bringing out stacks of bills. While the teller started counting the money, the manager brought over a check and a form that he wanted me to sign. *Uh, oh, here we go. As soon as I sign this the cops will slap the cuffs on me.*

I looked at the signature line and immediately saw a problem. My real signature wouldn't match the one they had on file. If they compared the two the jig would be up for sure. I took the pen from the manager and tried to make my signature look like the one on the account application. The manager took the form from my hand, looked at it, and then at the file. Apparently satisfied with my forgery of a forgery, he put the form into the file and handed me the check while Onofre stuffed the stacks of bills into a small bag.

If they're going to arrest us, now's the time. We've accepted the check and the money.

But nothing happened. Onofre and I looked at each other with a "let's get the hell out of here" look. So we shook hands with the manager and started walking casually towards the door. My heart was beating a mile a minute as I waited for the glass security doors to slide open. *If they were going to arrest us the best time would be just before we got out on the street.* But the doors slid silently open and the three of us stepped out onto the sunny sidewalk. *Of course. If they wanted to make the charge stick, they needed to let us get outside with the loot before arresting us.*

We walked as quickly and casually as we could muster down the sidewalk away from the bank. I kept expecting someone to shout "HALT!" or "ALTO!" or whatever the Spanish police shout just before they gun down fleeing bank robbers. But there was no shout, no cop cars screeching up onto the sidewalk in front of us, not even a tap on the shoulder. When we turned the corner at the end of the block, the three of us picked up the pace and started walking faster while still trying to look calm and cool. We must have been quite a sight, three grown men speed walking down the street, trying to look casual and failing miserably. Two minutes later we were in the car and racing down the street. We'd done it, and gotten away clean!

I couldn't believe it. I had just robbed a bank! Sort of. If you define "robbing a bank" as taking money out that you didn't put in, by force or deception, then I had just robbed a bank. But it was my friend Onofre's money that had been stolen from him. All I had done was cut through the red tape and gotten his money back sooner. At least that was my justification. The mood in the car was electric. We were all coming down off the adrenaline high and couldn't stop talking about the events at the bank. I was so relieved to be done with it all. It was like a giant weight had been lifted from my shoulders. I handed the check over to Onofre when he dropped me off at my hotel, still feeling great about pulling off our caper.

When I walked into our hotel room Cathy rushed up and threw her arms around me, obviously upset. When I asked her what was wrong she explained that while waiting for me to come back from my meeting she had gone out for a walk to get some coffee. When she got back to the hotel the clerk told her that a man had come looking for her. This really had her worried because she couldn't think of anyone in Palma who even knew she was there, let alone come looking for her. The only thing she could think of was that I had been arrested at the bank. It was a mystery. Who in the world would come looking for Cathy? This news made me even more paranoid than I was before. What had I gotten us into?

That evening over dinner, we told Onofre of Cathy's mysterious visitor. Onofre had a little bit of information of his own. After dropping me off and going home, the flight school manager had shown up at Onofre's apartment in a panic. Not knowing that Onofre and his partners knew about his stealing, the manager told him a story about how he had opened a bank account in my name. He told Onofre that the money was his mother-in-law's, and he was hiding it there to get around Spain's high tax laws. Apparently, when we left the bank to go see the notary, the teller called his brother to warn him that we were taking his money. But he was on the other side of the island. By the time he got to the bank we'd already made our getaway. His brother didn't recognize Onofre so the manager had no idea that he was on to him.

Onofre listened to the manager's story in apparent sympathy, and told him he hadn't been in contact with me for over a year. The manager was visibly upset, and told Onofre that he had contacted Interpol about the matter in order to keep me from leaving Mallorca. Onofre promised to let him know if he heard from me.

After hearing Onofre's story I really started to get worried. We weren't one hundred percent positive that Interpol had been contacted, but I didn't feel like finding out. I asked Onofre if he had any ideas on how I could get off the island without having to go through passport control at the airport. He told me that he might be able to pull that off but it would take a few days. In the meantime Cathy and I should just lay low, and try to enjoy our stay in Mallorca. Sure, I'm a bank robber on the lamb. So why not hit the beach? Cathy and I spent the next two days sightseeing on the beautiful island. We tried to look like normal tourists and enjoy ourselves but I was constantly looking over my shoulder. I felt like what I was, a fugitive.

Three days later, I was sitting in the crew lounge at Air Europa. The fact that Onofre was an Airbus Captain came in handy in getting me off Mallorca and back to the United States. Onofre talked to one of his fellow captains, and asked him if he could give me a ride in the jump seat of the Airbus he was flying to New York. The pilot was a good friend of Onofre and had no problem bringing me along. Unfortunately he wouldn't be able to get Cathy on the flight because she wasn't a pilot, and not allowed on the flight deck. The thought of leaving my wife behind, while I made a quick and easy getaway didn't sit well with me at all. How could I just leave, and let her fend for herself? Cathy told me it was probably the best plan we could come up with. She reasoned that even if Interpol was really looking for me, they weren't looking for her. And even in the unlikely event that they did stop her, what could they do? She wasn't the one who robbed a bank.

The next day Onofre snuck me into the airport through the employee's entrance. An airline captain in Spain has a lot of clout, and all Onofre had to do was tell the guard I was with him and we waltzed into the crew lounge. Once in the lounge I met the captain of the plane I'd be riding in. He led me through the maintenance exit and directly to the plane, bypassing security. I felt like a Russian defector being smuggled out of the old Soviet Union, all that was missing was the fake mustache and forged identity papers. The first officer met me on the flight deck and showed me the small fold-down jump seat I'd be riding in for my flight back to America. I couldn't believe it was going to be this easy to make my getaway. I kept thinking that at the last minute the police would come barging into the cockpit and haul me off in handcuffs. But nothing happened. The doors were closed and the crew started the engines. A short while later, when I saw the coastline disappear beneath the wings, I finally allowed myself to breathe easy.

When Cathy took our normally scheduled flight home the immigration official barely looked at her while he stamped her passport and wished her a good flight. We'd both gotten away clean. And now I can put "Bank Robber" on my resume.

THE SHAH'S REVENGE

"For us as pilots, the question is:
What do I do with this? Go or no go?"
- Wolfgang Langewiesche, as quoted in Weather Flying

In 1975, the Shah of Iran bought a new six passenger twin engine Cessna 310 and presented it as a gift to Anwar Sadat, the President of Egypt. It's unclear how much President Sadat flew in the plane before his assassination in 1981, but what was clear was that by 1997, it was a piece of junk. That was my first impression when Pete Demos and I walked into a dusty hangar in Cairo with Khalid Abdel Nasser, eldest son of Egypt's second president, Jabri Abdel Nasser. The red and white paint on the plane that Khalid was proudly showing us was faded and dull. The windows were cloudy from too much sun and the whole plane had the appearance of neglect. The longer I looked at the 310, the less I wanted to fly it. There was even a large area of the fuselage where someone had repainted it with, what looked like, house paint and a brush for crying out loud. If whoever worked on that plane was that clueless about basic aircraft maintenance what other surprises were in store for us? At this point in my flying career I'd flown enough planes to know that appearances can be deceiving. A shiny new paint job can hide a multitude of maintenance sins and an Alaskan bush plane might look rough, but have a brand new engine under its scuffed and dented cowling. Sometimes though, things are exactly as they appear.

The proud new owner of that piece of aviation history had arranged to have a maintenance shop in Minneapolis give it a complete overhaul. The 310 was scheduled to get new engines, avionics, paint and interior. They were basically going to turn it into a brand new plane, all we had to do was get it there.

Getting to Cairo had already been one hell of an adventure. Instead of flying to Egypt commercially, Pete had two beautiful matching Piper Senecas that needed to be delivered to Cairo, at the same time that the 310 needed to be brought back to Minnesota. Pete was going to save a ton of money on airfare. When it came to deciding who flew which plane Pete pulled rank on me and grabbed the brand new Seneca V. I would be flying the slightly older, but still nice, Seneca III. I really didn't mind having to fly the older plane vs. the new one, because when it comes to flying over the ocean I prefer an aircraft with a few hundred hours on it. My theory was that anything that was installed or manufactured incorrectly would have already failed by that time, and anything that was going to wear out should still last for a while. That was my theory at least. True to form, we'd been forced to turn back twice due to problems with Pete's new plane. Once with a faulty fuel pressure gauge and another time with a bad transponder. Each time Pete called to tell me that we had to turn around because he was having problems I couldn't help but smile because my older plane just kept humming right along.

Having two planes going to the same destination on one trip was a rare treat. Having Pete as the other pilot also guaranteed that there was going to be some good entertainment along the way. I didn't have to wait long for the first good belly laugh of the trip.

On the leg from Bangor to Goose Bay, I heard two Canadian pilots from Quebec speaking French on the frequency Pete and I were using. The Canadian pilots were having a nice long conversation that was, I have to admit, kind of annoying. I knew if they were bugging me they had to be driving Pete crazy. One of the first things I learned about Pete was that there was a long list of things he hated: the FAA, customs officials, female pilots, stupid people, and, strangely enough for the owner of an international ferry company, foreigners, especially the French. When I heard the French pilots jabbering away I knew it was only a matter of time before Pete spoke up.

"Hey, McCauley, can you understand a word these guys are saying?"

"Nope, not a word Pete."

"Kind of annoying isn't it?"

"Sure is."

The two French speaking pilots ignored our snide comments, and continued to chat away until Pete finally got to them.

"Hey, why don't you two learn to speak English?" Pete said over the radio.

"FUCK YOU!" One of the French speaking pilots replied.

Without missing a beat Pete replied, "Good! You're learning!"

I laughed so hard I nearly lost control of the plane.

With the Canadian pilots effectively silenced, we continued on over the endless expanse of lakes and trees, on our way to one of my favorite airports, Goose Bay, Labrador. Goose Bay, often referred to as Happy Valley, is a large civilian-military airport located three hundred miles north of Newfoundland. It's home to many NATO training squadrons. The military jets take advantage of its remote location to practice low level fighter operations without any neighbors to upset. The airport is also an ideal jumping off point for aircraft with limited range that need to stop in Greenland and Iceland before reaching Europe.

I love Goose Bay. It has that remote and exotic feel that feeds the sense of danger and adventure. Goose Bay is a serious airport, a working man's airport. There are no students putting around in the pattern doing touch and goes, or Sunday pilots taking the kids for a joy ride. All of the traffic at Goose Bay is either commercial freight, passenger service, military fighters or planes crossing the Atlantic. It's in the middle of nowhere, the weather is mostly terrible, and there's no screwing around. It's a pilot's paradise. Sitting in the run-up area makes you feel like you belong to an exclusive club. On any given day, you're likely to be in line with an ancient DC-4, a Twin Otter, and a group of Luftwaffe Tornadoes. All waiting to launch into the low clouds and mist. Manly pilots doing manly things.

We landed in Goose Bay late in the afternoon. Fueled the planes so they would be ready to go in the morning, dropped our bags at the hotel and headed to the bar for dinner. I walked up to the bar and got the bartender's attention.

"What will it be?" The bartender asked.

"What kind of beer do you have?"

"Labatt's Blue."

"That's it? Just Labatt's Blue?"

"That's it. It's been a long, cold winter. The inlet the cargo ships use to resupply us is still frozen," the bartender told me as he wiped the bar with a rag. "So all we have left is Labatt's Blue."

"Well, I guess I'll have a Labatt's Blue then," I said.

Our dinner choices were limited for the same reason there was only one kind of beer left in town. We settled on thin frozen steaks that we had to thaw in a microwave and grill ourselves. Two Dutch fighter pilots gave us the hot tip of smothering the steaks in butter while they cooked. They claimed this made the steaks slightly less tough than shoe leather. Apparently a Dutch fighter pilot who worries about dying from heart disease is an extreme optimist.

The bar in Goose Bay is also one of my favorite places. It's dark and dingy, with cheap log cabin paneling and a massive wood bar. The walls are covered with pictures of airplanes in flight, on the ground, and in pieces. Stuck to just about every flat surface are stickers from the hundreds of military squadrons and ferry companies who've passed through over the years. No matter how many times I go there, I always make sure our Orient Air sticker is still there. And of course, there are always a bunch of pilots sitting around the bar rehashing the day's flight, planning for the next one or just telling flying stories. It's heaven.

Early the next morning, Pete and I took off for Narsarsuaq, Greenland. With ferry tanks installed we had the fuel to go direct to Reykjavik, but the weather forecast in Iceland was for low ceilings and visibility. Knowing that the airport in Greenland was only a few miles out of the way, and had good weather, we figured we might as well stop in and get some gas.

Located on the southern tip of Greenland, the Narsarsuaq airport is the stopover for planes that don't have the range to make it all the way to Iceland. The first time Pete told me about the approach into Narsarsuaq, I couldn't believe that anyone actually flew it.

"What you do is fly to the Narsarsuaq NDB at 12,000 feet. Descend to 5,800, then fly outbound for nine miles while descending to 4,200 feet." Pete said as he traced the flight path on the approach chart he had out. I noticed the chart he was going to give me expired in April 1988. Only nine years out of date.

"At nine miles you make a standard rate turn to the left while descending to 3,600 feet. Then inbound down to 1,800 feet, that's your minimum descent altitude."

"A minimum descent altitude of 1,800 feet? Isn't that kind of high?" I asked.

"You won't think so when you see it in good weather. When you're flying outbound and making the turn, what you're doing is flying around a fifteen hundred foot mountain top, then descending into a fjord. The missed approach procedure is mostly a formality. If you drop into that fjord you either land or hit the wall. That's why I don't want you to try it unless the weather is really good, got it?"

Pete didn't have to try very hard to convince me that Narsarsuaq was only an option if the weather was good. I got scared just looking at that approach plate.

Approaching Greenland the first thing you see is the brilliant white ice cap that covers the huge island and reaches up to 10,000 feet. Surrounding the southern tip of the ice cap is a ring of sharp peaks and fjords full of icebergs that are spit out of the thousands of glaciers oozing from the ice cap. The visual approach to the airport was fifty miles up one of three, almost identical, fjords. I say almost identical because only one ends up at the airport. The other two are dead end traps. They look exactly like the correct one, but get narrower and narrower, until the poor unsuspecting pilot who blunders into one is trapped between steep rock walls too narrow to turn around in. Back during World War II, someone painted a large red cross on a small island in front of the correct fjord to help pilots who were unfamiliar with the route. Even with that crude but effective aid, the wrong fjords were littered with the wreckage of planes whose pilots chose incorrectly.

Even though this was my tenth trip to Narsarsuaq, and Pete's umpteenth, we were still slightly unsure if we'd picked the correct fjord until we saw the familiar sunken ship halfway in that marks the correct path. Once we were assured that we were in the correct fjord, I could settle down and enjoy the beautiful scenery. The high rock walls and crystal clear turquoise water filled with icebergs make this my favorite spot in the world to fly. In good weather the safest approach to Narsarsuaq was to come in high until you're over the airport then slowly spiral down. Or, if you're positive that you can select the correct fjord, you can follow it and enjoy the scenery of the fifty mile path, before descending to the runway. Those were the safe ways to get to the airport. In good weather I never chose either of those options.

As soon as I saw the sunken ship I pulled up sharply in a steep left bank and let Pete's plane pull ahead of me. I had enough speed and power to clear the rock wall on my left and continued the turn all the way around until I was high over the fjord. Pete was now two miles ahead of me. Officially this was a "spacing maneuver" designed to allow Pete to arrive at the runway ahead of me and land first. But I could have achieved the same result by simply slowing down and letting Pete pull ahead. The real reason for my maneuver was purely selfish. I was going to do a little low level flying. I think I actually giggled as I pushed the nose of the Seneca down toward the water. Leveling off at about fifty feet, I pushed the throttles forward and spent the next ten minutes buzzing icebergs and banking hard to follow the twists and turns of the fjord. I was having the time of my life. Flying a fast twin, in one of the most beautiful places in the world is truly a pilot's dream come true. The steep rock walls reminded me of the Death Star trench in Star Wars. But every party has to end sometime. If I hadn't been flying with my boss, I probably would've climbed back out and flown the fjord again. Knowing that Pete would probably kill me for wasting expensive fuel, I just pulled up when I reached the last turn and set up to land on the runway that was tucked into the steep valley at the end of the fjord.

The runway at Narsarsuaq is always fun to land on. One end of the runway starts close to the shore, and is eleven feet above sea level, the far end is 100 feet higher. The steep gradient makes for an interesting sight picture on landing. You actually had to be in a slight climb when you land and taxiing uphill requires a fair amount of power. At the far end of the runway the terrain continues to rise up to the ice cap. When you see the steep rock walls off either side of the runway you know why the airport directory states "Go-around not recommended."

As I dropped the landing gear and set up for landing, I noticed that there was a large iceberg grounded in the shallow water just off the end of the runway. That same iceberg had been stuck there for at least four years and from the looks of things it was going to be there for a long time to come.

The spacious ramp was mostly deserted except for our two planes with their beautiful matching paint jobs and one very unusual visitor. Parked next to the terminal building was a World War II era PBY Catalina flying boat. Inside the terminal, the airport manager told us the story about how the PBY came to be there. Earlier that summer four Europeans purchased the iconic aircraft and were ferrying it from the United States to Europe. None of the men had any flight time in a PBY or any experience flying over the ocean. Their lack of experience caught up with them on their flight into Narsarsuaq. Not taking the weather forecast for poor conditions over Greenland seriously enough, the men were caught by surprise when Julianehab radio informed them that the airport at Narsarsuaq was closed due to low clouds and fog. They circled over the airport for hours waiting for the weather to improve before low fuel forced them to try a desperate course of action.

Flying back out over the ocean the pilots descended slowly until they broke out of the clouds only two hundred feet over the North Atlantic. Then they utilized the unique capabilities of their aircraft by landing on the water and making the trip up the fjord to the airport on the water. Everything was going well until they hit a large chunk of ice halfway up a narrow, twisting fjord, and started taking on water. The hole was in the bow of the aircraft. The crew found that by increasing their speed the hull would raise enough to keep the hole out of the water.

Unable to stop or even slow down, the crew of the PBY drove the Catalina up the fjord as fast as they could. After a harrowing trip through the fog, they made it to the airport and were able to beach the flying boat on shore next to the runway. The next day they cleared a rough path to the runway threshold, lowered the landing gear and drove the damaged plane onto the runway and up to the ramp.

Once safely ashore, the crew of the PBY had to face the airport authorities who soon found a laundry list of violations. Not only didn't the crew have any survival gear, they didn't even have any maps of the area. They'd been relying solely on a handheld GPS for navigation. But the kicker was the fact that the fifty-year-old airplane hadn't been flown or inspected in years. The Danish aviation authorities refused to allow the plane to takeoff again until a complete inspection was performed and the aircraft deemed airworthy. If you had to pick the most expensive place in the world to get a plane like that worked on, Greenland would be it. Out of time and money, the crew was forced to return to Europe and no one in Narsarsuaq had heard from them in months. Pete and I shook our heads in disgust as we inspected the damaged plane. The PBY had always been one of my favorite planes and to see one treated like this broke my heart.

As our airplanes were being fueled Pete and I went into the weather office to get the forecast for Iceland and to file our flight plans. The news we got wasn't good. The area of low pressure was still making things miserable for the land of hot blondes and hot springs. The briefer was sure that things would be better the next day so Pete decided we should spend the night in Narsarsuaq and head for Reykjavik in the morning.

After checking in to the Hotel Narsarsuaq, with its huge Polar Bear statue in the lobby, we headed to the Blue Ice Café for dinner. The food was fantastic and seeing that we were only flying about four hours to Iceland the next day, Pete and I decided to stick around and shoot a few games of pool. Meanwhile, the bar started filling up with local Inuit men and women. About ten o'clock the party started to get a little rowdy, and the Danish workers who were in the bar got up and left. The two airport employees we were talking to told us that they never stayed at the bar very late because the Eskimos who frequent the bar had a tendency to get roaring drunk, and fights broke out almost every night. They suggested that if we wanted to drink any more we should go back to our hotel room to avoid any possible trouble. Just then the sound of an argument between two young men started to rise over the loud music in the bar. Taking that as our cue, Pete and I finished our drinks and followed the Danish workers out of the bar.

The scenery on the walk back to the hotel was magical with the arctic twilight casting a pale glow over the steep rock walls and random icebergs floating serenely in the fjord. I let Pete go on ahead while I walked down to the shore and took in the beauty of that faraway land.

The next morning we were halfway to Reykjavik, and I was bored. The departure from Narsarsuaq was interesting as usual, starting with the downhill takeoff over the grounded iceberg. The two of us then climbed up the fjord in a loose formation before flying up the glacier leading to the massive ice cap. The southern tip of Greenland is an amazing mixture of deep fjords, sharp, spire-like mountains and hundreds of icebergs dotting the coastline. I went through an entire roll of film taking pictures before leaving Greenland behind.

But there's not a whole lot to see in between Greenland and Iceland so I decided to be a good wingman and help keep my boss awake. I pushed the throttles forward and climbed to a high perch behind Pete's plane. "Pete, look over to your right, what do you see?"

There was a pause as I imagined Pete looking out the window of his plane and seeing nothing but endless ocean. "I don't see anything, what are you talking about?"

"Right at your three o'clock, tell me what you see." I said over the radio as I pushed on the yoke and dove my Seneca down below his plane, building up speed and overtaking him.

"Don't you see that? It's exactly at your three o'clock position."

Indicating over 200 knots I pulled up hard, pointed the nose at the sky and roared past Pete's wing tip going nearly vertical.

"GOD DAMN IT MCCAULEY! You scared the hell out of me!" Pete screamed over the radio. Sometimes I can be very immature.

After a brief stop in Iceland Pete and I took advantage of some unusual good weather over the British Isles and pushed on to Jersey, one of the Channel islands off the coast of France. After a forgettable English dinner the two of us retired for the night without the usual three or four nips from our travel bottles. We hoped for an early start so we could get into Rome early enough to enjoy a nice Italian dinner with Ricardo.

When we left the hotel the next morning our hopes for a quick getaway were dashed. A heavy fog had rolled overnight and the weather office threw out comments like persistent and mid-afternoon. The two of us went to the airport cafe for some coffee and sulking. If we were stuck on the ground until even late morning our gourmet meal and an evening in Rome would be replaced with Spam and crackers and Pete in his saggy whiteys.

As we sat and stewed there was one topic that we both failed to bring up. The possibility of a zero zero takeoff. The wet blanket of fog that hung over the Channel Islands was so thick and low that landing in those conditions would be nearly impossible and highly illegal. On the other hand there was nothing that said that we couldn't attempt a takeoff. Okay, there was something that said we shouldn't takeoff. Common sense.

A zero zero takeoff, while legal, was pretty damn dangerous. It wasn't the takeoff part that was difficult. (Any dummy can follow the dotted line down the runway.) It was what happened immediately after you broke ground that was the tricky part. Because the second you left mother earth you had to go on instruments, and if you so much as sneezed and dropped the nose for a moment you'd find yourself back on the ground, with predictably unfortunate results. What if you had some sort of problem that would normally require you to return to the airport? Well good luck. Hope you can keep your disabled aircraft in the air long enough to make it to an airport where a landing might be possible. it could be a long way. And then there's the worst possible situation, engine failure after takeoff. Normally if a pilot finds himself going down shortly after takeoff he at least has the luxury of seeing what he's about to crash into. Not so with a zero zero takeoff. With the fog right down on the deck you get to see what you're going to hit about one second before actually hitting it. Exciting.

So yes, a zero zero takeoff was dangerous, foolish and unnecessary. We're ferry pilots not bomber pilots. And we're delivering expensive toys to rich boys, not saving the world. So there's no reason to take such a risk. Except for the fact that I really wanted to do it! But I couldn't tell Pete that. I couldn't even hint at it. Because to do so would challenge my fellow pilot's courage. And that's not cool. I wouldn't want to influence Pete into doing something beyond his comfort level. But Pete's no wilting flower, he'll do what he wants to do. I took another sip of coffee and waited for Pete to make the first move.

"What do you think, McCauley?"

Aha! I told Pete that I could maybe be persuaded to possibly go out to the airplanes and have a look see. I pointed out that we were both pretty damn current on instruments and that our planes had been performing flawlessly. I told him as casually as I could that yes, I'd be willing to give it a whirl. For the sake of the team mind you. Not because I had some personal dragon to slay. And certainly not because I wanted to go to dinner in Rome. Pete agreed that he too could be persuaded to go have a look.

The man in the weather office raised an eyebrow when we informed him that we were leaving but accepted our flight plans without comment. Pete gave me the honor of going first. "After you" I believe he said. I lined up on the runway as straight as I could using the only two runway centerline markers I could make out over the nose of the Seneca. There might have been a momentary hesitation in my hands before they shoved the throttles forward but soon I was speeding down the runway. It was a lot harder than I thought it would be. I could barely make out the edge of the runway and the centerline stripes came at me faster and faster. My feet danced on the rudder pedals as I fought to keep the plane going straight down the runway. If things started to get away from me I'd have to jam on the brakes quickly to avoid running off the side of the runway. But I had it. The centerline stripes were coming at me faster and faster, straight and true. As my speed increased I lifted the nose of the plane slightly prior to takeoff, but when I did that the nose blocked the few centerline stripes that were my only visual cues to keep going straight. I was speeding down the runway with my main wheels still firmly planted on the asphalt blind as a bat. *Crap.* I hadn't thought of that. I was going too fast to stop so I locked onto the directional gyro compass and used that to hold my heading. An odd sense of calm came over me as I roared blindly down the runway. It was as if I just accepted the situation as unchangeable and could only do what I could do. Instead of trying to haul the plane off the ground early I let the speed build up normally and smoothly rotated into the air. I didn't feel the plane hit any runway lights so I assumed I'd managed to keep the plane going straight enough for government work. When I saw the altimeter start to climb I raised the landing gear and let out the breath I'd apparently been holding. Dinner was excellent.

* * *

The trip had been thoroughly enjoyable. It was with no small degree of sadness when I landed in Cairo, and climbed out of the Seneca for the last time. My mood didn't get any better when I saw the hunk of junk plane I was going to have to fly home. After Pete and I finished our initial inspection of Sadat's 310, we went to the hotel to get some rest and talk about the plane.

"Well, what do you think, McCauley?" Pete asked, taking a sip of Brandy he'd poured from his travel bottle. "We don't have to fly that piece of crap back if we don't want to. We could just tell him the plane's not airworthy, and go home."

"Yes, we could, but we haven't even really done much more than walk around the plane. We should at least open it up and see what kind of shape it's in before giving up." I said, not wanting to throw in the towel just yet.

"Okay, but if we find too much crap wrong with it I'm going to pull the plug, and we'll go home."

"Sounds good to me, I really don't feel like losing an engine halfway to Greenland."

We retired to the balcony with our drinks and talked about what needed to be done to get the 310 airworthy enough to fly across the ocean. After a while, our conversation dropped off as we sat there silently drinking and watching the nighttime boat traffic on the Nile. Each lost in thought about what lay before us.

The next day we walked into the hangar and met the mechanic who was going to be working with us on the 310. I was disappointed to see it was the same mechanic I knew from my last trip to Cairo. He was a wrinkled, old man with scratched coke bottle bottom glasses, who hadn't really impressed me with his vast knowledge of aircraft maintenance. His only tools seemed to be a crescent wrench, a pair of pliers and a rusty screwdriver. In fact, tools were in such short supply in Egypt the last time I was there I sold him the tools out of my flight bag because I couldn't stand the thought of him using that crescent wrench and pliers on an actual aircraft. Not having a first class aircraft mechanic to inspect the neglected Cessna didn't sit well with us. Pete and I both had a fair amount of experience working on aircraft, but neither one of us was a licensed mechanic.

Shortly after we started tearing the 310 apart for inspection, Mr. Nasser showed up to see how things were going. He informed us that the Egyptian Aviation Authority required that one of us hold an Egyptian pilot's license before we would be allowed to fly an Egyptian registered aircraft in Egypt.

"So what do we have to do to get an Egyptian pilot's license?" Pete asked.

"One of you will need to go to the Aviation Authority building and apply for a license. They will look at your logbook to ensure you are qualified to fly that type of aircraft, and if you pass the test, you will be given a license."

"Test? What kind of a test?" I said, not liking the sound of that.

"There is a written test on aviation regulations and procedures that you must pass in order to get a license."

Pete looked at me with a grin, "I guess that solves the question of which one of us is going to get the Egyptian pilot's license doesn't it?"

"Why me?" I asked knowing that I was fighting a losing battle, "You've got a lot more experience than I do!"

"That's true but you've studied the regulations and taken tests more recently than I have. And of course there's the biggest reason of all. I don't want to, and I'm the boss!" Pete said laughing.

Resigned to my fate, I left with Mr. Nasser to start the process of getting an Egyptian pilot's license. Our first stop was the home of retired Air Force General Ahmed Atef, a hero of Egypt's Six Day War with Israel. Mr. Nasser told me that General Atef was to be my shepherd through the mountain of red tape and official nonsense that would be involved in getting my license. The General's home was a small apartment in downtown Cairo, decorated with the things you would find in any former fighter pilot's home. Faded photos of smiling pilots standing around various military aircraft covered the walls and a model of a Mig-21 Fishbed sat on a shelf next to a battered flight helmet.

Mr. Nasser made his introductions, telling me that the General was a national hero for shooting down an Israeli F-4 Phantom during the Six Day War, and was essentially the best fighter pilot in the world. The General seemed slightly embarrassed by the attention and tried to shrug it off as nothing. But I could still see his face light up with pride, as the son of the president sang his praises.

The General drove me to the Egyptian Aviation Authority building to meet with the head of administration. Once in the building, I soon realized just how famous my guide was. It seemed we couldn't go more than a few yards without someone recognizing him, and stopping to talk and tell him how much they admired him. Apparently, the General was the Egyptian Chuck Yeager to the aviation community.

We were ushered into a large office and met the head of the Egyptian Aviation Bureau. I was a little intimidated by him. I was just a lowly ferry pilot looking to get an endorsement on my license. I didn't think it required such a high level of attention. But in the end it turned out that having friends in high places would come in handy. The Director and the General were old friends and spent a few minutes catching up before turning their attention to me. He told me that getting a pilot's license just required taking a written test and showing them my logbook ensuring that I had the proper training and instructor sign-offs. The written test worried me some, but when he mentioned my logbook, I saw a potentially big problem.

"Excuse me sir," I said rather meekly, "but I don't have my logbook with me."

"What do you mean you don't have your logbook with you?" The Director replied with a look of disdain.

From the minute I entered his office I'd gotten the feeling that the Director thought of me as a member of a lower class than himself and the General. But being called out for not having my logbook felt like I was in grade school, trying to explain that my dog ate my homework.

"Well sir, it's like this. I never fly with my logbook because if I lose it, it's irreplaceable. I just keep track of my flight time, and transfer it to my logbook when I get home."

The Director looked at me with cold eyes that clearly didn't like what they were seeing. "I am myself a certified Boeing 747 pilot with over twenty-five years of flying. I have never entered an aircraft without my logbook!" He paused and stared at the General with a look that said both Can you believe this guy? And what sort of trouble have you brought me?

"Excuse me sir, but just what exactly do you need to see in my logbook? My license and medical certificate are in my wallet, all you would see in my logbook are my flight times."

"I will need to see that you were checked out in that model of Cessna 310 by an instructor."

"But in the United States, a pilot with a multi-engine rating is legal to fly any multi-engine aircraft, up to twelve thousand pounds."

"That may be so, but this is Egypt, and I will need to see your sign-off before I can give you a license and allow you to fly that aircraft in Egyptian airspace. You do have a sign-off from an instructor in that make and model, don't you?" The Director asked, starting to get a little agitated. Now, of course I didn't actually have a sign-off to fly that model of 310, but I wasn't about to tell him that.

"Oh, yes sir, I certainly do have that sign off in my logbook."

"Well I will need to see it before you will be allowed to leave."

"If I had a copy of that page of my logbook faxed to you would that be satisfactory?" I asked, already formulating a plan in my mind of how to get the Director a copy of a sign-off that didn't exist, yet. He didn't look very happy with my suggestion but agreed that it would be sufficient. He then had an assistant escort me to a separate room to administer the written test I would need to pass in order to get an Egyptian pilot's license. I was more than a little worried about the test. I'd never even seen the Egyptian regulation book and had no idea what might be in it. When I opened the test book and started reading the questions I saw that I was right to be worried. There were a lot of normal questions about flying that I could answer, but when I came to the sections dealing with Egyptian airspace and commercial operations I didn't have a clue. There was a lot of guessing going on during the last part of that test.

If I thought the Director was unimpressed with me for not having my logbook with me, his opinion sure didn't improve when he saw how poorly I did on the test. He couldn't believe that I'd flown around Europe and Africa without knowing every stupid little regulation the International Civil Aviation Organization (ICAO) had come up with. At that point I didn't really care about his opinion of me. All that mattered was that I passed.

I soon found myself sitting in a small office next to the desk of a middle-aged clerk who sat silently hunting and pecking his way through my license form on an ancient typewriter. It was taking the little man a long time to type out my form so I put my left foot up on my right knee and tried to get comfortable. As soon as I did that, the little old man went berserk. He started shouting angrily at me in Arabic, while pointing alternately at my left foot, then back at my face. I had no idea why he was suddenly so riled up, but it seemed that he didn't like the fact that I'd crossed my legs. Trying to calm the guy down a little I slowly uncrossed my legs and put the offending foot back down on the floor. Apparently my left foot was the problem, because when I put it back down, the old man stopped shouting at me and angrily went back to banging on his typewriter. I found out later that in the Arab culture, showing the sole of your shoe to someone was the highest kind of insult you can give them. So when I crossed my legs and he saw the sole of my shoe he thought I was insulting him. He was still angry when he tore the form out of his typewriter. He shoved it at me and stormed off.

The General and the Director were still chatting away when I was escorted back into his office. I assured the Director that I could get my wife to copy the page in my logbook and fax it to him the next day.

When we returned to the airport, the General walked in with me to take a look at the 310. The plane was a mess. The cowlings were off the engines, and most of the access panels were open. Aircraft seats and random parts were strewn all over the hangar. The seventy year old mechanic, with his sweat stained t-shirt and coke bottle bottom glasses, completed the picture of maintenance excellence. After looking at the ferry tank Pete was installing, and poking his nose inside the cockpit, the General walked back over to me.

"Mr. McCauley I think I would rather dogfight a dozen Israeli Phantoms than fly this piece of junk across the ocean!" he said laughing. "You are a much braver man than I am my friend!"

"Either brave or stupid, take your pick, General!"

"That's a difficult choice," the General said as he shook my hand, "be careful and fly safe!"

The retired fighter pilot took one last look at the 310, and shook his head as he left.

While I was gone, Pete and the mechanic had found a long list of things wrong with the 310, but fortunately, or unfortunately, nothing that as yet would ground the plane. While the mechanic banged away with his hammer and crescent wrench at some defect, I helped Pete install the ferry tanks. We took the tanks and fittings out of one of the Seneca's and transferred it all to the 310. One difference; because the tip tanks out on the end of the wings are higher than the ferry tanks, we added an electric fuel pump in between the ferry tanks and the original fuel system to pump fuel to the tip tanks. The tanking was about half done when we quit for the day.

Instead of taking us back to our hotel that evening, Mr. Nasser and his business partner took us out for a night on the town. At dinner, Mr. Nasser asked how the preparations for the trip were coming along. Pete and I looked across the table at each other wondering just how we should answer him. We still hadn't made up our minds if we thought the 310 was in good enough shape to make the crossing.

"The tanking is going well," Pete said between mouthfuls of lamb, "it should be done by tomorrow if everything goes as expected. Kerry has been working with the mechanic, so he has the best information on the maintenance status of the plane itself."

All three men at the table looked expectantly at me for my assessment. *Thanks a lot, Pete.* I silently cursed him for putting me on the spot and making me be the bad guy that tells him that the plane he'd bought was a piece of junk.

"Well sir, we are making good progress, The plane hasn't been flown for quite a while, and we're finding a lot of things wrong with it that need to be fixed before we're willing to fly it across the ocean."

Mr. Nasser's face clouded over a bit when he heard what I'd said. "But you will be able to fix everything you find, is that not correct?"

He was really putting me on the spot. I didn't want to commit us to the trip just yet, but so far we hadn't found anything big that would ground the plane. On the other hand, if I told him that I thought his new plane was a piece of junk, and I wouldn't fly it over the ocean no matter how much he paid me, the trip would be over and both Pete and I would lose a lot of money. I did my best to split the baby.

"That's true unless we find something major or suspect that the engines are not reliable."

"But how could that be? The plane has only five hundred hours on it. The engines are supposed to be good for one thousand five hundred hours before being overhauled."

"It's true that the engines only have five hundred hours on them, but that's the problem. They only have five hundred hours on them in almost twenty years. It's not good for engines, or the whole aircraft for that matter, to sit for long periods of time. Rubber gaskets dry out, metal in the engine corrodes, and things break down." I paused wondering if I'd made my point yet. "An airplane needs to be flown regularly to stay in good shape."

"But we'll just see what we find," Pete interjected because he could see that his customer was a little distressed by what I'd told him, "I think we'll be able to get her into good enough shape to make the trip. Once the mechanics in Minnesota get a hold of her they'll turn her into a brand new plane!"

Looking slightly relieved the two Egyptian businessmen turned their attention back to their food. We spent the rest of the dinner entertaining them with our tales of daring, flying over the oceans of the world. Pete ignored the dirty look I gave him for basically telling the clients that we could do the trip. I hoped he wasn't committing us to fly the 310 before we had all the facts and could make an impartial decision about whether we should fly that plane or not.

Our first stop after dinner was a hookah bar where we smoked apple flavored tobacco out of giant hookah pipes. The bar was crowded with locals clustered around ornate pipes smoking and chatting away. The scene was exotic but I found the smoke bland and tasteless.

I gave Pete a little hell about our dinner conversation when we got back to the hotel.

"By the way Pete, thanks for telling Nasser that we can fix anything we find wrong with the 310 and would be flying it no matter what."

"That's not what I told him. I told him that if we didn't find anything we couldn't fix we would go, but you can still walk away anytime you want."

"Yeah, but you made it sound like there wasn't anything we couldn't fix." I said, still a little miffed. "I tell ya what Pete, this plane's a piece of junk and if we were smart, we would take a pass on this one."

"You're probably right McCauley. I'll tell you what. Let's give it one more day and if we don't like it any better we'll pack up and leave, okay?"

It sure sounded like he was just stringing me along, but I figured I could give it one more day. After all, what could possibly go wrong? (Man, I have got to get a new motto.)

That night I called Cathy and instructed her on how to forge a page in my logbook. I needed to show the Egyptians that I had received an instructor's checkout for the Cessna 310 before they would let me fly it. Trying to convey exactly what the logbook entry should look like over international phone lines and nine time zones took some doing but she managed to produce a pretty good forgery and get it faxed to the Director of Aviation in Egypt.

Things also started to come together for the plane that day. Pete and the mechanic were almost done with the inspections, and had yet to find anything that was too terrible. This news didn't make me happy at all. I had a bad feeling about that plane, and was really starting to have serious misgivings about flying it across the ocean. The problem was we hadn't found anything bad enough with the 310 that would give me an excuse to back out. That meant if I decided not to fly it, I'd have to admit to everyone, and myself, that it was because I was scared.

By the end of the day it was starting to look like I wasn't going to get the major mechanical problem I was hoping for. The inspections were complete, and any problems that hadn't been fixed weren't big enough to keep us on the ground. The ferry tanks would be plumbed the next day. After that we'd be all set to go. I was still waiting on final approval for my license, but with the forged copy of my logbook on the way, it would be coming soon. I spent that evening stewing in my hotel room, trying to come up with an excuse, any excuse, not to fly that plane.

The next day I had a shiny new Egyptian pilot's license in my wallet, and the plane as ready to go as we could make it. Everything was looking like the trip was a go, until Mr. Nasser walked into the hangar with a glum look on his face.

"The airport manager has informed me that he will not allow my plane to leave because he isn't satisfied that the inspections are sufficient to legally fly the plane in Egyptian airspace." He said. "He insists that the plane undergo a complete annual inspection, just like any other aircraft,"

Clearly frustrated, Pete spoke up, "You don't need an annual inspection if the plane is being moved for maintenance! All you need is a sign off from a mechanic saying the aircraft is airworthy!"

"That may be true in America, but in Egypt, the law is not so clear, and the airport director wants a full inspection."

"Well how long will that take?" I asked the mechanic who was standing with us.

"It is not so easy. The inspections are complete but the engines are too old to be approved."

"What do you mean too old? They only have five hundred hours on them!" Pete exclaimed.

"But they haven't been overhauled in the last ten years, as is required by Egyptian regulations."

"But that's why we're taking it to the United States!" I said, appearing to be upset at the news. "to get the engines overhauled!"

"Yes, of course, but that doesn't matter. They want what they want, no matter what kind of sense it makes. I'm trying to get an exception, but the director of that agency is not a good friend of mine."

It got quiet for a minute as all of us processed what we were hearing. If Mr. Nasser couldn't get a maintenance ferry permit for the 310, then we'd just wasted a week working on a plane that couldn't fly because there was no one in Egypt that could overhaul the engines. Everyone was unhappy, except me. Here was my way out! The government won't let us fly this piece of shit out of here? Bummer! Oh well, we tried. What time is the next plane to New York?

"There is one other option," Mr. Nasser said, "you could wait for the airport manager to leave for the day and then just takeoff."

Uh oh, I thought, *here we go again.*

"What about the guys in the control tower?" Pete asked, "I'm sure the manager has told them that the 310 isn't allowed to leave."

"The men manning the control tower aren't very bright. Just tell them you are on a test flight, then takeoff and go."

I wasn't crazy about the idea but I had to admit it did have a certain panache. And after all this is the Middle

East, you can get away with a lot in the Middle East as long as you don't get caught. But why was I even considering it? The perfect excuse for not flying the 310 had just been dropped in my lap. No one could blame me for not risking my license by making an illegal takeoff in Egypt, of all places. But somehow the thought of blasting off without permission and escaping the country before the authorities caught us made the flight more appealing, not less. *What the hell is wrong with me?*

We talked about the plan for a while, and Pete and I agreed that it was worth a shot. Our alternative was to leave the plane, and come back if they ever got the inspection done. I asked Mr. Nasser what was going to happen to him when the manager found out that we'd left and he told us not to worry. Even though he couldn't pull any strings to get the plane approved for flight they still wouldn't dare to arrest the son of the president for something so minor.

As Pete and I were planning our departure, I discovered a minor flaw in our great escape. The runway, and in fact the whole airport in Cairo was surrounded by tall office and apartment buildings. If we lost an engine on takeoff, a likely event in my opinion, we'd need to be as light as possible in order to be able to climb out on only one engine. That meant we could only take enough fuel to reach the nearest airport along our route, and that was Alexandria on the Mediterranean coast. And Alexandria is still in Egypt. That meant if the control tower in Cairo got mad and called ahead to report our illegal departure we might be in some serious trouble. But Pete assured me that if we didn't file a flight plan for Alexandria they wouldn't know where we had gone and wouldn't know who to call. I pointed out that there weren't that many airports in Egypt, and it wouldn't take a rocket scientist to figure out where we'd gone. In the end, Pete left it up to me to go or not, and I once again opted to go for it. I began to wonder if I might live longer if my motto was "better safe than sorry."

For the last two days Pete and I had been packing and checking out every time we left the hotel in the hope that we might be able to leave that day. So when the decision to go was made, all we had to do was throw our gear in the plane and put enough fuel in to make it to Alexandria. Late in the afternoon Mr. Nasser drove up to the hangar and told us that the airport manager had finally gone home for the day. Now was our chance. We hopped in the plane, casually taxied out to the runway and asked for permission to takeoff on a maintenance test flight. The tower took a long time deciding if they would approve our request but in the end they granted us clearance for the flight.

I lined up on the runway, said a little prayer and shoved the throttles forward. Pete had designated me pilot in command for the trip, so one of the duties I'd given him was watching the engine instrument gauges on takeoff. I told him that if he saw anything at all out of the ordinary to tell me, and I would abort the takeoff and keep that hunk of junk on the ground.

My heart was beating a mile a minute as the 310 accelerated down the runway. The engines put out a satisfying roar as I watched the apartment buildings get closer and closer. When we reached rotation speed, I pulled back on the yoke and the 310 climbed into the air for the first time in years. I quickly slapped the gear handle up and with a sigh of relief, felt the landing gear retract as our speed increased. With the gear up we easily cleared the buildings in our way and headed north toward Alexandria.

We told the tower we were departing the pattern to the north, and after receiving acknowledgment, turned the radio down. There was no sense listening to them yell at us because we weren't turning back. On the way to Alexandria Pete and I took stock of the 310 and its systems. There was a thankfully short list of squawks so far. The cylinder head temperature gauge for the right engine wasn't working and the number two radio was a little scratchy. All in all a good start. I just hoped the plane held together for the rest of the trip.

Arriving in Alexandria I contacted the tower and was relieved that no mention was made of our unauthorized escape from Cairo. We landed and informed ground control that we were just there for fuel, and would be leaving immediately. We hoped we could get out of there before Cairo had a chance to call around looking for us.

While I waited for the fuel truck, Pete went inside the terminal to file a flight plan for our next stop, the Heraklion Airport on the island of Crete. After an unusually long time, Pete came walking back across the sun baked ramp toward the 310.

"What's up?" I asked seeing the pissed look on his face. "Where's the fuel truck?"

"I don't know, something about it filling up at the tank farm on the other side of the airport."

"How long's it going to take?"

"I don't know, nobody seems to be in much of a hurry."

I sure didn't like the sound of that. The longer we hung around Alexandria the greater the chance of our little situation catching up with us. While we were waiting for the fuel truck an Egyptian Army jeep drove up and two soldiers with AK-47's got out. I was nervous at first but they didn't do anything but smile and walk around looking at the plane. Alexandria was a joint civilian/military base, and I guess they were there to keep us from stealing Egyptian military secrets. I noticed a row of Russian Mig fighter jets lined up on the other side of the ramp. I got out my camera to snap a picture of them. As soon as I raised my camera, one of the soldiers ran over and waved his hands signaling that I couldn't take any pictures. He didn't speak any English, but his purpose was clear, keep the American spies under wraps.

After waiting for almost an hour, the fuel truck finally arrived to top us off. We wasted no time in filling up and getting the heck out of there. It was with great relief that the tower gave us permission to takeoff and we left Egypt and headed out over the Mediterranean.

Shortly after takeoff we checked in with the Alexandria Air Traffic Control Center that would be monitoring us on the first half of our flight to Crete. They answered our radio call by telling us that we were in radar contact but that our transponder wasn't reporting our altitude.

Transponders in aircraft do two things, broadcast a specific code that identifies the plane on a controller's radar screen and send out a signal that tells the controller what altitude the aircraft is flying at. This altitude signal is called "mode C" and is required for all aircraft operating near large airports and flying in instrument conditions. Not having an operational mode C transponder is a big deal.

ATC will ask you to either fix it, or land as soon as possible.

I turned the transponder off and on a few times, the only fix a pilot can attempt in flight, but ATC informed us that our mode C was still inoperative. *Crap.* If there's one place in the world where it's virtually impossible to fly without a working mode C transponder, it's the tightly controlled airspace over Europe. I was sure that as soon as the first European controller saw that our Mode C wasn't working he would force us to land and get it fixed, no if's, and's or but's. Pete and I agreed on one thing, we weren't going back to Egypt. We would push on to Crete and then deal with the problem. Probably couldn't find anyone in Egypt who could fix it anyway.

Two hours later, Crete ATC started picking us up on radar and the first thing they did was ask us to turn on our Mode C. Instead of telling them that I knew it wasn't working, I decided to play dumb. I turned the transponder off and on a few times, trying to "fix" the problem. When ATC informed me that the transponder was still not working, I assured him that I would have it looked at after I landed. The controller seemed satisfied and handed me off to the control tower for landing.

Pete and I looked at each other and smiled. "You think we could get away with that again when we leave tomorrow?" Pete asked.

"Maybe. As long as we have a different crew in the control tower we can just act surprised again." I replied.

"What if it's the same guy?"

"Then we just tell them that we thought we had it fixed. If we stall them long enough we'll be so close to Italian airspace that they'll probably just let us go."

"You're right," Pete said, "It'd be easier to pass the buck than turn us around and deal with us again."

We landed in Heraklion, Crete, got two rooms at a small hotel, then went out to dinner to celebrate our "escape" from Egypt. The contrast of the beautiful Mediterranean city to the stench and filth of Cairo, was remarkable. Sitting at an outdoor restaurant drinking ouzo, I couldn't help but wish that we'd been stuck in Crete for a week, instead of Egypt.

The next day we took off for Rome and luckily got a new controller. So I went through my "Mode C not working? Really? Let me see if I can fix it" routine. I dragged out the procedure of turning the transponder on and off so long that we were almost one hundred miles west of Crete before ATC gave up and let us continue on to Italian airspace. We gave the Italian controllers the same song and dance and landed in Rome without too much trouble.

That night, we met up with our friend Ricardo for dinner. Those two men had spent years taking each other out to expensive dinners and fighting over the check. They each took it as a source of pride to play the great host whenever the other was in town. That night Pete thought he would be clever, and paid for dinner when he went to use the restroom. When Ricardo found out, he was pretty upset. I just continued to enjoy the fantastic meal as the two of them argued. It was very entertaining.

On the leg to Jersey Airport in the English Channel Islands, the 310 decided to up the level of difficulty. First the number two radio stopped working completely, leaving us with only one radio and one VOR receiver. Next, we discovered after we landed that the left engine had used almost two full quarts of oil more than the right one. That was a significant difference for only a nine hour leg. Using that much oil is a symptom of a possible serious problem. Without any maintenance facilities on Jersey, we decided to push on to Iceland the next day and see if the oil consumption stayed the same or got worse.

The leg to Iceland was an easy one, except that the ATC controllers responsible for the London airspace were not as understanding about our Mode C problem as the previous controllers had been. I pretended to try and fix the problem for twenty minutes as we flew through one of the busiest airspaces in the world. At one point the controller, who was starting to run out of patience, demanded that we turn around and return to Jersey because he couldn't let us continue on an IFR flight plan without a working Mode C. I stalled for time by telling him to standby while I consulted with my captain (me), and then didn't call him back for over five minutes, all the while getting deeper and deeper into his airspace.

When I finally called him back I asked if he could route us farther west around London or give us a lower altitude. The exasperated controller told us to descend down to 3000 feet where we would be out of the way of most of the traffic and signed off angrily. I sort of felt bad lying to all the controllers along the way, but only sort of. In all honesty I was having the time of my life. Using a little skill and deception to get the job done is in a ferry pilot's job description.

The rest of the flight went smoothly and we were soon treated to a rare sunny day over Iceland. Of all the times I've flown over the island, I have only been able to see the beautiful volcanic landscape a handful of times. Looking down at the vast black lava flows and barren mountains, it was easy to see why the Apollo Astronauts chose Iceland as a training site before heading to the moon. They say Iceland is where God put everything he had left over when he made the world. Apparently God had made just the right amount of trees, because there were none on Iceland.

After landing in Reykjavik Pete and I did a post flight inspection on the 310. Again, the left engine used a lot more oil than the right one. We didn't see any oil stains on the outside of the cowling to indicate a leak, so we guessed that the engine was losing oil past the piston rings, a common problem with aircraft that sit for long periods of time without flying. Pete and I discussed the implications of the high oil consumption of the left engine. If the engine continued to burn oil at its current rate, the twelve quarts it held should be enough to last us on the Iceland to Greenland leg. On the other hand, if the rate increased, we ran the risk of running out of oil somewhere over the iceberg strewn waters off the coast of Greenland. Not an appealing prospect. In the end we decided to keep rolling the dice. Because why wouldn't you fly a plane with a questionable engine over the Arctic Ocean?

Climbing out into the bright morning sun the next day, we left Iceland and headed for Greenland, a short 750 mile hop. Climbing through 4,000 feet Pete reached into his green nylon Orient Air flight jacket, pulled a half smoked cigar out his stainless steel cigar case and lit up. I glanced sideways at him in irritation, but didn't say anything. I'd been forced to put up with his smoking in the plane for years, and although I wasn't a big fan of cigar smoke in the cockpit, at least he'd stopped chain smoking cigarettes.

It wasn't a minute later that I caught a whiff of what smelled like aviation fuel. I looked around the cockpit for the source of the smell and didn't see anything. When I turned around to check the ferry tanks, my heart stopped. Gushing out of the filler neck of the ferry tank was a geyser of aviation fuel that would make Old Faithful proud.

"PETE, WE'VE GOT FUEL IN THE CABIN! PUT THAT DAMN CIGAR OUT RIGHT NOW!" I screamed as I realized the glowing ember of his cigar was less than three feet away from the fountain of highly explosive fuel. Pete looked around frantically before crushing out the glowing ember of his cigar in the palm of his hand. That had to hurt but his quick thinking probably saved us.

I turned around in my seat to try and stem the flow of fuel pouring into the cabin. I quickly tightened the wing nut that compressed the fuel cap and the flow of fuel slowed to a trickle, then stopped altogether. What prevented an explosion was the fact that we were still in a steep climb, and the nose high angle meant that the spilled fuel and highly combustible fumes flowed back toward the tail. With Pete's cigar out and the gas fountain stopped I turned the controls over to Pete and squeezed my body over the ferry tanks and into the rear of the cabin. I couldn't believe what I saw when I got back there. The entire back of the plane was filled with at least two inches of highly flammable, 100 octane aviation fuel. And I was kneeling in it, terrified that the fumes would ignite at any second.

"Pete, don't key the mike, don't flip any switches, DON'T DO ANYTHING!" I yelled over my shoulder.

I grabbed two rolls of paper towels and began mopping up the fuel. It took four grocery bags to hold all of the sopping wet towels. After I cleaned up most of the spilled fuel, I took out my knife and started cutting out the soaked carpeting. It had to go, or it would continue to fill the cabin with fumes for hours. The carpet was going to be replaced anyway. When I had all the fuel-soaked trash ready to go, I popped open the small cargo door, and kicked the mess into the slipstream. I held the door open for a few minutes to clear out the fumes, then secured it. I then sat with my back against one of the ferry tanks, thinking about how close we'd come to a very spectacular end.

After gathering my wits, I squeezed my way back up to the cockpit and into my seat. I put my headset back on, looked sternly over at Pete and told him in no uncertain words that the no smoking sign would remain on for the remainder of the trip. He didn't argue the point in the least.

Halfway to Greenland it was time to start transferring fuel from the ferry tanks to the main tanks so Pete turned around and reached behind his seat, and flipped the switch on the old, beat up transfer pump.

"God damn it!" Pete shouted over the engine noise as he was reaching over his seat flipping the power on the pump on and off. "The damn pump's not working!"

"Did you check the fuse?" I asked.

Pete didn't answer but awkwardly turned completely around on his seat. He got up on his knees and leaned over the seat back to reach down to the bottom of the pump where the fuse was located. He'd been working on the broken fuel pump for only a minute when we hit some turbulence and the plane bounced up and down quickly. Caught by surprise Pete's head smashed down on the sharp metal edge of the ferry tank he was bending over. He swore and straightened up, holding his forehead. I started to laugh at him but stopped when bright red blood started flowing out between his fingers.

"Holy crap Pete! You're bleeding pretty bad!" I said.

"No kidding genius, now get me something to stop it!" Pete yelled back angrily.

I grabbed what was left of the paper towels and told Pete to pull his hand away so I could take a look at the wound. I saw that Pete had a deep three inch gash in his forehead that was bleeding heavily.

"Wow Pete! Nice job! Want me to put a few hair plugs in there? Start a nice comb-over?"

"Screw you McCauley! Now fix me up."

I taped a big wad of paper towel to Pete's forehead then started working on the misbehaving fuel pump. After I got the fuse changed, I flipped the switch and . . . nothing. I wasn't surprised at all. Nothing on that piece of crap airplane worked, why should the transfer pump be any different? I gave the offending yellow metal box a few half-hearted whacks for good measure then started working the backup wobble pump handle. Intended as only an emergency backup, the hand pump moves very little fuel each time the little three inch handle is pumped back and forth. I was barely moving enough fuel to keep up with the two fuel hungry engines as the tip tanks stayed nearly empty.

For the next two hours I pushed the pump handle back and forth, moving the precious high octane lifeblood from the ferry tanks out to the wings. By the time the Greenland ice cap loomed into view my arm was already getting tired and my back was cramping from awkwardly bending over the seat for so long. Then Pete told me that we probably had enough fuel in the tip tanks to get us the rest of the way to the Narsarsuaq Airport. Exhausted, I turned back around in my seat and took the controls from Pete for landing. That was the third time I'd had a major problem with a ferry tank and my confidence in the jury-rigged fuel systems was starting to slip.

Miraculously, nothing new broke on the way from Greenland to Goose Bay. Even losing the alternator on the right engine as we flew into our last fuel stop in Val-d'Or, Quebec, didn't dampen our spirits. We did have a hard time ordering dinner in Val-d'Or because no one could or would speak English to us. Pete was fit to be tied. The two of us had been gone for almost two weeks and hoped that was our last night on the road.

By mid morning the next day our jolly, carefree mood was quite gone. The source of our latest discontent was a small stain of fluorescent pink dye creeping slowly down the left engine cowling. The only place pink dye could be coming from was the propeller hub. Pete and I looked at this latest development with a semi detached, almost indifferent, air that came from dealing with the nonstop mechanical problems from the 310. After experiencing so many problems over the last two weeks, we were numb.

"See that?" I said jerking my thumb out my side window.

"Huh" My partner said as he leaned over me to see the pink dye streaming down the engine cowling. "That's not good. Looks like the hub's leaking. Maybe it's just a blade seal going out." Pete said hopefully. "Or we could have a cracked hub that's about to give way."

"Could be," I replied trying to match Pete's cool. Right then, I really wished I smoked. What a great visual. The cool ferry pilot lights one up, calmly considering his options.

There weren't many things I really feared about flying twin-engine planes, but a hub disintegrating and propeller blades being thrown through the cockpit, was one of them. We had a big choice to make. We could shut the engine down or we could keep going and hope that it was just dried out seals or some kind of leak that wouldn't result in a catastrophic event.

If we shut the engine down there was no way we would make it home to St. Paul. We'd have to land somewhere in Canada, pull the prop off and have it overhauled. That would take weeks and cost thousands of dollars in hotel and travel expenses. On the other hand, we could just ignore the problem. The hub only had to hold together for another three hours and we'd be home free. Of course if we kept going, the propeller could come apart at any second and kill us. The two of us knew the options, and were experienced enough not to have to verbalize the ramifications if we chose wrong. We both just sat staring at the spreading pink stain for a few minutes, mulling over the decision, or just delaying it.

"Probably just a seal," Pete said, casting his vote.

I didn't answer right away but my delay was just a sham. I knew I was going to push on, but as captain I at least had to make a show of considering all the options carefully before making a decision. I think I was putting on a show as much for myself as for Pete.

"Yep, probably, but I'm gonna throttle back anyway, just in case." I said reaching for the throttles.

We spent the next three hours watching the bright pink stain grow steadily longer. By the time we crossed the Canadian border the stain covered the entire engine nacelle. Once back in the United States it would've been much easier to land at one of the many airports along our route and call it a day, but neither of us voiced that option. We'd brought the 310 that far and we were going to keep rolling the dice and make it to St. Paul.

When the tires finally squeaked on the runway in St. Paul, I half expected random parts to fall off the plane and go bouncing down the runway. Nothing so dramatic happened as we taxied to the terminal where the U.S. Customs agent waited for us. While the customs paperwork was being filled out, Pete and I inspected the leaking propeller hub on the left side. We couldn't tell for sure without taking the spinner off, but it looked to us that the pink dye was leaking from the base of two of the blades and not a crack in the hub itself.

"What do you think, McCauley?" Pete asked, running his fingers through the wet pink racing stripes of dye covering the left engine cowling. "She got fifteen miles left in her?" Pete asked, referring to the fact that we'd landed in St. Paul just to clear customs. Our final destination was a small airport just fifteen miles northwest where the aircraft would be overhauled.

"I don't know, Pete, It'd be pretty damn stupid of us to screw this up now after coming all this way."

"True, but if it lasted this long it'll probably make it through one more takeoff and landing."

I inspected the propeller blades for security and looked over the entire propeller hub trying to determine where exactly the pink dye was coming from. I didn't see anything obviously wrong, which didn't really make me feel any better.

"If we don't fly because of this and the feds find out, they'll ground the plane and we'll never get it out of here." Pete said.

"Yeah, and if a blade comes off on takeoff it will go right through the cabin and cut my head off!"

"Don't be so dramatic, it's just a ten minute flight. The blades seem tight, right?"

I nodded my head in agreement, still not convinced but starting to lean that way. Taking off in a plane with such an obvious discrepancy was beyond foolish, but I was so tired of that damn plane I just wanted to finish the trip and be done with it.

"All right, fine, what the hell. Why not?" I said. What's one more reckless decision on this trip going to hurt?

What could possibly go wrong?

You can add that ten minute flight from St. Paul to the list of the stupidest things I've ever done. But the propeller and hub held together on the short flight, so once again I got away with it. When we shut down the engines in front of the maintenance shop it was with a huge sigh of relief and a big sense of accomplishment. Pete and I put on the Arab headdresses we'd bought in Cairo and climbed out of the 310 for the last time. The owner of the shop got a big kick out of our joke, but when we told him what shape the plane was in he just shook his head. He really had his work cut out for him.

Afterword: When the maintenance shop finished their inspection of the 310 they came up with three full pages of major items that needed fixing. Both engines and propellers needed overhauling. The leaking propeller hub did indeed have a crack in it that could have let go at any time. And one of the main landing gear mounts was missing half of the bolts that held it onto the fuselage. The mechanic told us that if we'd side loaded the gear even a little bit on one of the landings it would've collapsed.

THE RESCUE OF THE STORMIN'
NORMIN

"Never fly in the same cockpit
with someone braver than you."
- Richard Herman Jr., 'Firebreak'

By 1997 things had started to slow down in the ferry flying business and I was only making two or three trips a year. Three years after the mid-air collision, the St. Croix Valley skydiving club broke up. A married couple bought most of the parachute equipment and opened up operations in Hutchinson Minnesota. At that time I decided that it was my opportunity to start a business supplying aircraft to this new dropzone. I borrowed some money from my grandmother, bought a Cessna 182 jump plane, and Skerry Air was born.

Skerry Air was an all encompassing aviation company that included aircraft leasing, skydiving instruction and pilot services. Within three years I had a fleet of four Cessna jump planes and was actually making some sort of a living. Despite having a full-time job and raising our two kids, Cathy took over management of the business, leaving me to do all the fun stuff. I definitely got the better end of that deal.

One day I was hanging around the dropzone talking with John, a fellow instructor, when one of the pilots told us that his mother had a condo on the island of St. Croix. I don't remember whose idea it was to start doing tandems down there but before I knew it we'd hatched a plan to start a small skydiving business on the island. Pushing tourists out of planes and landing them on the beach sounded like tons of fun. What could be better than spending all day skydiving and flying over beautiful turquoise water and all night drinking rum on the beach.

Because both John and I were full time skydivers, and had wives with real jobs, opening a winter skydiving operation seemed like the perfect gig. Jump in Minnesota during the summer and in the Caribbean in the winter. Who could possibly find fault with that plan? It turns out our wives could. Being the classic naive and clueless husbands we thought that our better halves would have no problem with our plan to spend the winter in paradise while they held down the fort with the kids and the cold weather. They weren't super excited but somehow, unbelievably, they let us go.

So we loaded up one of my jump planes, a Cessna 182, with all the skydiving gear needed to run the operation and headed south to seek fame and fortune. We didn't expect either but we were pretty sure we were going to have a good time.

We set up shop at the St. Croix International Airport in what was essentially a large closet in the corner of a large maintenance hangar. This tiny room became not only our office but our dorm room as well. John and I bought a couple of folding beds to sleep on that we could move out of the way during business hours. It was all very professional-ish.

THE RESCUE OF THE STORMIN' NORMIN

The skydiving business on St. Croix was so-so, at best. John and I handed out flyers, we made deals with all the local bars to advertise for us, we had stickers made and placed brochures in all the hotels. Nothing worked. It turned out that the cruise ships, that we'd hoped would provide most of our customers, rarely spent the night there. That meant that the tourists didn't usually have the time it took to go skydiving. We did make enough money to keep the doors open by taking the locals and expats for jumps over the beach. The Americans who moved to the island were especially glad to see us. It turns out you can only relax on the beach for so long before yearning for a little excitement to break up the monotony of paradise.

I loved island life. John and I traded a couple of jumps for scuba diving lessons. After that, whenever we weren't going up, we were going down. We also got to know a bunch of the locals who hung out at the beach bar each night watching the sun set. It was heaven.

It didn't take long for things to fall into a routine. Make a few jumps in the morning or early afternoon. Then a quick scuba dive before drinks on the beach with the laid-back club. I was starting to think that I could really get used to a life like that. It had been literally months since someone had asked me to risk my life flying in some hunk of junk over the ocean. So of course that had to change.

One day a man drove up to our office and asked John and me if we were the skydiving guys. We admitted as such and he introduced himself and said that he needed our help with a rescue. Now skydivers are not often asked to rescue anybody, so I was intrigued. I mean, what could we do? I suppose if his cat was stuck in the top of a tall palm tree I could land on it. But aside from that I was at a loss. His name was Cory and he told us he was the owner of a long line fishing boat that had become disabled out in the middle of the Caribbean Sea. The ship's name was The Stormin' Normin, and it had lost all power when its main fuel pump gave up the ghost, stranding them hundreds of miles from land. He said that the boat was in international waters so the US Coast Guard wasn't responsible and none of the South American countries were interested in helping either. The fix was simple, install a new fuel pump. The problem was that not only was the Stormin' Normin stranded, it was stranded smack dab in the middle of the Caribbean Sea, about as far from land as you can get.

So why was the owner of a disabled fishing boat approaching a couple of skydivers? Because we had a plane that you could drop things from, like people, or, in this case, a fuel pump. While John and I stood there in the parking lot with our arms crossed Cory proceeded to tell us his big plan.

Cory's plan was simple. We'd hop in my jump plane, fly out to the Stormin' Normin, and drop the replacement fuel pump to the crew. Easy peasy. Cory even came prepared; he opened the back door of his car and pulled out an oblong Styrofoam shell about twice the size of a football. It was spray painted bright orange and had 50 feet of nylon rope attached to one end; presumably to make it easier to grab once it was in the water. He even had a second dummy styrobomb made up so we could do a practice bombing run before dropping the real thing. Cory had apparently put some thought and effort into his plan. It all seemed simple enough.

Right. Just fly 300 miles out to the middle of the Caribbean Sea, find a tiny fishing boat in the middle of the ocean, drop down to an unsafe altitude, and bomb it with a fuel pump. Simple. Of course, when you're out in the middle of the ocean, the very last place you want to be is down low. Because if anything goes wrong you're in the water before you know it. Not enough time to prepare, and not enough time to call for help. Yep, the whole plan was pretty dangerous and stupid. So of course I said yes. I mean, how often do you get to risk your life for complete strangers for little reward and no benefit to yourself? Okay, all the time if you're me but that's beside the point.

To his credit the owner's plan for dropping the pump wasn't half bad. With the long nylon rope trailing behind the styrobomb there was a good chance that some part of the package would land within swimming distance of the Stormin' Normin's crew. And if I got lucky the rope might actually end up draped over the deck of the ship and no one would have to get wet or eaten by a Kraken or something. One thing we had going for us was that we wouldn't be relying solely on luck because I'd done this before. Well, not this exactly, but close enough. You see, I'm a Pumpkin Toss pilot.

Every Halloween the skydivers in western Wisconsin get together to jump out of planes, drink vast quantities of beer and bomb cars with pumpkins. Really. Leave it to skydivers to think that jumping out of airplanes isn't exciting enough. What happens at P-toss is we put a derelict car in the parachute landing area and the skydivers toss pumpkins out of planes and try to hit the car. Good fun. Of course jumpers being jumpers, there's usually a bunch of drunks standing on the car as it's being bombed. Wouldn't want things to get boring would you? It's not as dangerous as it sounds because from 500 feet hitting a car with a pumpkin is hard. Okay, standing on the car while it's being bombed with pumpkins is dangerous, but that's what makes it fun. Anyway, I'd done this sort of thing before.

So we had a plan and the mission was a go. Cory had been getting position reports on the boat from the U.S. Coast Guard. The Normin's crew had activated their emergency beacon and the Coast Guard was receiving up to date location data via satellite. Cory called to get the boat's latest latitude/longitude position while I got the plane ready to go.

As I was preflighting the Cessna, Rocky, the owner of the local FBO, came up and offered me the use of his handheld GPS. I immediately accepted because it was a brand new unit and much better than the old one I was going to use. I mounted Rocky's GPS on the yoke, punched in the Stormin' Normin's coordinates. I tossed my old one into the glove box as a backup.

It was at that point that John decided to come along to video the adventure. I told him no at first because the added weight would cut down the Cessna's speed and range. And why risk another life unnecessarily? But then I changed my mind. Because if it's not on video it didn't happen. So with little fanfare, and even less preparation, we took off to rescue the Stormin' Normin.

The 300-mile flight would take 2.4 hours one way and would require 62 gallons of fuel for the round trip. Luckily this particular 182 had long range fuel tanks that held 84 gallons. That gave me a reserve of just a hair over one hour of flight time. Not as much as reserve as I'd like but there never is.

As usual, it was a beautiful day for flying in the Caribbean. The turquoise waters surrounding St. Croix soon gave way to the deep blue water of the Gulf. As we got farther and farther from the safety of the islands my passengers became more and more nervous. Well, John at least. Cory seemed oblivious to the dangers of being out over a great big ocean in a small plane with only one engine. As a matter of fact, he fell asleep shortly after takeoff. But John and I had talked at length about just what we were getting ourselves into. We were not only flying far from land, but far from any help. The Stormin' Norman lay smack dab in-between Haiti and Venezuela. The chances of getting help from either of those countries if we ran into trouble were slim. But hey, if we went down and ended up in the raft it would at least be nice and warm. Kind of like taking a cruise. Sort of. Probably should've brought some rum.

After almost two hours of flying we arrived at the Stormin' Normin's location. I set up the perfect bombing run on the boat, dropped the fuel pump right on target and we were back home in time for happy hour. At least that was what was supposed to happen. What we really found when we got to where the boat was supposed to be was . . . nothing. Empty ocean.

I was mildly disappointed, but not terribly surprised. The lat/long position I'd entered into the GPS was at least three or four hours old by the time we got there and we'd been told that the boat was drifting to the east at about three knots. According to my monkey math, the Normin could be up to 12 miles east from our current position. Problem was, the visibility was near perfect and from our lofty perch the three of us could see at least 25 miles in any direction. And we didn't see a thing.

With cautious hope, I turned the Cessna eastward and started searching for the lost boat. I wasn't too worried. After all, we were only hundreds of miles out to sea with almost a full hour's reserve fuel to play with. Kind of makes you feel all warm and fuzzy having that kind of buffer between you and King Neptune.

After 15 minutes of searching for the Normin I really started to get concerned. With my excess fuel rapidly running out, I needed to find her soon, or admit defeat and head for the barn. Then something occurred to me. Cory had received the boat's coordinates from the U.S. Coast Guard. If I could somehow contact them maybe they could give me a current position report. I was too low and too far from land to reach the Coast Guard station in Puerto Rico, but if I could get a passing airliner to help it might be possible. I tuned my radio to the guard, or emergency frequency that every plane is supposed to monitor and put out a blind call for help.

A captain on a united flight passing overhead immediately offered to help. I gave him the details of what we needed then continued my search pattern while waiting with crossed fingers. The minutes slowly dragged by, and just when I was about to give up hope, a scratchy voice came up in my headset. He'd done it. The captain quickly read off the fresh set of lat/long coordinates for the Normin before he flew out of range. It was a close thing because I lost contact with him while saying thanks. I quickly punched the new numbers into Rocky's GPS, hit the GO TO button and looked at the results.

That's weird. This says the boat should be just north of us.

According to the Coast Guard's report, the Stormin' Normin was less than five miles from our current location. I pointed the Cessna north and told John and the owner where to look while I put the new numbers into the GPS a second time. Same result. No new heading and no fishing boat.

There's no way we couldn't see it if these coordinates are correct. And knowing the Coast Guard they're probably correct. So what the hell?

I started at Rocky's brand new GPS and tried to think what might be wrong.

Wait a minute.........New GPS?

Latitude/Longitude coordinates are traditionally expressed in hours, minutes, and seconds by pilots, sailors, and anybody who really knows how to use them. But apparently thinking in terms of hours and seconds is too hard for your average Joe, so somebody decided to make an optional method using degrees. It was a simpler method for simpler people.

What if Rocky had his GPS set to display the degree method instead of the traditional minutes and seconds?

That seemed unlikely. Rocky was a professional, he wouldn't do that. But then I remembered that the unit was brand new and that he hadn't even used it yet. I quickly brought up the setting screen and sure enough, the damn thing was set to degrees. *Unbelievable!* I changed the GPS to minutes and seconds, brought up the navigation screen again and, voila! It now said that the Stormin' Normin should be 50 miles west! I swore to myself as I banked hard over to the west.

I looked at the fuel gauges as we flew to what I desperately hoped would be the correct location and didn't like what I saw. We'd burned up almost all of our reserve screwing around in the wrong location and what we had left was going to be uncomfortably low by the time we got back to St. Croix. Oh, and the sun was starting to get a little low on the horizon as well. Keep going or play it safe and head back now? Wasn't really much of a choice.

We'd been flying at 10,000 feet to give us better visibility and longer range. I throttled back and started a slow fuel saving descent to what, I hoped, was the disabled boat's location. If it actually was in this new location, then I'd be set up to make the drop right away. If we got there and there was no boat, well…can't say we didn't try.

After a few minutes a small white dot appeared on the horizon. The dot grew and grew until we could tell it was what we'd been searching for. We'd finally found the Stormin' Normin.

I made one circle over the boat so Cory could positively confirm our target then flew out to set up the bombing run. My scan in the cockpit got busy.

Heading, altitude, descent rate, distance to target, fuel, airspeed, crew.

I turned around in my seat to see if the bombardier was ready to make the drop and saw that he was holding the dummy bomb we'd brought along so we could make a practice run.

"Put that down and get the real one ready" I shouted. "We're running low on fuel so it's going to be one pass and haul ass!"

I continued the descending left turn I was in, and lined up on my target. It felt like I was flying a WWII Dauntless setting up to dive bomb a Japanese aircraft carrier at the Battle of Midway. Everything was all set. John was sitting on the floor with his back to the instrument panel, video camera already rolling.

I yelled over my shoulder. "You all set?"

"All set!"

"Okay! DOOR!"

I reached down and pulled the locking pin allowing the in-flight jump door to swing up and latch under the wing. The warm ocean air swirled violently around the cabin as a few stray bits of paper flew around before being sucked out the open door. The profile of the Stormin' Normin grew in the windshield as we raced across the water. I dropped down to less than 50 feet over the wave tops, which was extremely hard and dangerous because it's difficult to accurately judge your altitude over open water. Pulling back on the throttle I slowed the Cessna down as much as I dared and bore down on my target.

Lineup, altitude, airspeed, distance, target, crew.

I quickly glanced back over my shoulder to see if everybody was ready and was horrified by what I saw. I was expecting Cory to be up on his knees, styrobomb at the ready with the long nylon rope neatly coiled in front of him. Instead, he was sitting on his ass with the package in his lap and the rope a jumbled mess, with loose coils and stray loops spilling out everywhere!

That was EXACTLY what I didn't want to see! If just one of those coils of rope caught on part of his body or part of the plane when he tossed out the fuel pump we'd be in the water before I could do anything about it.

15 seconds.

No time or fuel to close the door and go around.

"Get up on your knees!" I yelled. "And get control of that damn rope! John help him!"

Lineup, airspeed, altitude, distance.

10 seconds.

Watch what you're doing dumbass! Don't get distracted and fly into the water!

7 seconds.

Lineup, altitude, distance.

Getting a little slow, add a touch of power.

A quick glance back. He's up on his knees. The rope is sort of contained.

Should I go around and make another pass?

four seconds.

No. Screw it. Keep going.

Altitude, distance.

The ship is approaching rapidly. Its antennas are taller than I anticipated. I pull up. Just a little.

Not yet.........Not yet.........Almost there.........

"DROP! DROP! DROP!"

I winced as Cory tossed the jumbled mess of Styrofoam and yellow nylon rope out the open door. Moments later the Stormin' Normin flashes by underneath. Nothing snags on the plane, the package is on the way. Pulling up hard, I bank the plane to the right as the three of us lean out to watch the drop. The small bright orange comet with a long yellow tail streaks over the ship just missing the mast and splashing down on the far side. As I crank the Cessna in a tight circle, we see a crew member dive over the side of the boat to retrieve the package. We hooted and hollered at our success. High fives all around as I slipped the plane hard to close the door and head for home.

I could go on and on about how the trip back to St. Croix was fraught with peril as the sun disappeared below the horizon. About how the fuel gauges were bouncing on empty as the lights of the island came into view. Or how our fuel ran out just as the wheels squeezed onto the runway. But I can't. Because it didn't happen that way. I mean, it was close, of course, but isn't it always?

ST. ELMO'S FIRE

*"We had always worried about being near
thunderstorms in this airplane.
We had worried about being in the dark in this airplane.
And we worried most about being
in a thunderstorm at night in this airplane."*
- Dick Rutan, Voyager , 1987

Sweat was dripping into my eyes as I sat on a hot Arizona
tarmac reading the pilot's operating handbook for my latest
challenge. The plane I was melting in was a Piper Aerostar,
and it was looking like I had my work cut out for me. The
Aerostar is a sexy hot rod of a plane with a sleek bullet-like
profile and reputation for being the fastest piston powered
twin ever built. But it has a complicated fuel system and a
weird nose wheel steering system. I was studying the
handbook intently so I wouldn't make any stupid mistakes.
One of the things I love about being a ferry pilot is getting
to fly many different types of aircraft. But it was rare that I
received any kind of checkout, so I was used to teaching
myself how to fly them. But this time I was in a plane I'd
never even heard of before. I thought an Aerostar was some
sort of minivan.

"Are you sure you don't want me to just show you a
few things about the plane?"

"No thanks, I'll be okay" *Go away son, you bother me.*

"But the fuel systems can be tricky to figure out. You really should let me show you how it works."

The pain in my neck that afternoon was a particularly annoying flight instructor who was desperately trying to take me up in the Aerostar and show me a few things. But I really didn't want to go flying with that eager beaver, I just wanted to go.

I'd arrived in Arizona just that afternoon, and after seeing the Aerostar, I was eager to get it in the air and see if it was as fast as my boss said it was. That plane looked fast just sitting on the ramp! Also, it was already late afternoon and I had a long flight back to Minnesota ahead of me. If I was going to make it home that night, I had to get the show on the road. But the main reason I didn't want to go flying with the instructor was that I thought of myself as a veteran ferry pilot whose specialty was climbing into strange planes and figuring out how to fly them all by myself. It was a point of pride that I could climb into just about any aircraft and fly it anywhere on the planet (once I figured out how to start it). One thing I sure as hell didn't need was some snot-nosed kid trying to teach me how to fly that bird.

Leaving the frustrated instructor sulking in the pilot's lounge, I walked out to the ramp, opened the clam shell doors on the left side of the Aerostar and climbed in. It was love at first sight. The tight cockpit fit me like a glove. Looking out the left window I could see my reflection in the gleaming chrome propeller spinner just a few feet away. The cone shaped spinner elongated the reflection of the sleek plane's nose making it appear even longer. It made me look like I was sitting in the cockpit of an F-16. I was grinning from ear to ear.

The pilot's manual said the Aerostar would cruise at well over 225 knots and climb to 28,000 feet, not quite supersonic but still pretty damn good. I couldn't wait to takeoff and put the spurs to her. Steering with the thumb switch instead of the rudder pedals took a little getting used to but after weaving drunkenly down the taxiway I managed to get lined up on the runway, more or less straight. When I pushed the throttles forward the lightly loaded Aerostar practically leapt into the air. I couldn't help but give out a yell as I pointed the nose of the plane skyward and brought the gear up. I could really get used to this!

Two hours later I was approaching the heart of the Rockies at 19,000 feet and was facing a difficult decision. The sun had disappeared behind me and a powerful line of thunderstorms barred my way across the Rocky Mountains. I could try to find a way to get through those thunderstorms and sleep in my own bed that night or admit defeat and find a place to land. A bright full moon made it easy to see two towering thunderheads on either side of my flight path. It looked to me as if the large gap between the two giants was filled in with clouds that were lower than my current altitude. I intently studied the Aerostar's green storm scope watching lightning strikes in both of the thunderheads but saw nothing in the gap between them.

I sat in the dark cockpit, chewing my lip trying to make a decision. Thunderstorms are nothing to be messed with, besides producing heavy rain and strong turbulence, they can throw plane-smashing hail over forty miles away. Rain and turbulence I could handle. Hail was another matter entirely. Fly through a hailstorm at 200 knots and you'll come out looking like a golf ball. Hail is usually downwind of the thunder cells, so I checked the winds aloft and decided my path would keep me in the clear of that danger. What bothered me was the lightning. I'd already been struck by lightning once on a ferry flight and wasn't really looking forward to going through that terrifying experience again. But my cocky attitude and a bad case of get-home-itis once again got in the way of sound and safe decision making.

I've fought with thunderstorms many times over the years and won. I'd been banged around a few times, and had the crap scared out of me once, but had never gotten myself into a situation that I couldn't handle, so far. I admit my past victories have a tendency to cloud my better judgment and feed my ego. I'm Kerry McCauley, world famous ferry pilot. I can handle anything!

I stared intently at the storm scope and saw little green dots appearing on either side of the screen. Each green dot represented a lighting strike. From what I could tell there were plenty of strikes inside each of the cells, but the area in the middle looked clear enough to fly through. I looked again at the lower area of cloud in between the cells and thought if I climbed just a few thousand feet higher I would be on top of the clouds and could sail peacefully through the gap between the thunderstorms. That was the plan at least. The Aerostar's great high altitude performance and pressurized cockpit made my mind up for me. I was sitting in a high performance rocket ship that could climb over any storms and handle any weather, I was invincible.

"Denver Center November five three eight three Juliet, request climb to twenty-one thousand for weather."

"Roger, eight three Juliet, climb and maintain twenty-one thousand."

I pushed the throttles forward and the sleek twin responded, clawing for more altitude. As the twin towers of the thunderstorms got closer I started to doubt the Aerostar's ability to climb over the dark clouds that now filled the space between the thunderheads. I also started to doubt my decision. I was beginning to wonder if I'd succumbed to the biggest killer in aviation, overconfidence. Fear is a fickle tool for a pilot, too much, and he never leaves the ground, not enough, and his career might be a short one. As I approached twenty-one thousand feet the wall of darkness still loomed above me and it became apparent that I wasn't going to get high enough to clear the cloud tops. The two massive storms on either side seemed to expand, filling in the gap, hemming me in. It looked unlikely that I'd be able to turn around without flying into one of them. I was trapped.

Before I knew it the plane plunged into the dark gray mass barring my way. It wasn't too bad at first. The air was smooth and the strike finder was still showing only lightning strikes in the thunderstorms on either side of me. *Okay, not too bad. Nothing to worry about after all.* A slight hissing sound on the hull of the aircraft got my attention. Curious I flipped on the landing light and was rewarded with the sight of a million bright white comets hurtling toward my face at over 200 knots. I love turning on the landing light when flying through snow. The effect gives you an incredible sense of speed that you don't normally get while flying. *Warp factor 7 Mr. Sulu.* After fantasizing of piloting an X-Wing fighter on my way to blow up the Death Star I regretfully switched off the light and got back to business.

The strike finder showed a few bright green dots starting to ominously creep away from the edges of the screen and edge closer to my path. I frowned as I studied the display. If the strike finder started to show lightning strikes in front of me I could be in real trouble.

While I was staring at the strike finder I caught something out of the corner of my eye. Looking up I was startled to see two showers of sparks shooting out of the corners of the compass mounted on top of the glare shield. The shower of sparks was about three inches long and looked like multi-colored fans of fireworks coming from the screws on the upper corners of the compass. Suddenly, bright multi-colored tendrils of plasma filaments started weaving back and forth across the outside of the windscreen. I don't know if the hair standing up on the back of my neck was from the plane being electrically charged or from the terror I felt. Something else caught my eye and I looked out the left window and saw more St. Elmo's fire shooting two feet out from the propeller tips like a Christmas wreath of multi-colored fire. Thoroughly terrified, I looked back at the storm scope and was shocked to see a small green dot appear in the center of the screen, then another, then three more in quick succession.

Crap.

The gap between the two thunderstorms had started to produce lightning and I was flying right into it. I quickly jammed the throttles and propeller controls to the stops, pulled back on the yoke and desperately clawed for more altitude. I had to get out of the clouds before I got hit by lightning.

"Aerostar Five Kilo Bravo, say altitude," Denver Center was wondering what I was doing when my blip on their radar screen showed that I was climbing. I wasn't sure if transmitting would invite a lightning strike but I wasn't going to take any chances.

"Aerostar eight three Juliet, do you read Denver Center?"

Ignoring the persistent calls from ATC, I watched the needle on the altimeter move faster as I pulled the plane into a steeper climb, desperately trying to get out of the clouds. With only half a load of fuel left in the plane, the Aerostar was nice and light. I was climbing like a homesick angel for the safety of clear skies above. Seconds later I burst through the silver tops of the clouds like a rocket, shooting to the full moon in front of me. The thunderheads on either side towered high above me like two giant mountains shining in the moonlight. Finally clear of the clouds, I lowered the nose, let the Aerostar's speed build up and got the hell out of there. I was also brave enough to use the radio again. "Denver Center, Aerostar eight three Juliet."

"Go ahead eight three Juliet, we've been trying to reach you," came the terse reply.

"Aaaah yeah Denver, sorry bout that." I said doing my best Chuck Yeager imitation.

I was ninety percent sure she couldn't hear the quiver in my voice as I explained my reasons for changing altitudes and not answering their calls. (Well, seventy percent anyway.) The female controller's attitude and tone immediately changed. She completely understood my actions and said that she would have done the same thing. With a now warm, reassuring and almost apologetic voice, the controller approved my new altitude and then put out a pilot report, warning other aircraft of the St. Elmo's Fire I'd encountered.

The flashing thunderstorm clouds quickly faded. At 200 knots it's amazing how fast you can leave trouble behind. As I eased back into a comfortable cruising mode, I couldn't help but smile at my reflection in the spinner out my left window. Conquered another beast, slayed another dragon, got away with it again. But my smile didn't last long. Once the adrenaline wore off and the elation of not getting killed again faded, I couldn't keep one very powerful thought from ruining the party. *Well Kerry, that was pretty damn stupid.* Flying under a beautiful starry sky bathed in the comfortable glow of the instrument lights I began to take stock. I'd been taking a lot of risks lately. A lot of unnecessary risks. It seemed that the more dangerous things I got away with the more I became convinced that I was invincible. Every time I jumped out of an airplane, rode my motorcycle too fast, talked back to my wife or crossed the North Atlantic in a piece of junk airplane, I was reinforcing my "can't get hurt" attitude. Psychologist's call it the bubble of invincibility. Most people just call it stupid.

There was a good reason my friends called me "Scary Kerry". It had been acceptable when I was young and single. Who isn't convinced they're invincible when they're young? But now I was a family man with a beautiful wife and two young children who depended on me. Maybe it was time to start being a little more careful now and then. Or maybe, just maybe, I could just stop choosing the most dangerous option every time I had a choice. Maybe I could dial things back, just a little. Maybe.

But changing my attitude wouldn't be easy. Ever since I could remember I looked down on people who took the safe way out. In my opinion, if you weren't pushing it and living on the edge you just weren't living life to its fullest. I still remember when I was young telling my mother that I hoped that I would be dead by the time I was thirty-seven. My reasoning was that if my luck hadn't run out by that time, then I just hadn't lived the kind of dangerous, high-speed life I would be proud of. She responded that she thought I had a death wish and she hoped that I would grow out of it someday. In typical teenage arrogance I told her that it wasn't a death wish. It was just the only kind of life I personally thought worth living. Anything else would be less.

As I got older, and actually started doing some of the exciting and dangerous things that I'd dreamed of, I realized that people who got killed pushing the envelope fell into two categories: Those whose skill set and natural abilities were insufficient to keep them alive. Those whose luck just ran out at the wrong time. That's not to say that they were counting on luck to make it through and survive, rather that they had some bad luck at the wrong time. You can do everything right and still get killed if the wrong thing happens at just the wrong time. Normal people don't put themselves in such positions.

That realization had slowly crept up on me over the years and really hit me that night in the clouds. Should I begin to take fewer chances? Could I take fewer chances, and still be happy? One thing that I knew for sure was that I really had to stop flying single engine aircraft over the ocean. It was just too risky, and there just wasn't any reason to take that risk anymore. I'd done it enough times to prove that it wasn't just luck. And just who was I proving this to anyway? And risking my ass in a single engine plane over the North Atlantic just so some French flight school could get a new trainer just wasn't worth it. For that matter, even flying twin engine aircraft might not be worth the risk either. I spent the rest of that night flying home thinking about my life and wondering if this ferry trip might be my last.

When I got back home to Minnesota I told Cathy about the St. Elmo's Fire but I didn't tell her about the thunderstorms. She'd been really great and understanding about my ferry flying but I decided that bragging about my close calls might not be in her best interest. I also neglected to tell her my thoughts about retiring from the ferry flying business. I wanted to leave my options open in case I changed my mind.

I spent the next two days at home getting ready to take the Aerostar to Cyprus. Preparing for a long ferry flight had become routine. After years of ferry flying I'd finally figured out just how much cash I needed, what maps to bring and, most importantly, how many pairs of underwear to take along (four for Europe and six for the Middle East). Cathy and the kids drove me to the airport, and after hugs and kisses all around I climbed aboard. My time at home hadn't helped me decide if I was going to retire from ferry flying or not. Claire and Connor were getting older and soon they'd both be involved in sports, and lots of other activities. I knew it would tear me up if I missed seeing Claire's first dance recital, or Connors first baseball game, because I was gone on a trip. On the other hand I just couldn't see myself quitting the business and the adventures that went along with it. I'd been literally bouncing off the walls looking forward to flying the Aerostar to Cyprus. A trip like that is a pilot's dream, a great airplane that was fast, pressurized and had the extra safety of two engines. And to top it off, I got to fly it to another exotic location I'd likely never get another chance to visit if it wasn't for ferry flying. I had no idea what I was going to do.

The trip got off to a good start. Favorable winds allowed me to skip Maine and go directly to Goose Bay. The weather over Canada was perfect for flying and a 50 knot tailwind was helping the Aerostar eat up the miles to Goose Bay at a record pace. But flying east at two hundred and fifty knots in the middle of winter makes for a short day and it wasn't long before the growing shadows on the ground gave way to a moonless night thick as black velvet. Flying over northern Canada at night is magical. The complete lack of city lights reminded me once again of what astronauts must see when they slip the surly bonds of earth and rocket through space. As usual, when flying at night, I spent most of my time with the interior lights turned up high, allowing me to read a paperback to pass the time. At least once an hour though, I'd set my book aside, turn all the lights in the cockpit off and take in the star-riddled night sky. It's important not to let the pressures of the job make you forget why you became a pilot in the first place.

During the final hour of my flight I once again transformed my airplane into a spaceship and was rewarded with the magnificent sight of the Aurora Borealis dancing across the night sky. It pulsed and moved against the Milky Way in purple, green and yellow. Curtains of color folded upon themselves and exploded like silent fireworks as I stared in mindless wonder. Growing up in Minnesota I'd seen the Northern Lights many times before but never from an airplane at 23,000 feet. Everything seemed so close, so crisp, like I could reach out and drag my fingertips through the dancing lights. I left the lights off for the rest of the flight and brought the throttles back in order to slow the Aerostar and prolong the magic. But there was no stopping time, and soon the pale yellow glow of Happy Valley appeared on the horizon marking the end of the road and my brief escape from reality. *I'd have made a great astronaut.*

Goose Bay was Goose Bay. Frozen steaks with butter, limited beer choices and run-down hotel rooms. I loved every minute of it, but I couldn't shake the melancholy feeling that I might never pass this way again. The next morning I was once again sitting in line on the taxiway with ten military fighters from various countries. But this time, I was in an Aerostar. I think I caught a few of the fighter pilots looking at me with envy as I sat there waiting my turn to takeoff and fly that cool plane halfway around the world. Maybe. How was I going to get another experience like this if I stopped ferry flying? I decided to put the decision out of my mind and concentrate on the task at hand.

I was in a relaxed and content mood about halfway to Greenland when tall, white, beautiful cumulus clouds started to appear up ahead. I've never been able to resist such an inviting playground. With a huge grin on my face I put a favorite tape in my Walkman, cranked up the volume and kicked off the autopilot. I spent the next hour weaving in and out of the clouds and generally goofing off. Climbing and diving over the billowing white tops I pushed the Aerostar to its aerobatic limits to the pounding beat of some great classic rock. It was some of the most enjoyable flying I've ever done. As I neared the coast of Greenland I was ahead of schedule and fat on gas so I dropped down to wave top height and raced up and down the coastline weaving between icebergs like a slalom skier and having the time of my life. When I finally pulled up and pointed the Aerostar's nose towards Narsarsuaq I again had the sad feeling that I might never see that beautiful jagged coast again.

After a quick refuel in Narsarsuaq I took off to Iceland where I made one last visit to the Irish pub and the famous Blue Lagoon hot springs. It seemed that everywhere I landed on that trip there was something I was going to miss when I stopped ferry flying.

Landing in London the next day I was treated like a conquering hero by Mr. Neoklis Antoniou, one of the Aerostar's new owners. Mr. Antoniou's family swarmed all over the plane while he asked me dozens of nonstop questions about the trip. A Cypriot native who owned a successful printing business in London, Neoklis was almost crying as I showed him his new toy. Sitting in the pilot's seat his eyes shined brightly while I showed him where everything on his new plane was. He was doubly excited because he was going to accompany me on the last few legs from England to Cyprus. As our first ground training session wore on I began to get concerned. Not only didn't he have much in the way of multi-engine time in his logbook, he didn't have much total flight time at all!

The Aerostar is a very fast and complex airplane, not the kind of plane a novice should be flying. He told me that he had three other partners in the plane, and that this was the second twin that they'd bought together. The first plane, a Beech Baron, was destroyed when one of the other owners taxied it into another plane, starting a fire and burning both to the ground. That story didn't make me feel any better about the skill level of any of the pilots who were going to fly the Aerostar. But my job was just to deliver it, nothing more. If they killed themselves because they bought a plane that was way too much for them, it was none of my concern.

We stayed in London for two days waiting for the weather over Europe to improve. A cold front had moved in and covered most of the western continent in low clouds, rain and strong winds. The forecast also called for icing over most of the route, and even though the Aerostar was fully de-iced, I didn't see a need to push it. The weather finally improved enough to leave the white cliffs of Dover behind and head east. First stop, Zurich. I'd been to Zurich a few years prior on my first trip with Pete and still had some of the old approach plates and charts from that trip. They were way out of date, but they were better than nothing. Because, once again, Pete had sent me out on a ferry trip without current charts or approach plates for the region, and particularly the Zurich airport.

When air traffic control set me up on the instrument approach for Zurich, I dug out the folder that held photocopies of approach procedures for various airports around the world. All the ferry pilots in our company had a folder like this. When Pete sent us off to fly small planes all over the world, he rarely provided us with current charts or approach plates. It wasn't so much that he was cheap, it was because we never really knew exactly how we were going to get to our destination. Your initial plan could, and usually did, change. A large weather system might force you to fly hundreds of miles out of your way, forcing you to land in random countries just to keep moving towards your destination.

There were also constant problems with overflight permits for countries along your route. Some countries make it difficult, if not impossible, to get an overflight permit. Some are for very specific times and days. If you get delayed and miss your authorized day you might have to wait until another permit is issued or fly around that country. It all boils down to money. Sometimes it's cheaper to spend the fuel and fly around a country, rather than pay for food and hotels while you wait for a new permit. Another reason we all had our file full of approach plates is sometimes we were sent straight to pick up another plane without coming home. In that case there is no opportunity to get new maps or approach plates.

Either way, there are many times that a ferry pilot will be landing in airports that he didn't expect to. If he can reach into his magic folder and pull out the correct approach plate, he's way ahead of the game. Using an old approach plate, even if it's expired, is still better than admitting to ATC you don't have one. It can be downright embarrassing to ask them to read you the chart over the radio. So a good ferry pilot always updated his little bag of tricks whenever he had the opportunity. Either by copying charts along the way, or if two pilots happened to be in the Orient Air office at the same time we'd copy any we didn't have and those that were more current than the ones we had. Kind of like trading baseball cards. I know it sounds dangerous, shooting approaches using old charts, but they seldom change much, and they almost never move the mountains or other high stuff you might run into.

I looked at the approach plate for Zurich and saw that it was over three years out of date.

Geez. I hope nothing important has changed since then, like a radio frequency or minimum descent altitude. *Guess I'm going to find out.* Apparently not much had changed because neither air traffic control or the guys in the control tower yelled at me. We picked up a trace of ice on the approach and broke out of the clouds at three hundred feet with Zurich's long 10,000 foot runway stretched out in front of us.

While Neokilos was supervising the refueling, I went inside the airport operations building to check the weather, and file a flight plan for our next stop in Greece. I was also hoping to update my approach plates and departure procedures for Zurich.

Inside the MET office the man behind the counter was painting a gloomy picture of the weather along my proposed line of flight. Departing Zurich the clouds were low and thick and stretched all the way up to twenty-five thousand feet. The clouds themselves weren't the problem though.

"There are two pilot reports of light to occasional moderate icing on the climb out between four and twenty-two thousand feet," the weatherman said pointing to the weather chart he held in his hands as he gave me my briefing.

"If you can get over the mountains you can descend down to a warmer altitude to get out of the icing conditions. Once you clear the coast you should have good weather over the Mediterranean all the way to Greece."

I looked at the chart he was showing me and compared it to the navigation chart I had. "The minimum crossing altitude over the Alps is nineteen thousand feet, what's the freezing level on the other side of the Alps?" I asked.

"The freezing level over Italy is five thousand feet." He said consulting his chart. "Does your plane have anti-ice capabilities?"

"Yep, so we should be okay. If we pick up too much ice before we cross the mountains, we can always come back to Zurich or if we're on the other side, descend down to warmer air." I said confidently. The MET man agreed with my assessment and wished me luck as I left to go file the flight plan.

I went to operations, filled out the flight plan sheet and handed it to the man behind the counter so he could call it into the air traffic control system. A few minutes later he came back.

"Your flight plan was approved sir, but there is one change, you can expect the Zurich One Standard Instrument Departure Procedure."

"Okay, thanks." I said as I pretended to look through my flight bag for the current book that would have the departure procedure he referred to. It was all an act of course because I didn't even have an out-of-date copy of the Zurich One Standard Instrument Departure Procedure, let alone a current one.

"Say I can't seem to find the current book with that departure in it. I don't suppose you have a book I could copy it from, do you?" I asked innocently, trying to put on the charm and see how much help this guy could be.

Getting the people who work at airports to help you with whatever problem you might have is a skill that every good ferry pilot must have. You often encounter problems that you can't solve without their help. Some pilots barge into a situation like a bull in a china shop, demanding help with their problem and just being a jerk. This usually comes from the new guys who get frustrated with the nonstop problems and challenges a ferry pilot must deal with every day. They let the situation get to them, get angry and pretty soon they're yelling at some poor guy behind the counter for not giving them exactly what they want. Not surprisingly, the more of a jerk you are, the less cooperation you get. It's best to be really nice to everyone you meet right off the bat. You never know what problem might arise or who can help you solve it. One of my tricks to getting the people who work at the airports to like me is to compliment their country. Tell them that you can't wait to come back, maybe on vacation, because you just love it soooo much! Most people like Americans and telling them their country is fantastic goes a long way. Normally, when I turned on the charm I could get just about anything I wanted out of the guys in operations. That is, except when dealing with compulsive rule followers, like the Germans, Austrians and, unfortunately, the Swiss. The answer to my question about copying the departure procedure wasn't what I was hoping for.

"What do you mean you don't have a copy of the current departure procedures book?" The operations manager said, "Every pilot MUST have current copies of ALL arrival, approach and departure procedures for EVERY airport he lands at!"

Uh oh! This guy is pissed!

It's usually not a big deal to get a copy of something from operations but that guy could just not get over the fact that I didn't have the proper materials that every other pilot he dealt with had. Turning on the charm didn't work so I tried sympathy.

"I'm sorry sir, I wasn't planning to land here when I took off but strong headwinds caused me to come in here and to get some fuel." It was only a little lie.

"Zat is no matter. A pilot must have the proper materials for every flight he makes and prepare for every contingency along his route."

"I understand sir, I'll be better prepared next time." I left it at that and just stood there hoping that he'd get the hint that he was going to be stuck with me until he made me a copy of the departure procedure.

Option two when dealing with airport personnel, be a pain in the ass. They'll give you what you need just to get rid of you.

With a look of exasperation the operations manager walked back to the rack of manuals behind him, selected the correct one and goose stepped/walked over to the copy machine. He then angrily flipped to the page I needed, slammed it on the copy machine and hit print. When he was finished he handed me the copy and turned away without a word. His manner said it all, "Stupid American!" With the information in hand, I wasted no time getting out of there. It was a little embarrassing but I still got the job done.

Neokilos had the Aerostar all fueled and ready to go. I was a little concerned about the possibility of ice. We'd have to make it up to 19,000 feet to clear the mountains before dropping down to warm air of the sunny Mediterranean. But I had confidence in the Aerostar's excellent high altitude performance and de-ice capability plus, we had a light load with just the two of us in the plane. Shouldn't be a problem. I left out any mention of in-flight icing when I briefed my co-pilot because Neokilos was a low time pilot from a warm weather country. Even the mention of icing tends to freak those guys out.

Light snow was falling as we took off into the low hanging clouds. Right on schedule, at 4,000 feet, a thin layer of milky white rime ice started forming on the leading edges of the wings. I already had the pitot heat on, and when I saw the ice forming I hit the switches that turned on the heat for the windshield and the propellers. I was feeling pretty cocky in a well equipped plane.

"Aren't you going to use the boots to clear the ice on the wings?" Neoklis asked nervously as he looked out the window at the ice building up on the wings.

"Not just yet," I said calmly, "it's usually best to wait until the ice is a little thicker before using the boots. That way when you break it off it all comes off in big chunks that are less likely to stick to the rubber."

Neoklis looked skeptical but didn't press the point. When the accumulated ice on the wings reached about a half an inch of thickness, I hit the switch that inflated the rubber de-ice boots along the leading edges of the wings and tail. As soon as the black rubber boots inflated the ice broke apart into hundreds of small pieces and flew away into the slipstream. The smile on Neoklis' face showed how relieved he was to see the ice disappear from the wings.

As we continued to climb the ice started to accumulate at a faster rate than before. So much so that I stopped manually operating the de-ice boots and flipped the switch to the automatic setting that would cycle the boots once every minute or so. I looked out at the engines and saw ice begin to build up on the unprotected areas of the airplane like the front of the engine cowling and the tip of the propeller spinners. I still wasn't worried. I'd been in icing conditions many times before and the big globs of ice building up on the spinners were normal. My mood changed around 17,000 feet when the Aerostar's climb rate started slowing drastically. Because the de-ice boots were doing a good job of keeping the wings ice free, I assumed that the drop on climb rate was due to ice buildup on unprotected areas of the plane. When the climb rate dropped below 400 feet per minute, I really started to get concerned. We had almost 2,000 feet left to climb before reaching the minimum crossing altitude. And for the first time I wasn't one hundred percent sure we'd be able to reach it.

Flying with one hand, I looked at the map and did some quick calculations in my head. If our climb rate didn't get too much worse we should make 19,000 feet by the crossing point. That was a big "If". At 18,000 feet the Aerostar started to feel a little loose. It felt like the tail was getting heavy. A glance at the Vertical Speed Indicator showed that our climb rate had dropped down to just 200 feet per minute. There must be an ice buildup on the unprotected tail beacon. And from the feel of things it's gotta be the size of a basketball! *Crap!*

Things were beginning to look grim. If we couldn't reach 19,000 we'd have to turn around and descend back to Zurich. If we did make it to the minimum crossing altitude we'd have to be able to hold that altitude for at least 25 miles before being able to descend. We couldn't see them, but I knew just below us the jagged peaks of the Alps were waiting to tear us from the sky if we got much lower. *Maybe I pushed this one just a little too far.*

"What's going on? Why is our climb rate so low?" Neoklis asked, pointing to the needle on the VSI that was hovering just barely above zero.

"I think we're picking up some ice on the tail somewhere, maybe on the strobe light."

"Are we going to be able to make it over the mountains?" he asked, clearly very nervous about flying in icing conditions.

"We should be all right." I said, trying to sound confident. "Once we get over the mountains we can descend back down to warmer air and melt whatever ice we picked up." I hoped I sounded convincing. The last thing I needed right then was a co-pilot who was on the verge of panic.

The Aerostar stopped climbing at 18,700 feet. We were still 300 feet short of the minimum safe altitude depicted on the chart, but knowing that altitude was at least 1,000 feet above the highest obstacle I decided that I could live with being a little low.

"November five three eight three Juliet, Zurich Center, say altitude." Apparently that three hundred feet had not gone unnoticed.

"Zurich, eight three Juliet, level at eighteen thousand seven hundred and unable to climb any higher due to icing." The cat was out of the bag and my co-pilot gave me a panicked look.

"Roger eight three Juliet, advise if you need any assistance."

"Actually Zurich, we will need lower as soon as possible."

"Understood eight three Juliet, unable at this time, expect lower in two zero miles."

Twenty miles. Crap. I did some mental calculations. At our current speed of 135 knots it will take us about ten minutes before we can start descending. I glanced over at Neoklis who seemed to want to say something but thought better of it.

The ice on the propeller spinners continued to grow as the minutes ticked by. The ice must be building up on the tail as well. I looked at the airspeed indicator for the thousandth time and saw that it was getting dangerously low. The plane was wallowing in the air, and I desperately needed to lower the nose and pick up some speed before we stalled. Out of airspeed, and options, I reluctantly eased the yoke forward and started a slow one hundred foot per minute descent, trading some of our precious altitude for a few knots of equally precious airspeed. It's a deal with the devil, but one I must make.

My decision didn't go unnoticed. "We're descending!" Neoklis yelled excitedly over the intercom. "We're not supposed to be descending yet!"

"Don't worry, we're only a few miles from the lower minimum altitude point and I'm sure we're still way above the highest mountain in the area." (Probably.) *Come on baby, just a little farther!* My confidence in the situation wasn't rubbing off on my co-pilot but it didn't matter, the die was cast and all I could do was wait and see what happened. We were just above 18,000 feet when we got the call I'd been waiting for.

"November five three eight three Juliet Zurich Center, clear to descend to one seven zero."

Whew!

"Roger, eight three Juliet out of one eight zero for one seven zero." With great relief I thumbed the electric trim button on the yoke to start descending.

"See? Not a problem." I said to Neoklis with a grin.

"I'm never going to fly in ice again!" he said.

I agreed that staying out of ice was probably a good plan for him and his partners. It was probably a good plan for me as well. I'd really painted myself into a corner back there and there was no excuse. Once again, I'd let my ego, and an overconfidence in the Aerostar's de-ice capabilities, lure me into making one of the dumbest decisions of my aviation career. Instead of pushing on when the ice started to build up, I should have turned back immediately. Instead of sweating bullets over the mountains we could have been having lunch in some fancy restaurant, planning our next move. A nice glass of wine, cloth napkins, peace, safety. Of course I'd have had to deal with that pain in the ass of an operations manager again, but so what.

As we left the Alps behind and were cleared to lower and warmer air I could hear and feel the built up ice leaving the plane. Finally free of the excess drag the sleek Aerostar quickly picked up speed as the clouds cleared revealing the beautiful blue waters of the Mediterranean below us.

The rest of the day went quickly. A short turnaround in Corfu, Greece followed by a fast, two-hour night flight to Cyprus. It was on this leg that I hit my fastest ground speed in a piston aircraft. We'd started a shallow descent and were excited to be fast approaching the finish line. A nice strong tailwind was helping us along when I noticed that our ground speed was approaching 300 knots. Neoklis was at the controls and as our airspeed started to build up he reached for the throttles to slow us down.

"No, don't slow down." I told him, "Let's see if we can hit three hundred knots!"

"I don't know," he hesitated. "I'm not very comfortable going this fast."

"Look, you've got yourself a pretty fast plane here, and the sooner you get used to it the safer you'll be. You might as well get the experience of going fast with me sitting next to you rather than to do it by yourself some other time."

But Neoklis wasn't having any of it. He pulled the throttles back, slowing us down from our top speed of 295 knots, just five knots shy of the 300 mark. I was disappointed. Not only because I was cheated out of hitting the 300 mark but also coming to the realization that the Aerostar scared the hell out of Neoklis. It's good for a pilot to have a healthy respect for a new plane, but to be actually afraid of it can be downright dangerous. A pilot who flies a high performance airplane like it's a docile trainer can get himself into a lot of trouble. If he tries to pretend that his race horse is really a pony, he shouldn't be surprised when he's bucked off. I hoped I could get Neoklis and his partners ready to ride that thoroughbred before I left for home.

Early the next morning I went back to the airport to check out Aerostar's new owners. Neoklis had scored me a jump seat on a late afternoon commercial flight to London, so our time was limited. Six hours later, I was worrying that my efforts to bring four inexperienced pilots up to speed in the Aerostar had only been successful enough to get them killed. The middle aged businessmen had grasped the complexity of the plane's systems well enough but when it came time to actually fly the aircraft they all seemed way over their heads and way behind the aircraft. Each of them seemed to be terrified of how fast the plane moved across the sky, and how fast the ground came up at them when they tried to land. I did the best I could getting them used to the speed, and the maneuverability that was so different from what they'd been flying before. It was no use. They just didn't have the experience for that kind of plane. Just before leaving, I strongly advised them to hire an instructor and get some more training before blasting off on their own. I could tell my warnings fell on deaf ears. I hoped I wouldn't be reading about an Aerostar crash in the upcoming months.

After my brief stint as an Aerostar instructor was over, Neoklis rushed me to the main airport terminal where he introduced me to a good friend of his who was an Airbus captain. He was a tall, lean man who looked like he was born to wear his perfectly tailored uniform. The captain commanded instant respect, without the slightest effort. His gracious and confident manner made me instantly like and admire him. Here was exactly what I was striving to be, the perfect embodiment of a professional airline pilot. As he walked me into the huge Airbus cockpit it was like he was introducing me to my new life. My logbook was now filled with enough flight time to get me hired on at one of the small regional airlines. When I got home I'd really have a decision to make. It might be time to trade in my vagabond lifestyle for the gold stripes of an airline pilot.

The captain showed me the jump seat I'd be riding in, and introduced me to the co-pilot, who looked to be all of seventeen years old. I took my seat and buckled in as the captain and co-pilot started going over the preflight routine. It was fascinating watching the co-pilot call off items on the checklist and the captain confirm that the switch or knob was set correctly. It was a completely different atmosphere than my usual, jump in and go routine. I found it strangely appealing. Preflight complete and passengers loaded, the flight crew started the engines, got clearance from ground control and taxied to the end of the runway. After a last second check of the engine instruments, the co-pilot grabbed the yoke and pushed the throttles up to full power. I was pushed back in my seat slightly as the big Airbus started rolling down the runway. We picked up speed quickly and it wasn't long before the co-pilot eased back on the yoke, and we lifted off the runway at a steep angle and started climbing. *Wow! What a ride!* The whole takeoff was accomplished with the ease and precision that comes with a lot of practice and experience. It was exhilarating being in the cockpit, sitting in-between the pilots and witnessing firsthand the complicated technical dance that's required to get a fifty ton vehicle airborne. It was like being in the cockpit for the launch of the space shuttle.

The co-pilot flew the Airbus by hand for about fifteen seconds before leaning forward to flip on the autopilot. Relieved of immediate control of the aircraft the captain slid his seat back, took out a clip board and began working on the tons of paperwork airline management believes is necessary to make airplanes fly. Once the chores were done, both pilots turned their attention to me with just the occasional glance at the flight instruments. While the plane continued to climb to its assigned altitude, the captain started asking me nonstop questions about the Aerostar and what it was like to fly such a small plane over the ocean. As was usually the case, whenever I talked to airline pilots about ferry flying, they were at once impressed, scornful and jealous of my job. It seemed that most of them wished that they too could fly around the world, having grand adventures, free from the stifling world of constraints and rules. Many times such pilots would call me crazy in a vain attempt to knock me down a few pegs and make themselves feel a little better about being stuck in an unfulfilling job that relegated them to little more than a glorified bus driver. Fortunately, this captain wasn't such an insecure pilot. He was not only a confidant about his chosen profession but he was also a skydiver. The two of us spent the better part of an hour talking flying and skydiving.

But soon the conversion lagged, the captain turned to his newspaper while the co-pilot stared blankly out the side window at a thunderstorm flashing silently thousands of feet below us. I looked at the storm and thought that normally I'd be tightening my seat belt and getting ready to do battle with the elements. But up at 35,000, feet the flight crew was reading about the world cup standings, and daydreaming, without a care in the world. The flight deck was calm and quiet, with only the occasional radio call to break the peace.

It didn't look like anything interesting was going to happen for the next few hours, so I excused myself, went back into the cabin, and grabbed a couple of beers from the flight attendant. I found an empty seat and pondered my next move. I couldn't believe it. I'd spent years working toward my goal of being an airline pilot, and after less than two hours in the cockpit I was bored.

Two beers later I was back in the cockpit watching the pilots get ready for the approach into Heathrow Airport. They'd already set up autopilot to fly the instrument approach, so all they had to do was move their seats forward and monitor the systems as the aircraft flew itself through the clouds down toward the runway. As the plane got closer both pilots watched our progress on their multi-function display screens until the clouds parted revealing the lights of the runway stretching out before us. Then, seconds before touch down, the co-pilot put his hands on the controls then pushed a red button on the yoke to switch off the autopilot. There was a moderate crosswind on landing and the Airbus bounced and swayed a little as the co-pilot wrestled the big aircraft to the ground.

I didn't think the landing was that bad, especially since the co-pilot had his hands on the controls less than three minutes during the entire flight. But apparently, that wasn't an acceptable excuse, because the captain spent the next ten minutes berating him about his poor landing while we taxied to the gate. I felt like a house guest witnessing a husband complain about a new bride's cooking. I squirmed in uncomfortable silence as the co-pilot meekly accepted his tongue lashing in silence.

I was confused. I'd been really looking forward to leaving the purgatory of the piston engine world and moving up to the glamour of the jet world. A cockpit packed solid with lights, switches, moving maps and high tech gizmos was what I'd been working for all those years. I thought the powerful roar of jet engines rocketing the ship into a starry night sky would be the magical adventure I'd been dreaming of. But I'd just gotten a glimpse of the man behind the curtain, and I wasn't impressed. Instead of a glamorous world of fun and adventure, what I saw was a rigid and tightly controlled world where individuality and creativity were frowned upon. It was literally their job to be bored. The more I thought about the life of an airline pilot, the less appealing it was. Being gone from my family for days at a time would be bad enough. But flying back and forth between the same cities, spending all day either sitting in hotel rooms or in a sterile cockpit with a grouchy captain was . . . . Not for me?

On any given ferry trip, I'd be told to take a plane from point A to point B. That's it. How I got the job done was largely up to me. I picked my own routes, made my own weather calls and filed all the flight plans. I'd often make over a dozen landings in several different countries in a single trip. Along the way I could swoop and dive in the towering cumulus clouds. Fly as high as my lungs, or oxygen supply, would take me, or drop down to treetop level and see the sights. I could push hard and fly long into the night, or end my flying day early to enjoy a sunny beach and a cold beer. In those planes I was the boss. I was king. But a pilot on the line has all of his decisions made for him; a company dispatcher tells him where and when to go, how high and how fast to fly, and what hotel to stay at.

The more I sat and listened to the captain find fault with the poor co-pilot, the less I wanted to ever be on the receiving end of such a soul-crushing system. I realize why the airlines do things the way they do. Being responsible for hundreds of lives on each flight, there isn't room for swashbuckling pilots going around flying by the seat of their pants. Flight operations have to be done the same safe, standard way, every time, every day, period. And the more decisions you allow the pilot to make, the more trouble they can get into.

The young co-pilot managed to guide the Airbus to the gate and secure the engines without incident. With the aircraft shut down, the captain again had time to acknowledge my presence. I thanked him for inviting me into his cockpit and complimented him on his aircraft. Then I quickly made my escape. It felt like by spending any more time in his world than necessary, I might somehow be trapped.

During the rest of my trip home I tried to decide what to do with the rest of my life. I was pretty sure I didn't want to give up my life of adventure and become an airline pilot. But I also had to accept the fact that I couldn't continue to risk my life as a ferry pilot, with a family to look after.

I began to realize that my time as a ferry pilot had indeed ruined me as a pilot, or to be more precise, ruined my attitude or desire for anything less adventurous. Conquering the challenges of flying small aircraft around the world, alone and unassisted, was like doing battle every day. I'd literally become addicted to the feeling I got at the end of a day of ferry flying. Each night when my head finally hit the pillow my ears would ring from engine noise as my mind replayed the day's events. It would sometimes take hours for the adrenaline buzz to wear off. I was addicted. And like any addict, I couldn't quit looking for my next fix. I looked at the briefcase I used as my flight bag. The brown leather had been smooth and shiny when I tossed it into that Duchess so long ago. Now the leather was dull and faded. There was a small tear in the top and the corners were all soft and beat up. I was proud of the way that case looked. It made me feel like a veteran pilot. But I was 36 years old and I was starting to feel like that case. It was time for a change.

In the end I made a compromise. I'd put all my efforts into skydiving and see if I could make enough money to survive. If I was successful, great, I'd have a high-speed job that would also allow me to come home almost every night and see my family. But if I couldn't make a go of it, I'd surrender and get a job with the airlines. I was a little sad thinking that the Aerostar would be the last plane I'd ferry across the Atlantic, but in a way relieved to be getting out with my skin intact.

Back in Wisconsin I directed my energies at being a good father and husband, and to conquering my latest adversary, managing a small business. Running a successful skydiving school is every bit as challenging as ferry flying. Soon my wanderlust was muted, if not replaced, by the everyday high speed adventure that is professional skydiving. Oh, and there is still the tiniest bit of danger involved. So I had that going for me.

Two weeks after coming home from the Aerostar trip I finally got around to updating my logbook. Consulting my notes I carefully filled in the times and destinations of my last ferry flight. When I finally filled in the last landing in Cyprus, I was reluctant to close the book. I spent some time flipping through the pages filled with the dozens of different aircraft I'd flown (49). And foreign countries I'd landed in (56). Each one its own adventure. As I paged through the logbook, I wondered if I'd ever put anything as interesting as those flights in there ever again. It was not without a little sadness that I closed the book and put it up on the shelf.

ABOUT THE AUTHOR

Kerry McCauley grew up in central Minnesota. He began his career in aviation by becoming a UH-1H "Huey" helicopter crew chief and winter survival instructor in the Minnesota National Guard. He became a professional skydiving instructor and jump pilot before becoming an international ferry pilot. Kerry's career as a ferry pilot has taken him to 60 countries, over three oceans, and a dozen seas. Kerry has flown over 50 different types of aircraft, has accumulated over 9000 hours of flight time and over 20,000 skydives. He also starred in two seasons of the Discovery Channel series "Dangerous Flights." Kerry lives in Wisconsin with his wife Cathy where they own and operate Skydive Twin Cities, along with their children, Claire and Connor. He still flies and jumps almost every day.

Made in the USA
Monee, IL
13 January 2022

88894516R00197